# An Economic Analysis
## of
# Southern African Agriculture

*William R. Duggan*

## PRAEGER SPECIAL STUDIES • PRAEGER SCIENTIFIC

New York • Philadelphia • Eastbourne, UK
Toronto • Hong Kong • Tokyo • Sydney

Library of Congress Cataloging-in-Publication Data

Duggan, William R.
   An economic analysis of southern African
agriculture.

   Bibliography: p.
   Includes index.
   1. Agriculture — Economic aspects — Africa,
Southern.   I. Title.
HD2130.D84   1985         338.1′0968         85-12191
ISBN 0-03-003744-1 (alk. paper)

**Published and Distributed by the
Praeger Publishers Division
(ISBN Prefix 0-275)
of Greenwood Press, Inc.,
Westport, Connecticut**

Published in 1986 by Praeger Publishers
CBS Educational and Professional Publishing, a Division of CBS Inc.
521 Fifth Avenue, New York, NY 10175 USA

Printed in the United States of America on acid-free paper

## INTERNATIONAL OFFICES

Orders from outside the United States should be sent to the appropriate address listed below. Orders from areas not listed below should be placed through CBS International Publishing. 383 Madison Ave.. New York, NY 10175 USA

**Australia, New Zealand**
Holt Saunders. Pty. Ltd.. 9 Waltham St.. Artarmon. N.S.W. 2064. Sydney. Australia

**Canada**
Holt. Rinehart & Winston of Canada. 55 Horner Ave.. Toronto. Ontario. Canada M8Z 4X6

**Europe, the Middle East, & Africa**
Holt Saunders. Ltd.. 1 St. Anne's Road. Eastbourne. East Sussex. England BN21 3UN

**Japan**
Holt Saunders. Ltd.. Ichibancho Central Building. 22-1 Ichibancho. 3rd Floor. Chiyodaku. Tokyo. Japan

**Hong Kong, Southeast Asia**
Holt Saunders Asia. Ltd.. 10 Fl. Intercontinental Plaza. 94 Granville Road. Tsim Sha Tsui East. Kowloon. Hong Kong

**Manuscript submissions should be sent to the Editorial Director, Praeger Publishers, 521 Fifth Avenue, New York, NY 10175 USA**

for

Lynn Ellsworth

# ACKNOWLEDGMENTS

For institutional support in Southern Africa, I would like to thank the Social Science Research Council and the Ford Foundation. For institutional support in the United States, I would like to thank Columbia University's Department of History and Institute of African Studies, and the University of Wisconsin's Department of Agricultural Economics. For commenting on the manuscript, I would like to thank Marcia Wright, Graham Irwin, William Hance, Kenneth Shapiro and Morton Rothstein. For showing me the ropes in Botswana, I would like to thank David Jones, Selobatso Masimega and Gary Okihiro. For sharing with me some of her considerable knowledge of the economics of Southern African agriculture, I would like to thank Lynn Ellsworth, my wife.

# CONTENTS

# LIST OF MAPS, FIGURES, AND TABLES

## MAPS

## FIGURES

## TABLES

# 1

# Introduction

But the older agrarian regimes worked as interlocking
systems. It was difficult to take an axe to one part
without destroying the whole.

> — Marc Bloch,
> *French Rural History*

This book presents an economic history of Southern African agriculture from 1800 to 1980. It singles out "the commons" as the most
important factor contributing to the region's present configuration
of successful white farming and stagnant African agriculture. It presents the indigenous African agricultural system as supremely suited
to the economic conditions of the nineteenth century; the technical
requirements of modern commercial agriculture, however, argued for
major changes in this indigenous system. The most important requirement was some form of enclosure of the commons. The British colonial governments that ruled the region judged that sweeping aside
African agriculture was cheaper and easier than changing it. By granting African land to private white farmers, the British enclosed the
commons to produce the checkerboard plots so familiar to commercial farming throughout the world.

Official preference for private ownership over common rights to
farmland is a common feature of agricultural modernization.[1] What
is special about Southern Africa is the indigenous agricultural system's
extreme dependence on its commons and thus its extreme resistance
to full commercialization. Throughout the world's premodern agricultural systems, crop fields have tended to fall under some form of
private ownership while pasture for livestock remained a commons.[2]
There are solid technical and economic reasons for this that have
nothing to do with "traditional" attitudes to land or animals. In
Southern Africa, climate and soil and economic opportunity made
premodern agriculturalists depend overwhelmingly on their livestock

1

and thus on their pastoral commons. Economics, not tradition, prevented them from taking the leap from a commons to the private, enclosed fields and pastures that British authorities demanded. These British officials as well acted on sound economic principles in sweeping aside the thorny problem of adjusting African agriculture to fit their new commercial concerns. They chose the cheaper method of replacing the entire system with a new one.

This decision, to prefer enclosed white farms to the African commons, dates from the mid-nineteenth century. The authorities were unable to enclose all the land, however, for where would the people go? The new white farms could not employ them all, and the region's cities were very small. The mineral discoveries of the late nineteenth century, especially the Johannesburg gold mines, absorbed more of the dispossessed, but overall the British were forced to leave some of the African commons in African hands to accommodate a large part of the African population. On these enclaves, the authorities did try to move African agriculture toward their vision of commercial agriculture. The enormous technical difficulties of transforming so vital a commons, coupled with a population artificially swollen by refugees from enclosed white land, defeated these efforts. That is the Southern Africa we see today: prosperous enclosed white farms and overcrowded African enclaves.

This view of Southern Africa's agricultural history is susceptible to misinterpretation on two major points. First, some readers might see this view as an argument against the economic rationality of African farmers, that the British preferred white farming because Africans' commercial sense was poor. Second, some readers might judge that this view defends apartheid by arguing that technical considerations of agricultural development, rather than racist attitudes or white employers' desire for cheap African labor, motivated land alienation and territorial segregation by race.[3]

As a consequence, this book spends most of its time discussing precisely these two points. First, it takes elaborate pains to explain the economic logic of Southern Africa's indigenous agricultural system. It explains in explicitly economic terms why this commons-based system conflicted with what the British rightly judged to be the fastest route to fully commercial agriculture. Second, this book traces official agricultural policy in Southern Africa, showing how it indeed followed technical considerations of agricultural development above all. By no means is this a defense of the racial segregation that resulted. Rather, this book is valuable for precisely this point, to show how economic policies based on sound technical principles can create vast inequities such as those in Southern Africa.[4]

Demonstrating the first point, that African agriculture made economic sense but conflicted on technical grounds with full commercialization, required intensive field work in the region. No written records preserve enough detail to argue this point forcefully. Anthropologists and official records offer descriptions of agricultural practices and the organization of African society around these practices, but only in recent years have agricultural economists developed models to explain African agricultural systems in strictly economic terms.[5] Field work for this study comprised detailed interviews with the aged inhabitants of one rural area, reconstructing the precise practices and economic organization of agriculture in the nineteenth century, tracing changes in the agricultural system through the twentieth century, composing a descriptive, dynamic model using explicitly economic explanations. The commons emerges from this exercise as the central element of a complex and overwhelmingly sensible agricultural system, technically and economically rational, and well adapted to Southern Africa's grassland environment.

The choice of field work site was an important one. Although African agriculture in Southern Africa has never been homogenous, we can speak of one general indigenous system with these five characteristics: (a) an individual homestead grew grain on private fields and herded its privately owned livestock on pasture shared with others; (b) one homestead loaned livestock to and borrowed them from other homesteads; (c) grain likewise flowed from homestead to homestead through reciprocal arrangements; (d) all those sharing common pasture, centered on a permanent water supply, composed a chiefdom; (e) homesteads traded grain, livestock, and other goods with each other and with other chiefdoms. Although most of these features are still evident today, the alienation of African land for enclosure as white farms, severe overpopulation, significant if not full commercialization, and official efforts to transform African agriculture in the remaining African enclaves have combined to make the present agricultural system in most chiefdoms look quite different from a century ago. The field work for this study required a chiefdom relatively undisturbed, where the economic history of the local agricultural system was simpler to reconstruct because most of it remained intact. Botswana, formerly Bechuanaland, commended itself most strongly on these grounds. Its dominant agricultural system is typically Southern African, exhibiting all five of the main features listed above, and it suffered less alienation and enclosure than most of the rest of the region. The reason for this good fortune is that Botswana is drier and less productive than more densely farmed areas of Southern Africa. The best land became enclosed white farms, the poorest remained in African hands.[6]

The second issue, the technical basis of British agricultural policy, required both local and regional analysis. "Technical" here refers to the physical constraints of geography and technology and the economic constraints of financial costs and returns. Given an area's physical environment and available technology, different types of farming face different costs and returns. The local analysis involved an exploration of how the pressures of commercialization, population growth and official policy affected agriculture in Botswana. The lessons learned on this local level then informed a more general discussion of similar pressures elsewhere in the region, mainly in South Africa but also in Zimbabwe, formerly Rhodesia. Lesotho and Swaziland receive little specific mention but are covered by the general argument, while Mozambique and Namibia fall both outside British rule and under different agricultural systems.

These two points, the economic logic of African agriculture and the technical basis of official agricultural policy, are qualitative issues that defy the increasingly mathematical methodology of American and European economic history. Africa's lower level of economic activity, moreover, has generated far fewer hard data to suit quantitative historical analysis.[7] Yet Southern Africa is the continent's leading industrial region, and so affords more solid numbers than elsewhere in Africa. This study depends both on existing written records and on the reconstruction of African agriculture based on Botswana field work, guided by the theoretical principles of modern agricultural economics. The argument here thus comprises not mathematical or statistical proofs, but careful reasoning supported by a wide variety of evidence that includes quantitative data.[8] Because of the breadth and depth of its subject, this book must summarize most of its evidence rather than present it directly. Footnotes direct the reader to primary and secondary sources. A wide range of data is presented directly, however, in the text and in tables, maps, and figures.

Covering such a long period and a large area, delving in depth into the economic logic of African agriculture and the technical basis of official agricultural policy, this book cannot hope to be a comprehensive economic history of Southern African agriculture. Its purpose is analytic, not encyclopedic, and so it argues points rather than covers ground. Nevertheless, the themes it pursues are valid, indeed crucial, for the region as a whole.

Neither can this book do justice to the host of scholarly controversies that it touches. Some debates are mentioned in the text or footnotes, but overall this study sticks to its own point of view. Pausing to rebut opposing viewpoints would take years more writing and many more pages of what is already a very long project. Furthermore, the entire approach of this book takes sides in perhaps the most important ongoing debate in African economic history. Simply stated, the debate is this: Which economic theory is most appropriate for the historical study of Africa? Neoclassical economic theory now dominates the economic history of the developed world while scholars of other areas resist it. African historians, especially, avoid neoclassical theory for three reasons: first, hard data suitable for quantitative analysis are very scarce; second, many believe that this theory applies only to capitalist economies that generate detailed commercial records; third, some believe that the theory serves the interests of capitalists. Most African economic historians prefer some form of Marx's labor theory of value, arguing that it suits precapitalist or nonmonetary economies better than neoclassical theory does. Many argue further that choosing the labor theory of value serves the interests of workers and peasants rather than of capitalists.[9]

This book endorses neoclassical economics, or, more precisely, microeconomics. "Microeconomics" here simply refers to basic principles of price theory such as the laws of supply and demand and utility maximization.[10] Agricultural economists know that microeconomics can be applied to noncapitalist and nonmonetary economic systems, and that it is mute on the virtues of capitalists, peasants, and workers. This book benefits from my study of both African history and agricultural economics and can be viewed as an experiment in applying the latter to the former. Indeed, recent advances in applying household decision-making models to Africa find a descriptive parallel in this book's discussion of farming in Botswana. In general, this book poses the question, "How far can economic explanations take us in the study of African agricultural history?" This book tries to push economic explanations as far as they can go. Perhaps it is too far, but that is for others to judge.

Despite their focus on major technical issues, the following chapters do cover a very large subject in a very large geographical area over a very long period of time. The discussion is thus a very summary one. Chapter after chapter of summary sometimes makes the main points difficult to follow, so it would do well to outline them here. Chapters 2, 3, and 4 cover the period 1800 to 1900; Chapters 5, 6, and 7 cover 1900 to 1940; and Chapters 8 and 9 cover 1940 to 1980. Chapter 10 briefly discusses the implications of this book for the study of African agricultural economic history.

Chapter 2 introduces the modern world economy as it came to penetrate from the coast to the interior of every continent in the nineteenth century. Britain led the charge, no longer as a mercantile plunderer but as a capitalist free trader. Britain's advantage as the world's first industrial power was best served through open competition and the development of political institutions, both at home and abroad, to prevent the rise of protectionism. Technological improvements in transport, marketing, and communications accelerated in the second half of the century, pushing the modern economy deeper into continental interiors, including Southern Africa's. Where Britain was able to preserve free trade, the development of these new regions followed the principles of comparative advantage. That is, Britain was willing to buy or sell or invest in anything that showed a profit, protecting not even its home industries. The British goal was to let the market rule.

Britain's African conquests began and ended in Southern Africa and spanned the entire nineteenth century. Agriculture offered the first opportunity for commercial development, which poor transportation and communications at first confined to the coast. The extreme south featured a Mediterranean-type climate of dry summers and rainy winters, suitable for the commercial crops of wine grapes and wheat. The rest of Southern Africa, except for desert areas in the west, featured a subtropical or tropical continental climate, with rainy summers and dry winters. This summer rainfall zone was unsuitable for winter wheat and wine grapes without irrigation, while its African inhabitants produced summer sorghum and millet and cattle without irrigation. Because wheat had not penetrated the massive summer rainfall zone of tropical Africa, Africans had no grain suitable for the Mediterranean climate at the tip of the continent. This area was thus empty of settled cultivators and populated instead by nomadic herders when Dutch settlers arrived in the late seventeenth century. These Dutch Boers chased away, killed, or enserfed the nomads of the south and had only begun to expand against the densely settled summer rainfall zone when the British arrived at the beginning of the nineteenth century.

The British promoted free trade and fully commercial land and labor markets. The Boers had previously depended on a variety of racial restrictions to prevent free competition from Africans. Commercial wine farmers in the extreme southwest adjusted and prospered under the British, while southeastern Boers, in a zone of transition between the winter and summer rainfall zones, were unable to raise any grain, fought battle after battle against Africans settled just to their east, and depended on livestock herds that were easily stolen by these same Africans. The British government's final abolition of slavery and enforcement of a fully commercial land market moved these poorer, eastern Boers to escape the modern economy and strike out into the interior.

This 'Great Trek' into the summer rainfall zone faced no major African agrarian empire or state. The Zulu and their numerous offshoots and imitators were able to amass armies of thousands of warriors, but this was a phenomenon of the violent nineteenth century, unsupported by a strong historical economic base. Once defeated, these armies melted back into the landscape of small chiefdoms composed of a few thousand homesteads growing grain and herding cattle. The Boers sometimes negotiated with the heads of the larger armies, but overall their technological superiority, that is, guns and horses, enabled them to claim vast stretches of the summer rainfall zone.

An individual Boer located a permanent water supply, usually a stream or spring, and staked out an enormous claim around it. In this way the best portions of the African commons fell under private Boer control. But one Boer family was unable to farm such a huge spread, so the Boer struck a deal with the former African owners. They planted his field and herded his cattle in return for the right to plant their own fields and herd their own cattle on the land he now claimed. Indeed, he became something of a little chief, blending into the indigenous agricultural system, with his subjects rendering tribute in the form of labor. The Boers' fields and herds were thus scattered among their African tenants'. As the Boer farms were unfenced, the African commons remained unenclosed at least in practice.

The British, however, took advantage of the Boer penetration of the summer rainfall zone by claiming the new Boer territories as British colonies. Assessing the competing African and Boer claims to the land, the British awarded it to the Boers. They registered the Boer claims in record books, proceeded to map them out properly, and issued titles that could be bought and sold. Some Boers fled again this onslaught of a fully commercial land market, but many remained. The British likewise fixed the boundaries of African chiefdoms on the remaining land. Here they faced the problem of enclosing and issuing title to small, scattered crop fields and a sprawling pastoral commons.

Their tentative plan was a gradual one: to subdivide a chiefdom's land along clan lines, then further divide clan land by family, and then finally divide each extended family's allocation among individual members. Eventually no commons would remain, and every individual would hold a negotiable title to a plot of land.

Between the two methods of turning the land into private, enclosed plots, the British clearly favored the faster, cheaper, and simpler one. By recognizing Boer claims to the best land, the British obviated the task of gradually transforming the African agricultural system from an elaborate network of crop fields and communal pasture to a checkerboard of private farms. Subsequent chapters explain why a fully commercial land market of private, fully enclosed plots was impossible to impose on the African agricultural system. Chapter 2 simply points out that the British judged correctly that sweeping African agriculture aside on most of the best land was the fastest route to fully commercial agriculture.

This general British policy, to recognize Boer private claims and try gradually to enclose the remaining African enclaves, dates from the 1840s. The rest of Chapter 2 follows this policy through the century, as the British chased the Boers farther into the interior and then finally leapt ahead to establish Rhodesia. At each step some Boers went along with British demands for fully commercial land and labor markets, while other, generally poorer Boers resisted this imposition. The British demand for competitive markets included, at least at first, the abolition of racial restrictions in these markets. African citizens of Britain's coastal colonies, the Cape and Natal, were legally free to buy the enclosed plots that the Boers carved from the commons and which the British registered. The British pressed for the same rules when they annexed the inland Boer territories of the Orange Free State and Transvaal. Subsequent chapters explain why the British finally approved the reintroduction of racial barriers. Nevertheless, by the end of the nineteenth century most de jure white enclosed land was still de facto part of the African commons, with the indigenous African agricultural system still largely intact on it. Despite the legal enclosure of white commercial farmland, there was virtually no fencing in the nineteenth century and poorer Boer farmers clung to their African tenants despite British attempts to limit farm employment strictly to wage labor.

Chapter 3 introduces the Bechuanaland Protectorate, a drier summer rainfall territory in the deep interior. It became a British colony separate from its white-settler dominated neighbors, South Africa and

Rhodesia. Although a fair portion of Bechuanaland's best land was alienated for enclosed white farms, almost all its inhabitants retained possession of their fields and commons. The 1894 Glen Grey Act of the British Cape Colony, authorizing the survey and registration of all African land, automatically applied to Bechuanaland, but the remoteness of the area and the poverty of its administration postponed any attempt at enforcement. Bechuanaland offers the chance to examine the indigenous Southern African agricultural system in a chiefdom that remained relatively undisturbed by warfare, land alienation, or official land tenure policy. Moreover, the case of Bechuanaland illustrates the technical difficulties faced by a British administration that was immune to white-settler political pressure and committed to African agricultural development.

The chiefdom chosen for detailed examination is the Kwena of southeastern Bechuanaland. The last part of Chapter 3 presents its agricultural geography. Aside from its lower productivity, relative isolation, and undisturbed agricultural system, there was one important difference between the Kwena and most other Southern African chiefdoms. Most of the land recognized by the British as Kwena territory comprised the Kalahari, a sea of sand without permanent surface water. The well-digging technology of the nineteenth century did not allow significant occupation of the Kalahari, but as technology improved in the twentieth century the Kwena were able to expand into it. This movement relieved some of the population pressure that helped cripple agricultural development in most of Southern Africa's other African enclaves.

Chapter 4 presents the Kwena agricultural system as the British found it at the end of the nineteenth century. The entire range of established practices that affected agriculture, from the choice of crops planted to the rules of marriage, reflected the demands of the grassland environment described in the previous chapter. Above all, individuals participated in a host of economic exchanges that bound them intimately to each other in both the production and distribution of grain and livestock. Women, relegated to cultivation, knit themselves into a network of reciprocity that distributed the benefits and spread the risks of grain production widely through the chiefdom. Economic self-interest motivated them: A woman was free to withdraw and concentrate her efforts on only her own field, keeping her harvest wholly to herself. But the uncertainty of rainfall and its erratic spatial distribution made harvests uneven and unpredictable. One woman might do well while another woman's field miles away failed completely. If a woman worked alone and kept all her own harvest, no one would help her when her harvest failed. A woman plotted endless borrowing and lending to provide insurance against bad harvests, to be able to call upon the harvests of others when her own failed. And the smooth lending of hoes, seed, and labor enabled more fields to be planted, thus increasing the total grain harvest produced and distributed within the chiefdom.

Men monopolized herding, but depended on economic reciprocity as much as women did. Cattle depended on rain as much as crops did, not only for the pasture they fed on but also for water to drink. When summer rain fell, cattle herds spread over the land to eat new grass and drink from rain pools; the rainless winter dried these pools and forced the herds to retreat to a few permanent streams or springs. Men scattered their cattle among many herds, through lending and borrowing, as different neighbors occupied different parts of the countryside, which each year received varying and unpredictable amounts of rain. Poor rain or an outbreak of fatal disease in one place thus threatened only part of a man's herd. By spreading risks widely, borrowing and lending cattle followed clear rules of economic self-interest.

Reciprocity did not dictate equality, however. Southern Africa, and especially Bechuanaland, boasted larger, more stratified chiefdoms in the nineteenth century than most of the rest of Africa. Many large chiefdoms date only from that century, as war refugees sought safety in numbers and a strong leader to negotiate with the Boers and the British. Yet in much of the Southern African interior, the mix of crops and livestock, plus the scarcity of permanent water to last through the dry winters, had always argued for the larger settlements of chiefdoms. A close investigation of the rules of cattle lending and inheritance reveals that chiefs were less feudal lords extracting grain harvests from their peasants than descendants of large cattle owners who managed to hold onto their growing herds over generations. Drought destroyed chiefdoms by killing their cattle, and good years created chiefdoms and their chiefs by allowing them to stay in one place and prosper. The source of a chief's wealth was the herd he inherited from his father, multiplied over the years. A chief was a chief because he owned more cattle than his subjects. The natural reproduction of cattle, not a peasant surplus, gave a chief his wealth.

Marriage united women and men, grain and cattle, and again economics clearly motivated the prevailing rules. A woman who reaped consistently bountiful harvests was able to save grain and trade it for cattle, which her husband herded for a fee and which her daughters inherited in return for their labor on her field. This careful accounting between relatives gave young men and women a host of occasional partners, that is, regular borrowers and lenders, by the time they reached the age of marriage. The exchange of cattle to legalize a marriage constituted an elaborate loan from a husband's family to him, from him to his wife's family, rapidly immersing the new couple in a larger and more serious web of reciprocity. This marriage exchange was especially important for the high percentage of unions in the late nineteenth century that involved relative-poor refugees. The exchange of cattle, often as a loan from a sponsor, gave newcomers a family of lenders and borrowers that they had not had a chance to develop as they grew up.

All in all, the rural economy described in Chapter 4 reveals familiar features of premodern agricultural systems throughout the world. From technical details of how many seeds to plant in a field to social details of marriage and inheritance, the rural economy reflected the economic necessity of neighbors to work together to overcome nature. Individuals struggled to plant at the right time, borrow the right number of cattle, make the right marriage, and thus slowly build up the family fortunes until generations later someone would be wealthy enough to establish himself as chief. Self-interest led each and everyone to lend and borrow, but also to seek the best deal for themselves.

Southern Africa's agricultural economy was different from most other premodern rural systems, however, in depending more on livestock than on crops. This was not because the people had not yet evolved to intensive cultivation; rather, the soil was poor, rain was erratic, and cattle fared better. The chiefdom's pasture, its commons, sustained its wealth, its livestock. The entire economy depended on the free movement of herds throughout the commons, with men shifting animals from herd to herd. Drought and disease constantly reduced the herds, and the indigenous system described in Chapter 4 evolved to combat this threat. Dependence on cattle made a chiefdom's members more dependent on each other than in more agrarian societies.

Chapter 5 discusses how commercialization, imported technology, and population pressure changed the agricultural system described in Chapter 4. Overall, Bechuanaland agriculture commercialized quickly and smoothly, with very little disruption of the indigenous system. Fields and cattle had always been privately owned, cattle and grain had always been traded, individuals were free and willing to sell to the new markets. White and Indian traders bought these products and sold them to Southern Africa's growing cities. Three new items of technology especially aided this commercialization: ox-drawn plows planted larger fields; wells blasted with dynamite provided permanent water in new areas; ox-drawn wagons carried plows and grain to and from fields and market. Southern Africa as a whole became the only region of Africa where the plow replaced the hoe as the dominant tool of cultivation. Africans on the south coast began to plow early in the nineteenth century, the plow spread through Bechuanaland at the end of the century, and Africans in Rhodesia, even deeper in the interior, turned to plowing in earnest between the twentieth century's two world wars.

Chapter 5 describes in detail how commercialization changed Kwena agriculture. In addition to changes in cultivation and herding practices, the growing Southern African economy introduced formal wage labor on white farms, in cities, and in the new mines. The ability of young men to migrate to earn money when a harvest failed probably raised the population growth rate by insuring an alternative supply of food. Also, the fluid reciprocity of the indigenous agricultural system gave men, and also women, the flexibility to leave their fields and herds in the hands of relatives and friends in order to seek work for a time.

The most important feature of the agricultural system that did not change was land tenure. Commercial sales of grain and cattle did not create a commercial land market. Fields had always been privately owned, but crop land was plentiful. Every adult was guaranteed a field by chiefdom law, so none had to buy one. As population grew, land shortage first appeared not in grain fields but as overgrazed pasture, as more and more cattle filled it. The pastoral commons did not naturally divide into private plots for obvious reasons: there were not enough permanent water sources for every farm that would result; and every member of the chiefdom had a right to graze animals anywhere, so there was no pre-existing division to convert to full ownership. Land shortage might promote a land market in agricultural systems based on cultivation, but not in Southern Africa's livestock-based system. African agriculture commercialized above its commons, leaving land tenure essentially undisturbed.

In general, the members of the rural economy who prospered from this era of commercialization had already been better off in the previous era. Large cattle owners were able to sell their animals to buy plows, wells and wagons, thereby improving their productivity. Chiefly wealth became especially conspicuous in this era, but government salaries accounted for most of this. On enclosed land, Southern African governments collected a land tax, which was impossible on a commons. So men paid a per capita tax for the use of the chiefdom's land, and the chief collected it.

The adoption of the plow, the production of grain and cattle for sale, the endurance of economic reciprocity, and the strength of the commons were features common to most of African agriculture in the region in the late nineteenth and early twentieth centuries. Indeed, as Chapter 6 recounts, the agricultural system was so strong that it also dominated what the British had confirmed as enclosed white land. Boer farmers continued to depend on the fields and herds of their African tenants. The British promoted full commercialization, demanding that white farmers compensate workers only with wages, not with space to grow crops and herd cattle. Because the British insisted on free trade, grain and livestock imports from America and Australia kept prices low for Southern Africa's white farmers, reducing their ability to pay cash wages or to make the capital investments that the British advocated. Instead, white farmers let African tenants work their own plow teams and plant different plots at precisely the right time, when rain wet each one. The farm owner then collected part of the tenant crop as rent. African cattle moved freely across the invisible, unfenced property lines of white farms, so that the uncommercialized African agricultural system spread its commons across nominally enclosed land.

Chapter 6 discusses in detail the 1903-5 Native Affairs Commission Report, which addressed various official complaints about African agriculture. At this time the British ruled the Southern African territories of South Africa, Rhodesia, Bechuanaland, Swaziland, and Lesotho, all of which feature the same problems of African agriculture re-establishing itself on enclosed land or failing to commercialize fully. The commission acknowledged that Africans were better crop farmers than whites, but that livestock and land tenure were more important concerns. The vast interior grasslands of Southern Africa had exported wool and appeared able also to export beef. Competing on world markets in these products required an entirely different kind of production system than that of African agriculture. Wool and beef required fine rather than hardy animals. Yet better-quality commercial livestock died like flies when drought or disease struck. Producing these more delicate animals involved practices and investments very different from African agriculture's. A fence was crucial to keep the herd segregated and thus safe from disease infection or impregnation by poorer-quality animals from neighboring herds. A fence also enabled a farmer to control the number of animals on the pasture to prevent overgrazing. Disease control, breeding control, pasture control—these three features of modern commercial livestock production conflicted directly with African agriculture. The indigenous system had its own very different methods of managing breeding and disease, involving the selection not of fine commercial animals but of hardy ones, capable of pulling a plow or withstanding drought and disease. Every production practice, from the timing of calving, castration and culling to the scattering of one herd among numerous herders, conflicted with the commercial production system based on delicate, high-value animals.

Perhaps the most important conflict concerned grazing control. African agriculture left all free to herd as many animals as they wished on the commons. There was no indigenous system of controlling pasture to prevent overgrazing. The African agricultural system had evolved over centuries throughout which overgrazing was not a problem. The great population increase of the nineteenth and twentieth centuries, a phenomenon common to the Third World as a whole, raised the spectre of overgrazing. We shall never know whether African agriculture, left on its own, might have developed a solution. As it happened, the British fixed chiefdom boundaries and froze the political system by granting administrative powers to chiefs. The African agricultural system lost any flexibility in land tenure that it might have possessed.

The fence, essential to the kind of commercial production the British demanded, conflicted directly with the commons. Africans continued to breed hardy cattle rather than the fine, delicate creatures that fetched a high price for meat or wool. Where Africans bought enclosed farmland, they quickly reproduced their own system instead of the recommended one. Although most sold some livestock, they fared better by holding on to a large number of animals for plowing and as insurance against economic misfortune. They earned cash by sending out young men to work for wages.

Moreover, by crowding enclosed land with fields and herds of several families, Africans gained immunity from the very land market that the enclosure was supposed to promote. In theory, a land market insured the highest commercial output from a given piece of land, because a farmer who produced below this potential was either unable to pay a market rent or sold out to someone willing to invest in greater commercial production. Africans on private land responded to higher rents or land prices by sending more young men out to earn wages. Moreover, Africans had no incentive to fence the land, for their production practices and the hardy animals they herded made fences unnecessary.

The commission offered several recommendations to reverse African agriculture's encroachment on enclosed land. First, it proposed to end unrestricted racial access to land, a policy that the British had advocated through the nineteenth century. The commission recommended banning African ownership from most enclosed land, lest it all eventually revert to African commons. The British had occasionally acceded to Boer demands for racial restrictions on land purchase, and now the commission gave this policy solid technical support. The commission further recommended that Africans be allowed to purchase some enclosed land, but in limited areas that government authorities could supervise closely, in order to insure that the purchasers operated the farms on recommended principles rather than as an extension of the African commons.

In addition, the commission recommended a variety of legal measures to prevent white owners of enclosed land from simply inviting African tenants, and thus the commons, onto their farms. Africans would be allowed onto white land only as wage employees. On unenclosed enclaves, the commission endorsed the Cape Colony's Glen Grey Act, which promoted registered titles to African crop land but abandoned the hope of ever enclosing the pastoral commons. Several earlier attempts at full enclosure had failed completely. The Glen Grey Act granted each plotholder a permit to graze animals on the surrounding commons; by limiting the number of permits, the act attempted to limit overgrazing. Yet nothing prevented a permit-holder from herding an unlimited number of other people's cattle. The commission was unable to assess the act properly, however, because the act had been in force only a decade and had been applied as yet only to a very few areas.

These recommendations had serious political implications. The British had hitherto promoted nonracial democratic institutions in Southern Africa. All men above a certain level of income and education qualified to vote. In the Cape Colony especially, more and more Africans were managing to qualify. If nineteenth-century British policy continued into the twentieth, Africans would eventually gain enough votes to overturn the ban on African tenancy on and purchase of most enclosed farmland. They would permit the African commons to reconquer the countryside. The commission thus recommended that Africans be allowed to vote only in African areas and be denied the vote in white areas. Cities fell under white land. African areas were to be given parliamentary seats far below their representative proportion. African-elected seats would forever comprise a tiny legislative minority, regardless of the number of African voters.

The commission, then, offered a technically sound blueprint for promoting commercial agricultural development. The social inequity of their scheme was obvious. The British authorities endorsed the commission's report, but enacting it took decades. The rest of Chapter 6 discusses how a modern agricultural industry slowly took shape on enclosed land, despite the end of British rule in the most important territory in the region, South Africa, in 1910. Although a Boer Nationalist Prime Minister came to power in 1924, government policy before World War II conformed to the Native Affairs Commission recommendations. Chapter 6 delves briefly into South African politics to show that the Nationalists of this era opposed the British on issues of protectionism rather than of agricultural policy. The purpose is to argue that racial restrictions on land occupancy enacted during this period sprang not from Nationalist racism but from the technical proposals of the 1903-5 Native Affairs Commission, a creature of the British rather than of the Boers. Technical considerations of commercial development, above all else, motivated agricultural policy.

By World War II, however, official reports revealed that African agriculture still clung resolutely to white land. Fencing advanced rapidly, beef exports became important, but many white land owners still found illegal African tenants a more profitable business than commercial farming. Moreover, the steady growth of manufacturing between the world wars drew Boers into South Africa's cities, leaving their farms occupied entirely by African tenants. The land legally reserved for African occupation, on the other hand, ended the interwar period disastrously overcrowded and overgrazed. Glen Grey land registration and grazing limitation made minimal progress. There was simply too little land for too many people.

Chapter 7 returns to Bechuanaland. Here we can glimpse the commercial development of African agriculture relatively undisturbed by land alienation. The territory remained firmly in British hands before World War II, safe from white settler political influence. The extreme poverty of the Bechuanaland administration, in conjunction with the technical difficulties discussed above, dissuaded the British from expensive experiments to enforce the Glen Grey Act. More than elsewhere in the region, African agriculture in Bechuanaland was left alone.

Chapter 7 examines in turn the territory's participation in Southern Africa's growing cattle, grain, and labor markets. Although its cattle were among the lowest-quality and thus lowest-priced in the region, Bechuanaland did export large numbers to South Africa. Nationalist protectionism after 1924 forced most of these exports into illegal channels. Nevertheless, Bechuanaland was probably Africa's leading per capita exporter of cattle during the colonial era. These exports more than made up for a deficit in the grain trade, whereby Bechuanaland's grain imports consistently exceeded its grain exports. This grain deficit did not reflect a fall in grain production; rather, Bechuanaland producers had always traded cattle for neighbor's grain when their own harvests failed. Now this neighbor was the South African economy.

As for the labor market, Bechuanaland men and women were able to walk or ride the train across the South African border and look for work. The British had enacted severe vagrancy laws, which made unemployment grounds for eviction from town in order to keep the cities free of a potentially troublesome underclass and to promote docility among black workers by making them fear losing their jobs. Before 1940, however, the vagrancy laws were very poorly enforced in the Johannesburg area, which was South Africa's leading employer. By law a Bechuanaland citizen needed an official pass to travel to the city, but if he or she reached Johannesburg without it the city pass office would issue one on the spot. The Johannesburg area did nothing to keep out African workers until after World War II, with the major exception of the gold mines. The mines ceased hiring men on the spot in the early 1930s. Thereafter they relied exclusively on a network of rural recruitment offices that they had begun establishing early in the century. Men who did not want to risk the cost of travel to Johannesburg, and the cost of food and housing while they searched for a job, signed mine recruitment contracts that guaranteed them a fixed number of months work at a fixed wage, plus transport to and from the mine. The mines themselves preferred this contract system because it maintained a constant turnover in their mining barracks, rather than a stable working population that might form strong unions. Most mine work before World War II was so unskilled that the turnover did not hurt productivity. By 1940, after a severe drought in the previous decade drove hordes of men out to seek wage labor, a quarter of all Bechuanaland's working age men were on the mines. Another quarter had been to the mines at least once.

Low-quality cattle exports, sporadic grain surpluses, and unskilled migrant labor did not make for a robust Bechuanaland economy. With such a narrow tax base, the British administration was mostly confined to supervising these three markets. Its first capital investments in agricultural development were boreholes, that is, deep wells drilled with machines, to water cattle walking long distances to market. In 1929 the British Parliament passed its first Colonial Development and Welfare Act, so that grants and loans began to augment the Bechuanaland budget. The 1933 "Pim Report" by a special commissioner outlined a development plan to spend these public funds. This plan advocated the same type of investments in the livestock industry that South Africa had already delivered to its rural districts. The most important of these investments were veterinary services to oversee the cattle trade and expanded water supplies.

British budgetary assistance in the 1930s was too small to make a very large difference, but it initiated a planning process that became very important after World War II. To this very day, most former British African colonies, including Botswana, maintain a separate development budget to which foreign aid donors contribute. And indeed, the British colonial administration throughout the world was one large development agency, subscribing to the very same principles of comparative advantage and free trade as the World Bank does today. The difference of course is that the British colonial authorities did not consult the local population first.

The advent of state development assistance in the 1930s coincided with a boom in private transport in Bechuanaland. Of the territory's two major exports, cattle and migrant labor, the latter was easier to transport in bulk. While cattle continued to walk to the Bechuanaland railway or across the South African border, buses fanned into the countryside to carry miners to and from their home villages. Mine recruitment agencies delivered Bechuanaland's first bus services and built the territory's longest road, 500 kilometers from Maun to the Francistown railhead.

This boom in road traffic did not stimulate more trade in grain, which is easily transported by truck. No single farmer produced enough to fill his own truck, so they sold to traders. And so traders, rather than producers, reaped the transport and handling profits of the grain trade. Unable to help farmers capture a greater share of grain profits, the British tried to help farmers earn more profits by producing more grain. The British hired Agricultural Demonstrators, known as ADs, to promote intensive farming techniques. By 1938 there were 12 ADs in Bechuanaland, one of whom worked in the Kwena chiefdom.

The techniques that the ADs preached were first developed in Rhodesia in the 1920s. In many African enclaves in Southern Africa, overcrowding had already moved beyond overgrazing to an absolute shortage of cropland, a situation that these Rhodesian techniques addressed. Their goal was to raise yields per hectare, to grow more food on less land. They contradicted the principles of indigenous Southern African agriculture, which increased output by planting more hectares. The ADs encouraged farmers to invest money in their fields, to concentrate all their labor and all their capital on a small area. In general, this process required farmers to withdraw from the reciprocal network of borrowing and lending that sustained them through bad years.

Chapter 7 details the conflicts between the intensive, self-reliant techniques advocated by the government and the extensive, inter-dependent agricultural system of the pre-World War II Kwena chiefdom. These conflicts were common to Southern Africa as a whole; greater fertility reduced them, greater land shortage increased them. Before World War II, however, the region's governments spent very little to promote the intensive techniques, so their impact was minimal everywhere. In the Kwena chiefdom, borehole drilling was the government's only effective aid to agricultural development, and it did nothing to intensify agriculture. New boreholes merely allowed the Kwena to plant crops and graze cattle, extensively, in new parts of the chiefdom.

Chapter 8 follows Bechuanaland agriculture into the post-World War II era. Wartime technological advances, especially in the internal combustion engine, combined with a boom in the world economy to stimulate Bechuanaland's struggling agricultural industry. More efficient trucks, tractors, borehole drills, and pumps improved production and marketing to meet rising world demand for agriculture commodities. With greater tax revenue from exports, and more grants and loans from a wealthier postwar British Parliament, the Bechuanaland administration began in earnest the planned agricultural development that the 1933 Pim Report had proposed. The result reveals the priorities and the limitations of a British South African administration committed to free trade and comparative advantage, free of Boer settler political demands. Aside from delivering basic infrastructure to assist agricultural production, marketing, and processing, the postwar Bechuanaland administration renewed its commitment to enclosing the commons.

The livestock industry continued to offer the most promise for commercial development. Bechuanaland's scattered blocks of enclosed white farmland invested in fences, boreholes, trucks, and tractors to achieve a semblance of modern ranching. The government enclosed more Kalahari grassland, adjacent to these older white areas and newly opened up with deep-drilled boreholes. In the early 1950s the volume of medium-quality cattle was large enough for the government to open a modern abattoir in the southeast, along the railway. Value added from this meat factory helped raise prices to producers and allowed the export of beef, frozen and chilled, beyond Southern Africa. Bechuanaland's enclosed farms geared their production expressly for the abattoir, accounting for a proportion of its volume far in excess of their share of the national herd. The government redoubled its efforts to encourage African herders to produce and sell more animals of commercial grade.

Most new government and private boreholes in the Kalahari were in African rather than enclosed white areas. The administration tried to develop rules that would at least partially enclose the commons around them by limiting the number of cattle and cattle owners at each one. A program of fencing and private land registration in these new areas would have been expensive, complicated, and time-consuming, whereas the government was concerned to keep costs down and expand production quickly to fill the abattoir. Therefore, instead of waiting to develop a full enclosure program, the government drilled boreholes and gave them to the chiefdoms. The official rules to limit cattle numbers proved impossible to enforce. The commons simply expanded deeper into the Kalahari. Overgrazing followed closely behind. The government still hoped to establish fully enclosed fenced ranches in the deep Kalahari, but a severe drought in the early 1960s reduced the national herd by one-third. The overgrazing problem suddenly vanished, albeit temporarily. The administration postponed any major enclosure program until the national herd had recovered and there were enough animals to fill new ranches in the Kalahari.

Chapter 8 further explains why African cattle owners on the commons proved unable to benefit from improved marketing and processing facilities as much as ranchers did. Despite high prices paid by the abattoir and government promotion of marketing cooperatives, the percentage of African cattle offered for sale remained virtually unchanged. The requirements of herding on the commons, the demand for cattle for plowing, and the place of cattle in a household's budget combined to prevent commons cattle owners from producing the right kind of animal and selling it at the right time to meet an abattoir quota. They were very small operators in an industry that throughout the world boasts vast economies of scale, especially in drier areas. They could not compete with the large enclosed farms elsewhere in Southern Africa, including Botswana itself.

Postwar financial solvency also allowed the Bechuanaland administration to deliver services for grain marketing and production. Careful study of the grain market, however, convinced the government that a local marketing board would only duplicate the storage facilities that the South African economy already provided. An open customs border between the two territories permitted Bechuanaland to sell grain when it had a surplus and to buy from South Africa in deficit years. Private traders had been making these transactions for decades. The government did try to develop local processing by subsidizing a maize mill alongside the abattoir. The drought of the 1960s immediately eliminated its Bechuanaland maize supply.

Again and again, official attempts at agricultural development faced the economic logic of the status quo. The delivery of marketing and processing services had little impact on an African agricultural system already adapted to the modern economy of the twentieth century. A greatly expanded extension program for grain production likewise had little effect in Bechuanaland, except in the extreme southeast. A combination of economic circumstances, such as the most temperate climate in the country, a low population density because of the absence of permanent surface water before dynamite-blasted wells, and proximity to South African towns, enabled Rolong grain farmers to expand production as the ADs recommended. These successful farmers then moved on to purchase tractors and trucks, which greatly increased their efficiency of planting and transport. Elsewhere in the territory, farmers in crowded districts began to hire tractors for plowing, replacing the cattle that no longer thrived on the overgrazed commons.

Chapter 8 concludes with a profile of the rural poor of Botswana, the independent country that Bechuanaland became in 1966. Surveys of the 1970s reveal the rural poor to be overwhelmingly women. As overcrowding crippled commons agriculture and South African wages rose, men depended less and less on agriculture for their income. Women were less valuable as economic partners. Agricultural success came from owning a private borehole in the Kalahari or owning a tractor, not by supporting a cultivating wife. Men who succeeded in agriculture were generally older and had saved their salaries or wages to invest in boreholes or tractors. Even without men, women struggled to plow and harvest and send their children to school. It is they who depend most on the old system of reciprocity. Wage labor, the self-reliance of the wealthy, and the crowding of the commons have seriously eroded the networks of borrowing and lending in agriculture. But a survey in 1980 in one of the oldest Kalahari villages in Kwena territory reveals that in some places reciprocity is still the rule, with producers borrowing and lending plow cattle, labor, and tools without a cent of cash changing hands.

In Bechuanaland, then, the postwar economic boom brought prosperity primarily to the large enclosed farms despite the government's greater financial ability, and thus willingness, to assist African agricultural development. In addition to the enduring technical conflicts between the African system and fully commercial agriculture, the commons was now so crowded that there was not enough pasture or cropland for each household to produce enough to subsist. Wages from migrant workers kept farm households alive. The Kwena and a few other Bechuanaland chiefdoms relieved some of the pressure by expanding into the Kalahari, but elsewhere in Southern Africa it was simply too late.

Nevertheless, the South African and Rhodesian governments, the richest in the region, set out to transform African land tenure once and for all. In 1954, the Tomlinson Commission offered a development plan for the African enclaves of South Africa. This plan proposed removing half the population from the land and settling them in large villages at the margins of the enclaves, where they could easily migrate for wage jobs. The remaining population would be allocated land in parcels large enough to produce a household's food requirements plus a commercial surplus. Crop fields would be surveyed and registered, each houshold would receive a permit to graze a limited number of animals on the surrounding commons, and, in a program worked out by government agricultural authorities, a subchiefdom would control breeding, pasture, and disease almost as one large communal ranch. This was a compromise between the original British conception of enclosure in the 1840s and the 1894 Glen Grey system.

The all-white South African Parliament rejected the Tomlinson plan because of its cost. The plan required grants and loans from the central government. Instead, its technical program became official policy but proceeded in bits and pieces, funded by the dismally low tax base of the African enclaves themselves. The technical program made technical sense; indeed, its system of private cropland and a defined, enclosed commons occupied communally by a subchiefdom fit well the indigenous agricultural system. The administrative costs of organizing such a tenure system were enormous, however, and by the post-World War II era South Africa's African enclaves were hopelessly crowded. Hence the Tomlinson Commission's chillingly practical recommendation to eliminate half the population from the land. The Tomlinson formula might have worked in the 1840s, obviating British endorsement of Boer land conquests, encouraging the British to leave the land in African hands. But the British government was in no financial position then to absorb the tremendous administrative costs. No, the British chose the simpler, cheaper, faster route.

The Rhodesian government proposed a plan similar to Tomlinson's in the 1950s, but its enduring status as a British colony prevented anything as drastic as removing half the population from the land in the African enclaves. Instead, the government proposed to fix the farming population at its current level, allowing no further crowding, and to redistribute land within the enclaves. The future population excluded from the land would live in villages on the margins of the enclaves where they could migrate to wage jobs, as in South Africa. The government hoped that taking land from large farmers in the enclaves and giving it to sub-subsistence households would enable everyone to become subsistence-plus-surplus farmers as in the Tomlinson model. But the current population in the enclaves turned out to be far greater than the government had estimated, so that giving each farm household equal shares would have made everyone sub-subsistence farmers. The process of registering and redistributing land stirred up nationalist resistance in the African countryside. In the early 1960s the government abandoned the plan.

The postwar success of Bechuanaland's ranches was replicated, and bettered, by the large enclosed farms elsewhere in Southern Africa. In South Africa especially, the tractor at last turned white farms into the fully commercial enterprises that the British had envisioned long before. White landowners no longer needed a myriad of African ox-plow teams to guarantee them a large crop. Hardy plow oxen gave way to more delicate beef animals, one man on a tractor replaced several plow teams. Africans were no longer needed as farmers. They became wage laborers once and for all. The United States achieved a ratio of one tractor for each farm in 1955; South Africa achieved a ratio of one tractor per white farm in 1957.

The success of enclosed farms and the costs and conflicts encountered by postwar attacks on the Southern African commons convinced the independent Botswana government to concentrate its agricultural development efforts on the former. The national herd recovered from the drought of the 1960s, raising again the question of whether further increases in cattle numbers would graze commons or enclosed land. Diamond discoveries and an influx of foreign aid swelled the government's budget, enabling it to bear the administrative costs of further enclosure. In 1975 a new Tribal Grazing Land Act authorized the enclosure of land in the deep Kalahari for ranch development. The new ranches were available for leasing by any Botswana citizen.

Chapter 9 concludes the case study of Kwena agriculture with a glimpse of the new enclosure's progress in the chiefdom's western pastures. The ranch program bypassed the overcrowded commons to enclose land only lightly grazed, which boreholes were still opening up. Even in independent Botswana, then, with an African government and a healthy treasury, there emerged no solution for the overgrazed African commons. Modern technology advanced in leaps and bounds from the early nineteenth century to the 1970s, but the conflicts between the indigenous African agricultural system and fully commercial modern agriculture remained remarkably similar. Again and again, African farmers and government officials faced insurmountable technical and economic problems in the commercialization of African agriculture.

Chapter 10 discusses the implications of this study for African agricultural economic history. Its most important methodological point is that microeconomic theory need not yield to variations of the labor theory of value in explaining noncapitalist economic systems or the political economy of colonial and independent Africa. Agricultural economists routinely analyze nonmonetary resource allocation and state agricultural policy. This study shows how these concerns of agricultural economists apply to Southern Africa.

The above summary presents the main arguments of this book. Before moving on to the detailed discussion in the following chapters, the reader is reminded once more that this study is not a comprehensive economic history of Southern African agriculture. There are gaps in the evidence and gaps in the argument. Overall, the book's purpose is to pursue themes and suggest a synthesis for a wide and complicated subject. It does not pretend to be the last word.

## NOTES

1. See, for example, E. Gonner, *Common Land and Enclosure*, London, 1912; B. Slicher von Bath, *The Agrarian History of Western Europe*, London, 1963; M. Bloch, *French Rural History*, London, 1966; M. Turner, *English Parliamentary Enclosure*, Folkestone, 1980.

2. See K. Parsons et al., *Land Tenure*, Madison, 1956; H. Ruthenberg, *Farming Systems in the Tropics*, Oxford, 1980; A. Duckham and G. Masefield, *Farming Systems of the World*, New York, 1969.

3. "Conservatives" argue that Africans' commercial sense was poor: for example, D. Houghton, *The South African Economy*, London, 1964, and L. Gann, *A History of Southern Rhodesia*, London, 1965. "Liberals" argue that the British bowed to white racialism: for example, M. Wilson and L. Thompson, *The Oxford History of South Africa*, 2 vols., 1969 and 1971, and R. Horwitz, *The Political Economy of South Africa*, London, 1967. "Radicals" argue that the British bowed to white employers: for example, R. Palmer and N. Parsons, *The Roots of Rural Poverty in Central and Southern Africa*, Berkeley, 1977; C. Bundy, *The Rise and Fall of the South African Peasantry*, London, 1979; S. Marks and A. Atmore, *Economy and Society in Pre-Industrial South Africa*, London, 1980.

4. D. Goodfellow made precisely these two points in the 1930s, in *Principles of Economic Sociology*, London, 1939, and *A Modern Economic History of South Africa*, London, 1930.

5. For a review of recent economic research, see C. Eicher and D. Baker, *Research in Agricultural Development in Sub-Saharan Africa*, Michigan State University, 1982. African cattle herding especially has defied formal modeling until recently: see E. Ariza-Nino and K. Shapiro, "Cattle as capital consumables and cash: Modeling of age-of-sale decisions in African pastoral production," in J. Simpson and P. Evangelou, *Livestock Development in Sub-Saharan Africa*, Boulder, 1984.

6. These same factors helped Isaac Schapera, an anthropologist of colonial Bechuanaland, to assemble "the most comprehensive body of knowledge relating to the history, the social and political life and the contemporary situation of any single group of African people. . . . " M. Fortes, "Introduction," in M. Fortes and S. Patterson, *Studies in African Social Anthropology*, London, 1975, p. 3. This present study benefited especially from Schapera's *Handbook of Tswana Law and Custom*, London, 1938, and *Native Land Tenure in the Bechuanaland Protectorate*, Lovedale, 1943.

7. The great difficulties of producing statistically significant results with African agricultural data can be seen in P. Mosley, *The Settler Economies*, Cambridge, 1983.

8. See R. Fogel and G. Elton, *Which Road to the Past?* New Haven, 1983, for a discussion of the use of economic theory in historical research.

9. A succinct summary of these arguments against the use of neoclassical theory in African agricultural economic history is found in C. Meillassoux, "From reproduction to production," *Economy and Society*, 1, 1972. The "radical" Southern African histories cited above, note 3, subscribe to this viewpoint. See also G. Kitching, *Class and Economic Change in Kenya*, New Haven, 1980, and F. Cooper, *From Slaves to Squatters*, New Haven, 1980.

10. The most outstanding use of neoclassical theory in African agricultural history remains A. Hopkins, *An Economic History of West Africa*, New York, 1973, which employs a macroeconomic vent-for-surplus model. See also P. Curtin, *Economic Change in Pre-Colonial Africa*, Madison, 1975, and J. Hogendorn, *Nigerian Groundnut Exports*, New York, 1979.

# 2

# British South Africa, 1800–1900

This chapter explains how the expansion of British commerce during the nineteenth century brought Southern Africa into the world economy. The first part of the chapter singles out some features of the world economy that were to prove important for the region's agricultural development. The second part describes the development of commercial agriculture in the region up to 1860, when British commerce was still confined mostly to the coast. The third part charts Britain's commercial conquest of the interior. This chapter shows in general terms how Britain promoted enclosure and a commercial land market and how local conditions prevented the full implementation of this agricultural program.

## THE WORLD ECONOMY

The world economy in the nineteenth century was largely British. As the world's first industrial power, Britain roamed the seas buying raw materials, selling manufactures and industrial equipment, and investing in commercial enterprises. Its rules of commerce came to follow those prescribed by Adam Smith in the last quarter of the eighteenth century: free trade and comparative advantage increased the wealth of nations, and none more so than Britain's. Other countries bought British machinery and began to industrialize as well, but this competition grew severe only in the last quarter of the nineteenth century. Even then it was these newcomers who protected their infant industries against British products, not the reverse. With a large initial competitive edge, Britain defended open competition—if necessary with its army and navy. Its last domestic barrier to free trade fell in 1846 upon the repeal of the Corn Laws, which had protected British farmers from foreign competition. By 1860, after the forcible opening of China and Japan, Britain's commercial empire extended to every region of the world.[1]

Beyond free trade, Britain demanded that local governments finance and otherwise promote rapid commercial expansion. This spared Britain the cost of direct overseas administration. Where governments proved unable or unwilling to cooperate, Britain set up its own colonial administration. As the nineteenth century progressed, more and more territories failed to satisfy Britain's demands, and so became British colonies. In Africa, most of whose local governments were extremely small and weak, Britain's first and last colonial acquisitions were in the south. There were two British colonies on the Southern African coast as of mid-century. In the 1870s and 1880s Britain's new European industrial rivals, France and Germany, rushed to claim parts of the continent still beyond British influence, moving Britain to do the same. Britain came out the winner by far, owing largely to its conquests in the interior of Southern Africa.[2]

The conquest of the Southern African interior was aided by railways, which pushed into most of the world's continental interiors during the same period. At first exclusively of British manufacture, these railways enabled large-scale world markets in many agricultural products. The greatest expansion of this sort took place in the American Midwest, which railways opened up to extensive wheat production in the 1860s. The loss of men during the Civil War then hastened their replacement with mechanical equipment, especially in reaping and threshing. Milling was quickly mechanized as well, first by joining more and more millstones and speeding the passage of grain through the mill, and then, in the 1880s, by replacing millstones with metal rollers. The main markets for this midwestern flour were the growing cities of eastern America and Britain, although some reached other parts of the world as well.[3]

The new American railways also carried cattle from the vast Great Plains to midwestern slaughterhouses, from which chilled beef packed in ice and salt traveled by rail to eastern cities and then by ship to Britain. Refrigerated railcars and steamships took over this trade in the 1870s. Other areas suitable for extensive livestock production, chiefly Australia and Argentina, were so far from Europe that even refrigerated meat would spoil, and so these two countries pioneered the frozen meat trade. In 1861 the world's first meat freezing plant opened in Sydney; Argentina's first successful shipment of frozen meat arrived in France in 1877 and Australia's arrived in England in 1880.[4]

These technological developments in the world grain and meat markets were to prove important for Southern Africa, whose climate is suitable for both products. Roller milling was especially important, for the region's chief grains were maize, sorghum, and millet, all of whose structures made them difficult and expensive to grind with a millstone into commercial flour. Maize roller mills were introduced at the turn of the century, whereas the commercial milling of sorghum and millet flour was developed only during World War II.[5] Other technological advances were also important for Southern Africa during this period. Dynamite, invented in 1875, sped the development of the region's many mines. The first transatlantic cable was laid in 1865: The telegraph brought instant communication to the world, including Southern Africa, permitting rapid business transactions and modern administration over vast distances.[6]

By later standards, however, the industrial technology that spread through the world in this period was cumbersome, expensive, and inefficient. The steam engine, developed in the eighteenth century, still dominated industry at the end of the nineteenth. It powered factories, railways, and the steamships that eclipsed the sail only in the 1880s. In agriculture, plows and other equipment were still drawn by horses and oxen, which also pulled wagonsful of produce to the new railways. Although the world economy reached every corner of the globe, only Europe, North America, and a few other smaller regions developed very successful manufacturing and agricultural industries.[7] Southern Africa's position is illustrated by the opening of its first railway in 1860. This event put the region far ahead of other parts of sub-Saharan Africa, which received their first railways decades later, beginning with French West Africa in 1881. This 1860 railway was only three kilometers long, however, showing the limits of the region's industrial economy.[8]

As part of the Southern African interior, Botswana became a full member of the world economy only after 1860, when railways pushed inland and the territory became a British colony. Before 1860, however, British commerce in the region had already assumed many of the characteristics that were later to prove important throughout the interior. Perhaps most important, the agricultural policy that Britain applied to the interior was developed in its coastal colonies before 1860.

## COASTAL COLONIES, 1800-1860

As in most of the world, agriculture offered the first opportunities for commercial development in Southern Africa, and the first determinant of agriculture is always the natural environment.[9] The only parts of the African continent lying outside the tropics are the southern portion of Southern Africa and the wide stretch of North Africa, historically and economically part of the Mediterranean and Middle East, although its ties to sub-Saharan Africa are also strong. Latitude is important because temperatures drop as distance from the equator increases, so that most of Southern Africa has a warm subtropical or temperate climate rather than a hot tropical one.

Maps 2.1A and 2.1B give a closer view of the region. Map 2.1A shows its present-day political boundaries, including South Africa's four provinces, namely Transvaal, Natal, Cape Province, and Orange

**Map 2.1A.** Southern Africa: Political Divisions

500 km.

▥ Land above 1500 m.

■ Land above 3000 m.

**Map 2.1B.** Southern Africa: Altitude

Free State. Note that the Tropic of Capricorn divides the region roughly in half, with South Africa almost wholly outside the tropical zone. Altitude is another important determinant of climate, and most of Southern Africa is a rolling plateau, the highest parts of which are shown in Map 2.1B. Higher altitudes have lower temperatures, so that these upper plateau areas are even more temperate than the rest of the region. This is especially important in Zimbabwe, which is entirely within the tropics. The hotter coastal plain below the plateau is narrowest on the west, and widens on the south and east. Natal's coastal lowland is far enough outside the tropics to keep its temperatures relatively low, whereas Mozambique is very much a hot tropical lowland. Lesotho, as Map 2.1B suggests, is very high: Its mountainous slopes are mostly too steep for agriculture.

Map 2.2 shows Southern African rainfall. We can see immediately why the Zambezi is a reasonable boundary for the region. Rainfall increases north of the Tropic of Capricorn toward the equator: Southern

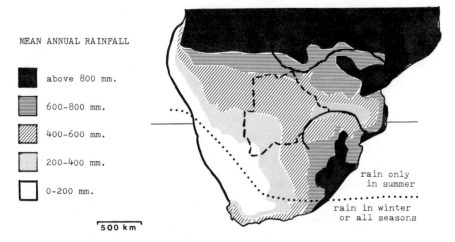

MEAN ANNUAL RAINFALL

- above 800 mm.
- 600-800 mm.
- 400-600 mm.
- 200-400 mm.
- 0-200 mm.

500 km

rain only
in summer

rain in winter
or all seasons

**Map 2.2.** Southern Africa: Rainfall

Africa is drier than equatorial Africa, and this, along with its cooler temperatures, makes the region suitable for livestock. Hot wet weather promotes livestock diseases, which in Southern Africa are greatly reduced, especially at higher altitudes. Also, grass is the dominant vegetation of the world's drier regions, so that Southern Africa is mostly one vast pasture, although most areas have trees and shrubs as well. The crops that thrive in such conditions are also grasses, otherwise known as grains.

Map 2.2 also shows rainy seasons. In all but the southwest, rain falls in the summer and the winters are dry. The main grains of this summer rainfall zone, which includes Botswana, are millet, mostly in wetter areas and in the north; sorghum, mostly in drier areas and in the south; and maize throughout the entire zone. Summer rain in the southwest coast is too slight to support these summer grains. There is winter rain here, however, so that the climate of this coast resembles its mirror image across the equator on the northern coast of the continent, along the Mediterranean.

At the beginning of the nineteenth century, the vast summer rainfall zone had long been occupied, probably for more than a millennium, by Africans who combined hoe cultivation and livestock herding. The densest settlement was in Natal and eastern Cape Province, where rainfall is high but temperatures are lower than in the tropics, so that both cattle and crops fare unusually well. Cultivation is difficult below 400 millimeters rainfall and summer crops cannot grow in the southwest, so that Africans in these areas relied entirely on herding, hunting, and gathering. The winter rainfall zone of the south coast was thus occupied by Africans, but not by cultivators, when the first white settlers arrived there in 1652.[10] These settlers brought a winter grain that had long been a staple of Mediterranean agriculture, but that had been unable to penetrate the thousands of kilometers of summer rainfall lying between North Africa and this southern coast. Now it arrived by ship. When planted in a hot rainy summer, this grain rots in the field. It requires lower temperatures, or lower rainfall, or both. The cool rainy winters of the south coast of Africa suited it well.[11]

The settlers were Dutch, their new capital was Cape Town, and the grain they introduced was wheat. The Dutch established Cape Town, in the extreme southwest of the continent, as a way station to supply fresh food and wine to their ships traveling between Europe and the Indian Ocean. Their settlers, known as Boers, expanded east from Cape Town for more than a century, until they approached the summer rainfall zone, thickly peopled by African cultivators and herders. The roving African hunters, gatherers, and herders of the south coast were no match for the Boers. Even in the African cultivation zone there were no large states to oppose them, but only scores of small chiefdoms.[12] Indeed, the parts of sub-Saharan Africa with the longest histories of large centralized states were the temperate highlands of Ethiopia and the dry southern fringe of the Sahara. These areas had access to the domesticated horse, from Europe and Asia. This item of military technology was far more susceptible to disease than cattle, sheep, and goats, so that the wet tropical zone blocked its southward penetration to the drier temperate areas of Southern Africa. Large kingdoms also arose in the wet tropics and in the south, but these were more difficult to sustain without horses.[13] One of the largest of these was located in southern Zimbabwe, but it had declined by the time the British arrived at the Cape.[14] Like wheat, therefore, the domesticated horse reached the more hospitable climes of Southern Africa in Dutch ships.

Imported horses and imported guns, whose quality was poor at first but improved over time, gave the Boers a direct military advantage over Southern Africa's Africans, who walked and carried spears.[15] They expanded along the south coast, buying and stealing African cattle and driving away the Africans themselves, or pressing them into service as field workers or herders. These servants eventually became known as Coloureds. (The Dutch imported slaves as well, mostly from Madagascar.) The Boers also ranged out northwards, grazing their herds on the dry fringe of the southern coast.[16]

In 1778-81 the Boers fought their first major skirmishes with the African cultivators and herders, known as Xhosa, on their eastern frontier along the coast. They drove the Xhosa east across the Fish River, which the Dutch now declared to be the colony's eastern border. The Boers did not settle permanently on the western side of the river, however, for it was very much a zone of transition between the winter rain area to the west and the summer rain area to the east. Here summer rain was too erratic for summer grains and winter rain was too heavy for winter wheat. Total rainfall was adequate for a good cover of grass, however.[17] Boers from the west and Xhosa from the east both took their cattle to graze there, but neither could establish permanent settlements. Both remained mobile, clashing over pasture and raiding each other's cattle.[18]

In 1795 the British seized Cape Town from the Dutch, in order to secure the strategic Cape sea route. After handing back the colony briefly to the Dutch, they took over its administration completely in 1806 and set about expanding commerce in the region. Although the Boers numbered only 25,000 at the time of the British occupation, their horses and guns made them the likeliest British allies.[19] Yet many Boers proved openly hostile to Britain's attempts to establish its new commercial order. Their grievances were many, and we can divide them into the two general categories of labor and land. As for labor, in 1807 the British abolished the slave trade throughout their empire, including the new Cape Colony. Then in 1828 they declared freely contracted wage labor to be the only legal terms of employment, that is, employers had to offer a specific wage before signing a contract, which could not exceed one year. Servants were free to seek the best contract they could find, from any master. Once signed on, however, breach of contract by a servant was a criminal offense. Then the British abolished slavery in 1833, although the slaves would remain apprentices to their masters until 1838.[20]

The British goal was a free labor market with full racial equality under the law to all citizens of the colony. The Boers had always paid their servants irregularly, and often only with clothing and food. The cost of regular wages was more than many Boers could afford, and many servants elected to remain illegally with their masters, as the alternative was usually no employment at all.[21] Boers themselves feared falling into debt and being forced to seek labor contracts as servants.

Moreover, in 1820 the British landed 4,000 British settlers in the transitional rainfall zone west of the Fish River. These settlers planted wheat, which rotted in the fields, driving most of them off their new farms. Some took work as artisans, many became traders, but all possessed the same vital commercial skill: literacy in English. In 1822 the British declared English to be the sole official language of commerce, education, and administration.[22] The Boers thus faced a labor market in which they had little competitive advantage; its desirable occupations were filled by English-speakers, whereas most Boers possessed no more commercial skills than their former servants or slaves did.

Consequently, the Boers tried to stay outside the labor market by remaining independent farmers. Yet they faced new troubles on the land as well, and not only from higher labor costs. In 1829 the British established a farming settlement of 2,000 Coloureds beyond the Fish border, as a defensive buffer against the Xhosa, on land the Boers wanted for themselves.[23] Other Coloureds had settled on their own beyond the colony's northern border, and in 1834 the British made a treaty with the chief of the Griqua Coloureds across the northeast border, where the transitional rainfall zone shaded into the drier summer rainfall zone.[24] They paid this Griqua chief a salary to keep order and to oversee commerce in the region. War broke out on the Fish border at the end of 1834. Driving back the Xhosa, the British annexed a large area east of the river. Boers hoped to settle this land, but at the end of 1835 the British canceled the annexation. Instead, they began making treaties with the Xhosa chiefs, recognizing their rights to the land, and invited a group of Africans that had not fought in the war to occupy land between the Fish and Keiskamma rivers. These African settlers, known as Mfengu, had settled only recently among the Xhosa. They were refugees from Natal, where the rise of a new African state, the Zulu, spread warfare through most of the summer rainfall zone in the 1820s and 1830s. With no land rights among the Xhosa, the Mfengu had nothing to lose by taking up the British offer, and 17,000 eventually did so.[25] Now if the British extended the colony's border in the future, to the east or to the northeast, thousands of Mfengu and Griqua would join the thousands of former Coloured servants and slaves as the Boers' legal equals. Competition in the land and labor markets would certainly be fierce, with no guarantee that the Boers would emerge as winners.

Boer discontent was greatest in the eastern districts.[26] Government troops now defended these border areas from Xhosa cattle raids, and this sudden safety drew poorer Boers from the west, where only a few valleys were suitable for the production of wine, the colony's only significant export. Cultivation remained difficult in the east, and so these areas remained pastoral. More and more Boers needed more and more land for their herds, attracting more raids, and thus requiring more protection. The Boers here depended on government troops to keep them on the land and out of the labor market; as of 1835, however, the British demonstrated that they were merely keeping order along the colony's borders and had no intention of favoring the Boers in the colony's economy.[27]

In the 1830s, commercial agriculture came to the eastern Cape. The Dutch had tried more than once to introduce Spanish merino wool sheep in the colony. In 1804 they began breeding them on a government farm, which the British continued.[28] Eastern settlers began to buy merinos in the early 1820s.[29] In 1828 the colony exported 40,000 lbs. of wool; in 1835 it exported 216,000 lbs., 80,000 of which came from the east; in 1841 the colony exported 1,017,000 lbs., 611,000 of which came from the east. In the early 1840s, wool surpassed wine as the colony's leading export. In the east during the early 1830s, Boer and British settlers invested large sums of money in wool production. One of the wealthiest eastern Boers, Andries Strockenstrom, spent £2,624 in 1832-34; one eastern British firm spent £4,945. The minimum requirement seems to have been about £750.[30]

For most Boers, however, £750 was a sizable sum, especially in the east, where there had been no previous opportunities for commercial agriculture. Moreover, those unable to invest in merinos suddenly faced losing their farms, because the British also attempted to enforce a commercial land market. The Dutch had granted land on easy terms in the east, at a fixed rent of less than £5 per year. In 1813 the British declared all land in the colony to be government quitrent, that is, the government collected a rent according to the value of the land, and a farmer could be evicted for failure to pay it. The right to use the land could then be bought and sold. Proper surveys and diagrams were required for all farms, at the farmer's expense. A survey cost £80, in advance, and rents were computed by determining the value of the land fully cultivated and fully stocked. That is, an eastern farmer faced a rent assessed according to its value in wool, whether or not he actually owned any merinos.[31]

Surveying so much land was a huge task, however, and a farmer did not have to pay rent until the process was completed. In ten years, the government was able to convert to quitrent only one quarter of the old Dutch titles.[32] This changed in 1828, when the British declared that they would now charge rent on all land, surveyed or not. Land policy changed again in 1832, when London instructed the Cape government to sell all land at public auction, whether held by Dutch or quitrent tenure. That is, a farmer would keep his land only if he was the highest bidder. The Cape government immediately modified this rule to exempt all land applied for before 9 January 1832; nevertheless, this new policy closed the Cape land frontier.[33] For those Boers unable to invest in wool, rents rose above what they were able to pay, and their children faced the prospect of being unable to afford to purchase any land at all.

This is a familiar scenario in the commercialization of agriculture, but the Boers gave it an unusual twist. From 1835 to 1837, some 5,000 of them escaped the colony altogether, accompanied by thousands of Coloured servants, striking out across the northeast border to the temperate highlands of present-day Natal, Transvaal, and Orange Free State. Almost all came from the eastern wool districts. At the end of 1835, a British officer in the border areas reported that one of the most serious grievances of the departing Boers was the "very insecure tenure of their lands. Four-fifths of the landholders are without their title-deeds. . . ."[34]

This Great Trek succeeded not only because the Boers had horses and guns, but also because the summer rainfall zone had recently suffered severe dislocation following the rise of the Zulu. The Boers rode into the breach and defeated the Zulu and their chief rival, the Ndebele, by 1839. After these battles, more than 5,000 more Boers left the Cape. One of the trek's largest parties turned southeast to the Natal coast, seeking independent access to the sea. They carefully chose the best land and staked out farms on the plateau just south of Zulu territory, above the small port of Durban, which a handful of British settlers had established in 1824. British troops now arrived and the British annexed the area that the Boers had claimed. They immediately declared that this new colony of Natal would follow Cape laws, and most of the Boers left in disgust for the deeper interior. The British then signed a treaty, in 1843, recognizing full Zulu ownership of the land north of the colony. In the same year, the British signed two treaties on the northeastern Cape frontier: the first renewed the earlier Griqua treaty; the second enlisted an African chief, Moshoeshoe of the Sotho, in maintaining order and overseeing commerce in his territory. In 1844, the British signed a treaty with the Xhosa as far east as the new Natal border. In 1845, British troops attacked Boers in Griqua territory, defending the 1843 treaty there. As of 1845, within the two colonies of Natal and the Cape there was full racial equality under the law; outside the colonies, the British recognized that surrounding land belonged fully to its Griqua, Xhosa, Sotho, and Zulu occupants.[35]

These were very much emergency measures, however. The Great Trek suddenly forced the British to confront the question of what economic policies to adopt in the vast summer rainfall zone beyond the Cape Colony's borders. The policy they now adopted in Natal guided their actions in later decades throughout this zone, including Botswana. The new colony's first British governor arrived there in December 1845, and in March 1846 an official commission met to decide government land policy. The land commission confirmed as commercial land all the farms that the Boers had staked out and declared them quitrents. The few Boers who remained in Natal did not have to buy their titles, but they did have to pay quitrents. All other farms went up for public sale. As for the area that the Boers claimed but did not stake out, the British declared this Crown Land, also to be offered for sale as quitrents. If they did so, however, Natal's 100,000 African inhabitants would fare poorly at the auction. Indeed, many Boers had sold their farms to British speculators before quitting Natal, and these speculators were eager to buy up more of Natal as well. Africans had even less capital than Boers. Fearing massive dislocation, with Africans rebelling or rushing into Natal's small towns, the government exempted one quarter of the colony from the land market and allocated it for African occupation. These "locations," later known as reserves, were mostly poorer land in the coastal lowland, below the plateau where the Boers had staked out farms.[36]

The British planned to protect the locations from the land market only temporarily, however. As with the Cape Dutch titles before 1832, landholders would first purchase titles to the land they already occupied, that is, without public auction. These titles would then circulate on the market. The Natal government would not charge rent until the survey and registration was completed. In the meantime, African landholders would pay a per capita tax. The government found location title conversion a very difficult task, owing to the nature of African land tenure. One African household both hoed crops and herded cattle; although the crop field was individually owned, it could not be sold, and no rent was charged. Thus, poor farmers could not be evicted to let someone with more capital use the land, as in the British commercial land market. Furthermore, the crop fields were so small and scattered as to make surveying them a very expensive operation. Grazing rights were even more difficult, for the pasture that a household's cattle grazed was not individually owned, but communal.[37] As in most of Southern Africa, each chiefdom claimed a part of Natal as its commons.[38]

Dividing a commons into smaller individual holdings was enormously complicated, expensive, and constituted a drastic change in the African rural economy. This was why the British confirmed the Natal Boer farms as commercial quitrent rather than hand the land back to its former African occupants. In wresting vast areas of good land away from African tenure and staking out large private farms, the Boers accomplished a rapid enclosure of the common. This was a crucial step toward commercial agriculture. Although fences and modern farming methods came much later, eventually these large private farms came to resemble the extensive grain and livestock farms of similar ecological zones in North America, South America, and Australia.[39]

This does not mean that Africans were not responsive to commercial opportunities. On the whole, Africans throughout Southern Africa welcomed British commerce, selling skins, ivory, livestock, and crops for consumer manufactures, clothing, tools, and utensils. Chiefs willingly signed free trade agreements. As we shall see in subsequent chapters, African agriculture operated on rational economic principles that made its producers responsive to commercial incentives. African land tenure made consummate sense in its precommercial economic climate, whereas the British suddenly demanded a system based on private ownership and commercial rent. Again, this is a familiar scenario in the commercialization of agriculture.[40]

In 1860, Natal's governor outlined the first step toward commercial tenure in the African locations. He proposed selling location land at half the current market price for Natal: At two shillings an acre, the locations would sell for a total of £100,000. Each household eventually would receive 25 acres. Fearing "the advances of speculators," he filed this report to his superiors:

> . . .the lands which have been set apart for the Natives of Natal, and which are termed locations, are, generally speaking, so rugged and broken, that they could not be indiscriminately divided into small farms, while at the same time, it is to be observed that the pursuits of the Natives are and will long continue to be pastoral, and large tracts of land, such as they now hold in common, are best suited for the pasturage of their herds. Under these circumstances, the minute division of the locations amongst

individuals, or the granting of unfettered titles to such lands, are at present impracticable. . . . The Secretary for Native Affairs and myself have frequently discussed this subject, and we have concluded that the first step should be the issue of legal or documentary titles to each tribe, or, where the tribe is divided and under different chiefs, to each branch of a tribe. These titles should be vested in trustees, one of which should in all cases be the chief of the tribe. The lands ceded should not be a gift, but each tribe, or branch of a tribe, should be required to purchase the land at a moderate sum per acre, payment for which should be made in yearly instalments extending over a period of about six years; the trustees to have power to divide the land into smaller tracts, and apportion it amongst different sections of the tribe, and, when practicable or expedient, into family holdings and unfettered titles. The trustees should also be enabled to lease or sell portions to individuals of the same tribe, or to lease or sell portions to other natives or colonists with the consent of the majority of the tribe. By this scheme the land would ultimately be divided into farms as small as the physical features of the country will permit, and the Natives be placed in their land tenure on the same footing as the civilized colonist.[41]

The secretary of state in London accepted the governor's plan, while reminding him to take care to avoid excessive cost, popular discontent, and "the aggregation of the natives as distinct masses of population."[42]

As of 1860, therefore, the British had decided upon a land policy in the Southern African summer rainfall zone. They would recognize Boer land claims, thus moving the land one step closer to commercial tenure. Within the commercial land market, land would go to the highest bidder, whether Boer, British, African, or Coloured. Land occupied by Africans beyond the private farms would become reserves, temporarily exempt from the land market, to be moved in steps toward private tenure. Eventually, all land would be commercial, open to purchase by any buyer.

The British quickly took their preference for private tenure beyond Natal into the rest of the summer rainfall zone. In 1848, they annexed all land between the Orange and Vaal rivers, where Boers were still fighting for Griqua and Sotho land. The British awarded the Boers titles to the land they claimed, for which they would now pay quitrent, as in Natal. The British then carved out an area on the Sotho-Griqua border, north of the Orange, as commercial farmland. The remaining areas recognized in the 1843 treaties became Sotho and Griqua reserves.[43] This southern slice of the land was the most valuable in the area at that time, because it was an extension of the wool zone north from the coast.

The British soon found, however, that the cost of administering such a vast area remained greater than the revenue the quitrents yielded. The distant Transvaal, with no opportunities for commercial agriculture, would certainly not pay its way if the British annexed it. In 1852 the British signed a treaty recognizing the independence of the Transvaal Boers, and in 1854 they canceled the 1848 annexation of the area between the Orange and Vaal Rivers. This area became the Orange Free State, whose ownership the British turned over to the Boers. These Boer republics promised to prohibit slavery, and the British promised not to interfere in the republics' internal affairs. The British thus endorsed Boer ownership of the best land in the summer rainfall zone. Although the British did not assume that the land and labor policies of these republics would conform to British desires, in later decades, when they began to show more commercial promise, the British intervened directly in their land and labor markets. In the 1850s, the British were content just to have the Boers stake out their large, privately owned farms, which they bought and sold among themselves.[44]

As for the Cape, another border war ended in 1847 with the British finally annexing a large slice of the densely populated Xhosa summer rainfall zone. The area between the Fish and Keiskamma rivers became part of the Cape, and the area between the Keiskamma and Kei rivers became a separate colony. The latter area, later known as the Ciskei, also joined the Cape in 1865. War raged again in the Ciskei from 1850 to 1853, and the British now embarked upon a full military occupation, building access roads and bridges and carving out one-fifth of the territory for an army settlement.[45]

In the seventy-five years since their first major skirmish with Boers, the Ciskei Xhosa had been denied more and more of their communal pasture across the Fish River, where enclosure as private commercial farms was greatly speeded by the rise of wool in the 1830s and 1840s. The cattle on which the growing Xhosa population depended were confined to a smaller and smaller commons. More and more cattle on less and less pasture left the Ciskei virtually grassless, and now the British marched in to take away even more land. There was nowhere left to graze cattle. British traders offered to buy the herds. Although a few Xhosa sold their cattle, most refused. They killed them instead, in 1856 and 1857. Throughout the Ciskei, Xhosa slaughtered their livestock rather than see them sold and grazed on the very pasture that had once been their commons. Unable to resist any longer, they destroyed the last of their wealth, and thus many of themselves. In

January 1857, the Ciskei Xhosa numbered some 100,000: By June, only one-third remained in the Ciskei; the other two-thirds fled west into the Cape, east across the Kei, or died.[46]

## THE CONQUEST OF THE INTERIOR, 1860-1900

In the mid-1860s, most of Southern Africa's quarter million white residents were still outside the summer rainfall zone: 180,000 were in the Cape Colony; 50,000 were in the two Boer republics; and 18,000 were in Natal.[47] The price of wool fell during the 1860s, slowing its penetration inland, and cotton failed in Natal. The British had hoped for cotton cultivation to raise the value of the small crop fields in Natal's African reserves, and thus speed the development of a commercial land market there.[48] Natal's coast proved well-suited to sugar instead. Large sugar mills of the era required a constant, carefully controlled supply of cane, so that mill companies bought surrounding farm land, leased it out to planters, and then accepted only bulk deliveries at fixed times. Sugar takes eighteen months to ripen in Natal, whereas tropical sugar takes twelve; Natal planters thus faced longer periods of waiting before they received income from a first crop. These demands kept sugar plantations very large and beyond the means of most white farmers, let alone Africans.[49] African location residents did not seek work on the plantations, for they proved able to pay their tax with cattle sales. In 1860, the first Indian contract laborers were imported to work on the new estates.[50]

In the late 1860s, three mineral discoveries drew British commerce inland. Two of these finds were gold, in the eastern Transvaal and near the Tati River in northeast Botswana. The third was diamonds, near the confluence of the Orange and Vaal rivers. The gold proved minor, but the diamonds proved spectacular. The town of Kimberley grew up quickly to service the new diamond fields, where South Africans and European immigrants and capital, mostly British, now flocked. Prospectors spread through the rest of the interior in search of more gold and diamonds. Britain annexed the Kimberley area as a new colony and then, in 1872, granted self-government to the Cape, which was now able to finance its own administration with customs revenue from imports flowing through its ports to Kimberley.[51]

In anticipation of future mineral discoveries, the British proposed a self-governing, self-financing federation from Namibia through Botswana and all of South Africa. The Boer leaders of the Transvaal took out a loan from a Cape bank in order to finance a proper government of their own, but the money dissipated. Africans in the eastern Transvaal then routed a Boer government force, in August 1876. The British responded by annexing the Transvaal in 1877, intending to set up an administration that could oversee the orderly expansion of commerce in the area.[5][2] Toward the same end, in 1879, they turned finally to disband the Zulu army, which fought back and routed the British army once before losing the war.[5][3] Another war flared in 1880 when the Cape government tried to disarm the Sotho, who had acquired a considerable number of rifles.[5][4] Transvaal Boers also began fighting the British in 1881. These rising costs of direct involvement moved the British to abandon their federation plans and to rescind the Transvaal annexation. The British then extended Cape land and labor laws to the Transvaal, including the right of Africans to buy land, and also began to set aside reserves; the Transvaal Boers promised to continue these policies when the British returned their independence in 1881, but they did not.[5][5]

Southern Africa's first railway opened in Durban in 1860, running three kilometers from the port to the town. In the 1870s, the Cape's new legislature financed lines from all three of its ports, in the hope of stimulating commerce in their hinterlands. Natal quickly followed suit. Map 2.3A shows Southern Africa's railways in 1885, the year they reached Kimberley. The Cape trains carried imports inland and picked up a little wool and wheat on the return trip to the coast. Natal's line

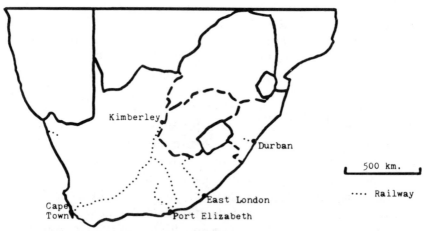

**Map 2.3A.** Southern African Railways: 1885

fared better, carrying coal to Durban for export. Agricultural exports still exceeded mineral exports: The diamond fields were not wealthy enough to sustain this extensive transport system, and this knowledge reduced Britain's willingness to incur further expenses in the region.[56]

As for the domestic market, the railway flooded Kimberley with American wheat flour. Cape farmers were able to sell some wheat to small local water- and steam-powered mills, but summer rainfall farmers found little demand for their sorghum or maize, which millstones could not grind into commercial flour.[57] We have already noted that maize roller mills were not developed until the turn of the century.[58] Moreover, both the Cape and Natal governments refused to grant local produce any advantage in customs tariffs; that is, they refused to protect domestic farmers from overseas competition. Their inland railway rates, on the other hand, gave a small preference to local products.[59]

In 1886, the largest gold fields in the world were discovered in the southern Transvaal. The previous railway investments suddenly paid off, and South Africa's four ports boomed. Ox wagons carried a full range of imports, from mining equipment to flour, from the Cape and Natal rail lines to Johannesburg, the new city at the center of these

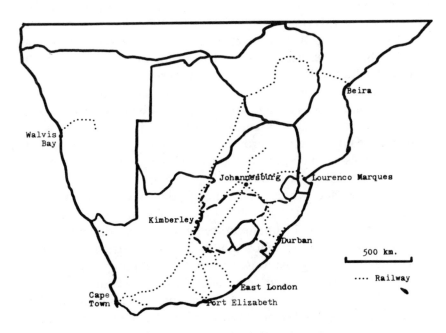

**Map 2.3B.** Southern African Railways: 1902

Rand gold fields. Again, South Africans and European immigrants flocked into the South African interior. The Transvaal Boers hurried to set up a proper administration to oversee the region's development, and their economic policy was severely protectionist. At first they tried to postpone the extension of railways from the four British ports until they could build their own railway, in conjunction with a German-owned company, from the old Portuguese port of Lourenço Marques due east of the Rand.[60]

By 1896, railways linked Johannesburg to all five ports. The Transvaal government insisted that a large percentage of traffic travel over its own Lourenço Marques railway, whose revenues it shared. It charged high tariffs and railway rates on imports, thereby taxing indirectly the gold mines. These policies kept the price of most items considerably higher than free trade and world market prices would have allowed. The mine owners invested vast amounts of European and Kimberley capital in their new companies and objected to the Transvaal government's inefficiency and protectionism. One of their leading complaints was the high cost of dynamite, whose local production the Transvaal government was trying to promote and protect. Because the Rand's surface gold was quickly dug out, deep shafts and tunnels were now required. The Transvaal was probably the world's largest consumer of dynamite at this time.[61]

Meanwhile, the British annexed the rest of Southern Africa outside the Boer republics, with the two major exceptions of Namibia and Mozambique. British annexation proceeded slowly until 1884, when Germany claimed Namibia. As we can see from Maps 2.1 and 2.2, Namibia includes a large area of temperate highland suitable for cattle. Low rainfall makes cultivation very difficult here, however. Namibia's main attractions proved to be minerals, copper in the north and diamonds in the south, although neither rivaled South Africa's mines. In the 1890s, the Germans began to promote ranching on the temperate highland, which they linked to the coast by rail in 1902.[62] In 1904-7 they solved the problem of the African commons by driving out the Herero and Khoi herders in a war of extermination.[63]

As for Mozambique, whose boundaries were settled in 1890, Portugal's claim to its coast was centuries old, although the Zambezi Valley was the only inland area under Portuguese control before the end of the nineteenth century. Mozambique had no valuable minerals, and as a hot, wet tropical lowland, it was poor cattle country. The port of Lourenço Marques was its only apparent asset.[64]

In 1885, the British annexed as a separate colony the present-day northern Cape Province and declared a protectorate over the southern half of present-day Botswana.[65] The leading Tswana chief, Khama of the Ngwato, several times had requested British protection from Boer cattle raids. When the British announced their 1885 annexation, Khama and two other chiefs offered land for British settlers along their borders with the Transvaal, so as to strengthen Britain's commitment to preventing Boers from crossing this border to raid or to claim land. It became increasingly clear to African chiefs that they would soon lose their independence to someone, and the British were known to set aside reserves safe from Boers.[66]

Interior chiefs faced similar pressures from prospectors, speculators, and commercial agents clamoring for a free hand in their territories. In selling a concession to one company, the highest bidder, so to speak, a chief reduced the onslaught to a more manageable scale. Refusal to allow access to some company was out of the question, of course, given the British insistence on open trading borders. The most important concession of the era was in present-day Zimbabwe, where the Ndebele settled after their defeat by the Trek Boers. Prospectors had long pressed north even beyond the area of the 1885 Protectorate, and in 1888 the Ndebele chief, Lobengula, sold a concession to agents of Cecil Rhodes, Kimberley's leading millionaire. In the next year, Rhodes founded the British South Africa Company (BSAC), which the British government now declared its official agent throughout both present-day Botswana and the area claimed by the Ndebele, that is, present-day Zimbabwe, which the BSAC now dubbed Rhodesia.[67]

In 1890 the BSAC marched several hundred white horsemen into the temperate highlands of eastern Rhodesia, which the Ndebele claimed but did not control. Their chief offered this area to the BSAC in the hope of keeping it out of his own chiefdom in the western highlands.[68] The BSAC had wanted control of Botswana, where prospecting failed to yield any valuable minerals, mostly as a base from which to launch this march, and so it now lost interest there. The British government rushed into the breach to set up its own spare administration in the region, in 1890, uniting northern and southern Botswana into the Bechuanaland Protectorate.[69]

The eastern highlands of Rhodesia quickly proved to contain only a few scattered minerals, and so in 1893 the BSAC conquered the Ndebele chiefdom in order to prospect freely there. By the end of

1894, this area also proved disappointing. The BSAC had begun railways to Rhodesia from Kimberley and from the Mozambique coast, but now it stopped their construction. The BSAC had promised land to its settlers, and now more frustrated prospectors turned their eyes to agriculture and began to stake out farms. The BSAC assisted this land grab, also seeking an alternative to mining. In the west, they took the temperate highlands from the Ndebele and gave them two reserves at lower altitude to the north, where disease would soon weaken their cattle. In the east, where chiefdoms were very small and numerous, the BSAC had yet to allocate any reserves at all. The BSAC's main interest shifted back to South Africa, however, which its owners now knew for sure to offer the greatest commercial potential in the region. BSAC investment was intertwined with Rand gold companies and depended on their prosperity now that Rhodesia had failed to pay off.[70]

The BSAC suffered a minor setback in 1895, when Britain handed over its northern Cape colony to the Cape Colony proper, and moved to turn over Bechuanaland's administration to the BSAC. The Protectorate's three leading chiefs sailed to London with their missionary advisors to protest BSAC reserve policy in Rhodesia. The BSAC hastily agreed to recognize the reserve boundaries that the three chiefs demanded, in return for immediate transfer of the land they had offered in 1885 for British settlers. Three strips along the Transvaal border thus became BSAC property, and from one of these, on the last day of 1895, BSAC horsemen attacked the Transvaal.[71]

On one hand, this raid was a disaster for the BSAC. The Transvaal government arrested the invaders before they even reached the Rand. London now halted the transfer of Bechuanaland to Rhodesia. Hearing of the BSAC defeat, Africans in Rhodesia seized the moment to revolt. At this time, rinderpest was spreading through the territory. This was a deadly livestock disease that for several years had been pushing south from Ethiopia. Rinderpest prevented the BSAC from sending horsemen or ox wagons of supplies to reinforce its Rhodesian police. The BSAC now hurried to complete the railway from Kimberley through Bechuanaland to Rhodesia, in 1897.[72] The revolt ended with BSAC troops using dynamite to blast out rock caves where rebels hid.[73] The massive investment required to reconquer Rhodesia committed the BSAC to a long-term policy of making the colony pay, or at least break even, and in 1899 it completed the railway from Mozambique.[74]

On the other hand, the BSAC raid hastened the final confrontation between the British and the Transvaal government. Businessmen of all nationalities agreed that Boer protectionism was strangling the Rand's commercial development. One of the raid's chief backers was a German mine owner, Alfred Beit.[75] Although the Transvaal government made a few adjustments after the raid, the demands of its businessmen were too many. The Boers began to import large numbers of automatic rifles. Full-scale war broke out in 1899, and in 1900 the British annexed the Transvaal and the Orange Free State, whose Boers knew that this final British offensive would revise their position as well. Some Boers from the Cape also joined the fight. The British seized the railways and Boer horsemen ranged the countryside. This was Britain's bloodiest and costliest African colonial war, and it ended with Boer surrender in 1902.[76] Map 2.3B shows Southern Africa in that year, when the conquest of the interior by railways and British commerce was now complete.

In conclusion, then, we can see that the world economy arrived in the Southern African interior in conjunction with a British legal system that promoted commercial land and labor markets. Subsequent chapters describe these markets in greater detail: Here we need only note that the British consistently preferred the private pastures of Boer agriculture to the communal pastures of African agriculture, first at the coast and then in the interior. They exempted the reserves from this market only reluctantly, anticipating their enclosure and commercialization when circumstances permitted. Until then, they left African land laws in the reserves substantially intact. The next chapters follow the penetration of British commerce into the heart of one such interior reserve, describing how it adapted to the new British commercial economy.

## NOTES

1. For England, see P. Deane, *The First Industrial Revolution*, Cambridge, 1965; E. Hobsbawm, *Industry and Empire*, Hammondsworth, 1968, pp. 131-50. For Africa, see J. Gallagher and R. Robinson, "The imperialism of free trade," *EHR*, 6, 1953; R. Robinson and J. Gallagher, *Africa and the Victorians*, London, 1961; R. Louis, *Imperialism: The Robinson and Gallagher Controversy*, New York, 1976.

2. Robinson and Gallagher, *Africa*; Hopkins, *Economic History*, chs. 4-5; P. Cain and A. Hopkins, "The political economy of British expansion overseas, 1750-1914," *EHR*, 53, 1980.

3. E. Hobsbawm, *The Age of Capital*, New York, 1975, ch. 3; F. Talbot, *The Railway Conquest of the World*, London, 1911; H. Fornari, *Bread Upon the Waters: A History of United States Grain Exports*, Nashville, 1973, ch. 3; A. Olmstead, "The mechanization of reaping and mowing in American agricul-

ture, 1833-1870," *JEH*, 35, 1974; J. Storck and W. Teague, *Flour for Man's Bread*, Minneapolis, 1952.

4. J. Critchell and J. Raymond, *A History of the Frozen Meat Trade*, London, 1912, pp. 19, 28-32, 386; T. Morris, "Management and preservation of food," in C. Singer et al., *A History of Technology*, Vol. 5, Oxford, 1958, pp. 47-49.

5. S. Matz, *Cereal Technology*, Westport, 1970, p. 17; O. Brekke, "Corn dry milling industry," in G. Inglett, *Corn: Culture, Processing, Products*, Westport, 1970, p. 262; R. Hahn, "Dry milling and products of grain sorghum," in J. Wall and W. Ross, *Sorghum Production and Utilization*, Westport, 1970, p. 573. Commercial flour milling required removing the grain's germ so that the flour would not spoil during storage and shipment.

6. J. McGrath, "Explosives," p. 293, and C. Jarvis, "The distribution and utilization of electricity," p. 226, in Singer et al., *History*.

7. Hobsbawm, *Age*, pp. 42-60, 174-75.

8. For technical details, see J. Day, *Railways of Southern Africa*, London, 1963; S. Katzenellenbogen, "The miner's frontier, transport and general economic development," in P. Duignan and L. Gann, *Colonialism in Africa: The Economics of Colonialism* (Vol. 4), Cambridge, 1975.

9. The following outline will be familiar to African geographers. See W. Hance, *The Geography of Modern Africa*, New York, 1975, ch. 2; J. Wellington, *Southern Africa*, Cambridge, 1975, vol. 2, Part II; J. Phillips, *Agriculture and Ecology in Africa*, London, 1959. For South Africa proper, see South Africa, Department of Agriculture, *Agro-Economic Survey of the Union*, 1948. Historical geographies include N. Pollock and S. Agnew, *An Historical Geography of South Africa*, New York, 1963; A. Christopher, *Southern Africa*, Folkestone, 1976.

10. See M. Wilson, "The hunters and herders," "The Nguni people," and "The Sotho, Venda and Tsonga," in Wilson and Thompson, *Oxford History*, vol. 1.

11. For a description of cultivation in the early eighteenth century, see P. Kolb, *The Present State of the Cape of Good Hope*, New York, 1968, vol. 2, pp. 67-74.

12. See M. Katzen, "White settlers and the origins of a new society," in Wilson and Thompson, *Oxford History*, vol. 1; L. Guelke, "The white settlers, 1652-1780," and R. Elphick, "The Khoisan to c. 1770," in R. Elphick and H. Gilliomee, *The Shaping of South African Society*, Cape Town, 1979.

13. J. Goody, *Technology, Tradition and the State in Africa*, London, 1971, pp. 32-37; H. Fisher, "'He swalloweth the ground with fierceness and rage': The horse in the Central Sudan," *JAH*, 14, 1973; R. Law, "A West African cavalry state," *JAH*, 16, 1975.

14. P. Garlake, *Great Zimbabwe*, Aylesbury, 1973.

15. S. Marks and A. Atmore, "Firearms in Southern Africa," *JAH*, 12, 1971.

16. Katzen, "White settlers"; Guelke, "White settlers"; J. Armstrong, "The slaves, 1652-1795," in Elphick and Gilliomee, *Shaping*. During this period, German and French immigrants joined the Boers, who also intermarried with Coloureds and slaves.

17. H. Leppan, *The Agricultural Development of Arid and Semi-Arid Regions*, Johannesburg, 1928, pp. 11-12; Goodfellow, *Modern Economic History*, p.

47; J. Chase, *The Cape of Good Hope and the Eastern Province of Algoa Bay*, London, 1843, pp. 20-21, 150.

18. M. Wilson, "Co-operation and conflict: the eastern Cape frontier," in Wilson and Thompson, *Oxford History*, vol. 1; G. Theal, *History of South Africa*, London, Vol. 4, ch. 5.

19. The 1805 census reported 26,000 "Europeans," 30,000 slaves, and 20,000 Coloured servants. Theal, *History*, vol. 5, p. 188.

20. S. Newton-King, "The labour market of the Cape Colony, 1807-1828," in Marks and Atmore, *Economy*; Theal, *History*, vol. 6, ch. 24.

21. Guelke, "White settlers," pp. 58-71.

22. I. Edwards, *The 1820 Settlers in South Africa*, London, 1934; G. Butler, *The 1820 Settlers*, Cape Town, 1974; Theal, *History*, vol. 6, ch. 16.

23. T. Kirk, "The Cape economy and the expropriation of the Kat River settlement," in Marks and Atmore, *Economy*; Theal, *History*, vol. 6, ch. 22.

24. For the border of African cultivating in this area, see M. Legassick, "The northern frontier to 1820," in Elphick and Gilliomee, *Shaping*.

25. J. Galbraith, *Reluctant Empire*, Berkeley, 1963, chs. 3-7; Theal, *History*, vol. 6, chs. 25-29.

26. H. Gilliomee, "The Burgher rebellions on the eastern frontier, 1795-1815," in Elphick and Gilliomee, *Shaping*.

27. H. Gilliomee, "The eastern frontier, 1770-1812," in Elphick and Gilliomee, *Shaping*; J. Voigt, *Fifty Years of the History of the Republic in South Africa*, London, 1899, p. 123. Gilliomee, p. 317, reports that only one quarter of eastern married male Boers held title to land in 1812.

28. Theal, *History*, vol. 5, p. 158.

29. A. Strockenstrom, *Autobiography*, Cape Town, 1887, Vol. 1, p. 206; C. Henning, *Graaf-Reinet*, Cape Town, 1975, pp. 28-29.

30. Chase, *Cape*, pp. 170-89; S. Neumark, *Economic Influences on the South African Frontier*, Stanford, 1957, pp. 165-71; L. Knowles, *The Economic Development of the British Overseas Empire: South Africa* (Vol. 3), London, 1936, p. 19. Theal, *History*, vol. 6, p. 207, reports Cape exports as follows:

Average Annual Exports (£000)

|         | Wine | Wool | Total | % From Port Elizabeth |
|---------|------|------|-------|-----------------------|
| 1836-40 | 92   | 53   | 259   | 18                    |
| 1840-45 | 30   | 100  | 300   | 37                    |

31. Theal, *History*, vol. 5, p. 265; L. Duly, *British Land Policy at the Cape*, Durham, 1968, chs. 3-4.

32. Duly, *British Land*, p. 69, Table 1.

33. Theal, *History*, vol. 6, p. 13; Duly, *British Land*, ch. 7.

34. Theal, *History*, vol. 6, ch. 32. These districts were Beaufort, Graaf-Reinet, Somerset, Albany, and Uitenhage. The most complete study of this exodus is E. Walker, *The Great Trek*, London, 1934.

35. For a summary of these events, see L. Thompson, "Co-operation and conflict: the high veld," and "Co-operation and conflict: the Zulu kingdom and Natal," in Wilson and Thompson, *Oxford History*, vol. 1.

36. Natal Commissioners for Locating the Natives, "Report," in "Papers relating to the settlement of Natal," Great Britain, *Parliamentary Papers*, 42, 1847-48. That the British had no plans to annex African land in the summer rainfall zone before the Trek is apparent from an 1836 London meeting in which land policy for the Cape was discussed: "Report from the Select Committees on the Disposal of Lands in the British Colonies," *Parl. Papers*, 11, 1836.

37. Lieutenant-Governor Scott to Secretary of State, October 1860, in "Despatches from the Governor of Natal," *Parl. Papers*, 36, 1862.

38. For a general survey of Southern Africa, see B. Sansom, "Traditional economic systems," in W. Hammond-Tooke, *The Bantu-Speaking Peoples of Southern Africa*, London, 1974.

39. For technical details, see Leppan, *Agricultural Development*; W. Spafford, *Agriculture in the Temperate and Sub-Tropical Climates of the South*, Adelaide, 1936; A. Duckham and G. Masefield, *Farming Systems of the World*, New York, 1969, chs. 2.4, 2.8; P. Laut, *Agricultural Geography: Mid-Latitude Commercial Agriculture* (Vol. 2), Melbourne, 1969, ch. 2. But see note 3, ch. 9 below.

40. Compare with Gonner, *Common Land*; Turner, *English Parliamentary Enclosure*; Bloch, *French Rural History*, ch. 6; Slicher von Bath, *Agrarian History*, pp. 318-22.

41. Scott to Secretary of State, 1860, "Despatches," *Parl. Papers*, 36, 1862.

42. Secretary of State to Scott, 4 January 1861, in "Despatches," *Parl. Papers*, 36, 1862.

43. Theal, *History*, vol. 7, chs. 54-55.

44. Theal, *History*, vol. 7, chs. 56-59; Thompson, "The high veld," pp. 405-24. For the fate of the Griqua, see R. Ross, *Adam Kok's Griqua*, Cambridge, 1976. As we have seen in the eastern Cape, and shall see again in later chapters, the Boers did not necessarily use the land as private plots, but rather moved their herds over a wider countryside in much the same way Africans did. *De jure* private ownership, however, was a crucial step toward *de facto* private use.

45. See Theal, *History*, vol. 7, Chart 11, for a map of these new boundaries.

46. Theal, *History*, vol. 7, ch. 50. For a missionary's eyewitness account of the cattle-killing, see C. Brownlee, *Reminiscences of Kaffir Life and History*, Lovedale, 1896. For cattle sales during the panic, see J. Rutherford, *Sir George Grey*, London, 1961, p. 349. A lung-sickness epidemic spread from the Cape and began to kill Ciskei cattle in 1855: the Ciskei is good sheep country as well, so perhaps the Xhosa here were clearing their pastures in order to fill them with valuable merinos, which Brownlee in fact distributed to them after the cattle-killing.

47. D. Houghton, "Economic development, 1865-1965," in Wilson and Thompson, *Oxford History*, vol. 2, pp. 1-7.

48. Natal Commissioners, "Report," *Parl. Papers*, 42, 1847-48.

49. South African Railways and Harbours, *Farming Opportunities in the Union of South Africa*, 1926, ch. 2; Houghton, "Economic development," pp. 1-9; Theal, *History*, vol. 8, ch. 70.

50. F. Wilson, "Farming, 1866-1966," in Wilson and Thompson, *Oxford History*, vol. 2, p. 118.

51. T. Barnes, *The Gold Regions of Southeast Africa*, London, 1877; Theal, *History*, vol. 9, chs. 84-85; L. Thompson, "The subjection of the African chiefdoms," pp. 253-57, and T. Davenport, "The consolidation of a new society: The Cape Colony," in Wilson and Thompson, *Oxford History*, vol. 2.

52. Theal, *History*, vol. 10, ch. 11; Thompson, "Great Britain and the Afrikaner republics," in Wilson and Thompson, *Oxford History*, vol. 2, pp. 292-300.

53. Theal, *History*, vol. 10, chs. 13-14; Thompson, "Subjection," pp. 261-67.

54. Theal, *History*, vol. 11, ch. 17; Thompson, "Subjection," pp. 267-71.

55. Theal, *History*, vol. 11, chs. 19-20; Thompson, "Great Britain," pp. 298-300; C. deKiewiet, *The Imperial Factor in South Africa*, New York, 1966.

56. J. van der Poel, *Railways and Customs Policy in South Africa*, London, 1933, ch. 1; C. Schumann, *Structural Changes and South African Business Cycles*, London, 1938, p. 44.

57. Wilson, "Farming," p. 114.

58. There was enough winter rain to grow wheat in the cool uplands of the area that the British had recognized briefly as Sotho land in 1843. This area is unique in Southern Africa for its natural fertilization: Rain water washes minerals from the local lime phosphate rocks into the soil. Thomas, *Agricultural and Pastoral Prospects*, p. 228.

59. Van der Poel, *Railway*, p. 17.

60. The Transvaal government also collected high direct taxes from the mining companies. Van der Poel, *Railway*, chs. 2-6; J. Van-Helten, "German capital, the Netherlands Railway Company and the political economy of the Transvaal," *JAH*, 19, 1978.

61. Van der Poel, *Railway*, chs. 2-6; "Papers relating to the complaints of British subjects in the South African Republic," *Parl. Papers*, command 9345, 1899, especially p. 7.

62. R. Logan, "Land utilization in the arid regions of Southwest Africa," in L. Stamp, *A History of Land Use in Arid Regions*, Paris, 1961.

63. On the agricultural origins of the German assault, see H. Bley, "Social discord in South West Africa," in P. Gifford and W. Louis, *Britain and Germany in Africa*, New Haven, 1967, pp. 613-18.

64. E. Axelson, *Portugal and the Scramble for Africa*, Johannesburg, 1967; Van der Poel, *Railway*, pp. 53-54. Some of the original Trek Boers had aimed at Lourenço Marques as an alternative port to Durban, but livestock disease prevented them from establishing a trade route.

65. For the northern Cape, see A. Dachs, "Missionary imperialism—the case of Bechuanaland," *JAH*, 13, 1972.

66. A. Sillery, *Founding a Protectorate*, The Hague, 1965; A. Sillery, *John Mackenzie of Bechuanaland*, Cape Town, 1970, pp. 55, 129-30; A. Dachs, *The Road to the North*, Salisbury, 1969.

67. J. Galbraith, *Crown and Charter*, Berkeley, 1974, chs. 4-8.

68. R. Brown, "Aspects of the scramble for Matabeleland," in E. Stokes and R. Brown, *The Zambesian Past*, Manchester, 1966, pp. 86-90.

69. Galbraith, *Crown*, chs. 4-8; A. Dachs, "Rhodesia's grasp for Bechuanaland," *RH* 2, 1971; Sillery, *Founding*, chs. 11-12. Also in 1890, the BSAC bought a concession from a prominent chief across the Zambezi, and the British soon annexed this area too, which eventually became part of Northern Rhodesia.

70. I. Phimister, "Rhodes, Rhodesia and the Rand," *JSAS*, 1, 1974; R. Palmer, *Land and Racial Domination in Rhodesia*, Berkeley, 1977, pp. 66-71. The BSAC set aside these reserves only at the insistence of the British government.
71. Sillery, *Founding*, ch. 18.
72. Phimister, "Rhodes"; C. van Onselen, "Reactions to rinderpest in Southern Africa," *JAH*, 13, 1972.
73. T. Ranger, *Revolt in Southern Rhodesia*, London, 1967, p. 298.
74. Phimister, "Rhodes."
75. G. Blainey, "The lost causes of the Jameson Raid," *EHR*, 18, 1965. For Boer and American opposition to the Transvaal government, see C. Gordon, *The Growth of Boer Opposition to Kruger*, Cape Town, 1970, and T. Noer, *Briton, Boer and Yankee*, Kent, 1979.
76. See the comprehensive volume edited by P. Warwick, *The South African War*, London, 1980.

# 3

# The Bechuanaland Protectorate

This chapter introduces the case study of a Southern African rural economy. It describes the natural resources of the Bechuanaland Protectorate, situates its chiefdoms on the land, and then explains how the new British administration applied its coastal land policy to Bechuanaland. Finally, it presents the Kwena chiefdom and its territory, the Kweneng.

## CHIEFDOMS

"Bechuanaland" is an anglicization of "land of the Tswana," rendered in the Tswana language itself as "Botswana." In the nineteenth and twentieth centuries, the name Tswana came to denote the chiefdoms of most of Botswana, northern Cape, western Transvaal, and northwest Free State, whose language and economic organization were very similar. The northern and southern Sotho who occupied the Free State, Transvaal, and Lesotho were also closely related to the Tswana. Although most of Southern Africa shared the general characteristics of the Kweneng economy, such as cattle herding on communal pasture, many of its details were common to a large portion of the region as well.[1]

We can see Botswana's position within Southern Africa by returning for a moment to Maps 2.1 and 2.2. As the country lies astride the Tropic of Capricorn, the north is more tropical and the south is subtropical. Map 2.1 shows that Botswana's plateau does not contain any temperate highlands. Map 2.2 shows that Botswana is on the drier end of the summer rainfall zone. Botswana is dry enough for live-stock diseases to be reduced and for grass to dominate the natural vegetation, yet it is not far enough outside the tropics, nor is it high enough, to qualify as prime cattle country like the temperate high-lands around it, where livestock diseases are much less prevalent. Botswana is thus more dependent on cattle than most of the rest of the Southern African summer rainfall zone not because its climate is more hospitable, but because its lower rainfall makes crop cultivation more difficult.[2]

Map 3.1 shows the geography of Botswana in greater detail. The most striking feature that this map shows is the cover of sandveld in all but the southeast. This sandveld is a surface layer of coarse sand, a hundred meters deep in places, covering what would otherwise be

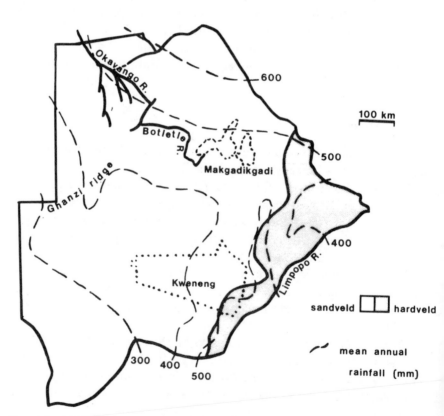

**Map 3.1.** Botswana: Rainfall and Hydrology

surface rocks. Because rainwater sinks quickly into this deep sand, there is no river or other perennial surface water in the sandveld, with one unusual exception. The Okavango River rises in the distant Angolan highlands and pours vast volumes of water into the sands of northwest Botswana, feeding as well the Botletle River and occasionally the Makgadikgadi salt lakes. This well-watered but still sandy northwestern part of Botswana is known as Ngamiland. The southern fringe of the Okavango and the Botletle provide water for cattle to drink, but the delta itself is so wet that livestock diseases thrive there. The moist hot climate above 550 mm. or so across the northern tip of Botswana also supports diseases and keeps livestock numbers low.[3]

Another important sandveld feature is the Ghanzi limestone ridge in the west, rising up through the sand to hold water very near the surface. Beyond the Okavango and Ghanzi, the vast sandveld south of 500 mm. rainfall is known as the Kalahari Desert. This is not a true desert, which must receive less than 250 mm. annual rainfall. The Kalahari receives enough rain to support a continuous cover of grass and low scattered trees, except in the extreme southwest of the country and on into Namibia and South Africa, where rainfall drops below 250 mm. and sand dunes are found.[4] Rather, the Kalahari is called a desert because it has no permanent surface water. Rainwater does collect in pools and depressions in the sand during the summer, only to evaporate during the dry winter. Indeed, the name Kalahari comes from the Tswana verb *go kgala*, which means "to dry up," and in the nineteenth century it earned the English name "Great Thirstland."[5]

In the hardveld shown in Map 3.1, the surface rocks are covered by a normal layer of soil, as in the rest of the Southern African summer rainfall zone. Some of the rocks press above the surface, in some places to form small chains of low hills. The rain that falls here in summer soaks into the soil right down to the rock layer, forcing some water to run off, forming streams and small rivers flowing east into the Limpopo. Although none of these hardveld rivers flows all year round, many have bends and twists where pools of water remain through the dry winter. The same is true of the Botletle, whereas the Okavango never stops flowing.[6]

The soils of Botswana follow the same general hardveld-sandveld division shown in Map. 3.1. Most of the country fulfills the minimum requirements of arability: soil deep enough to raise a crop, with a suitable chemical composition; slopes that are not so steep that the soil washes away when disturbed by a hoe or plow; sufficient rain for a crop to grow. Almost all the sandveld above 400 mm. or so is thus arable, although barely so. The hardveld is more hospitable for cultivation, but even here soils are often rocky or sandy and almost all are very old, and thus worn out.[7] Africa as a whole is a very old continent, that is, its surface has not been renewed in recent geological time by volcanic flows or inland lakes dropping sediment and then drying to leave deep beds of new soil. Most of the nutrients in African soils have washed away over the centuries, and in drier areas, such as Botswana, the sparse vegetation returns very little humus to the soil. The hardveld's flat terrain and poor but arable soils are characteristic of most of Southern Africa.[8]

The vegetation of Botswana is almost exclusively savanna. Woody trees and shrubs are scattered through a coarse cover of grass, which absorbs rain water quickly and leaves little excess for more woody plants to grow. Wetter savannas, as in Botswana's extreme north, have more trees and shrubs because there is more rain for these woody plants, whose leafy canopies block sunlight from the shorter grasses. If there is enough rain, as in the Congo forest far to the north, woody plants will eliminate grasses altogether. Human exploitation favors grasses in the wetter savanna, where burning and clearing fields help to keep the woody plants at bay.[9] In drier savannas below 600 mm. rainfall, as in Botswana, human exploitation tends not to assist grasses but to eliminate them. Around water points with excessive livestock populations, grasses are eaten so fast as to deprive woody plants of rainwater, so that shrubs encroach quickly onto the pasture. In extreme cases, so many animal hooves trample grass and shrubs alike that they leave only a bare expanse of soil or sand.[10]

We can see from this geographical review that water has always been the most crucial determinant of agriculture in Botswana. Rainfall helped determine the level of cattle diseases, the amount of grass for pasture, and of course, the reliability of cultivation. Surface water determined whether human and livestock populations could occupy an area: Despite its arability and grass cover, the Kalahari had no surface water for cultivators, herders, or herds to drink. Sand wells dug in Kalahari depressions supported some permanent settlement, but these were unreliable and very few. After the summer rain, rain pools and wells began to dry up throughout the dry savanna. Only the Okavango and pools in the hardveld rivers and the Botletle reliably bore water through the dry winter.

At the beginning of the nineteenth century, the hardveld and southern Ngamiland were the only parts of Botswana with sizable populations. The northern tip of the hardveld was occupied by Shona-speakers, the dominant language group through most of present-day Zimbabwe and on into southern Mozambique. Southern Ngamiland and the rest of the hardveld were occupied by Tswana chiefdoms. Both the Shona and Tswana herded livestock and planted crops. The northern tip of the country was sparsely cultivated by groups spreading south from Central Africa, but disease prevented cattle-keeping here. Most of the rest of the sandveld was occupied by scattered bands of Sarwa, commonly termed "Bushmen," who hunted game, gathered wild foods, and participated not at all in agriculture. The eastern fringe of the sandveld was occupied by Kgalagari-speakers, whose ancestors had occupied the hardveld before the Tswana arrived a few centuries before. Although they planted a few crops, the Kgalagari were chiefly herders. Their language is very similar to Tswana, although the two are not mutually intelligible.[11]

Except for the Tswana in southern Ngamiland, we can describe Tswana territory as the southeast quarter of Botswana. They remained mostly on the hardveld, but also ranged out to herd their cattle at sand wells in the sandveld. This pushed some Kgalagari farther into the desert, but some remained in the eastern sandveld as herders of Tswana stock. The Tswana claim always to have lived in large villages: Every member of a chiefdom was supposed to have a house in its capital village. Although we do not know whether this was always the case, the first missionaries and travelers to visit the southernmost Tswana, in present-day north Cape, reported that this was so at the beginning of the nineteenth century. We do not know how many Tswana chiefdoms were present in Botswana proper at this time, for before visitors could count them the Zulu and Boers exploded into the interior.[12]

Although the hardveld suffered repeated raids, neither African nor Boer raiders found the area desirable for permanent settlement, and so the Botswana hardveld was safer than areas to the east and south. Thousands of refugees, most but not all Tswana-speaking, fled to the margins of the Kalahari, where most of them joined one of the three Tswana chiefdoms that rose to prominence during this period: the Kwena of the Kweneng, the Ngwato north of the Kweneng, and the Ngwaketse to the south. The Tawana chiefdom of southern Ngamiland also drew refugees.[13]

English- and Dutch-speaking ox-wagon traders followed in the 1840s, pushing north along the eastern hardveld to exchange ivory and skins for simple manufactures and guns. Missionaries pushed north as well. In the 1850s, the Kweneng's big game was shot out, and the gun-game-goods trade moved on into Ngwato territory. Then Tati in the northeast hardveld became the site of one of the two minor gold discoveries in the late 1860s that drew prospectors deep into the Southern African interior, along the hardveld wagon road. Moreover, Ngamiland to the northwest and Zimbabwe to the northeast still teemed with game. In the following decades, the northernmost entrepot of this booming trade route was the capital village of the Ngwato, whose chief Khama used his position to pull together several times more guns, refugees, game products, and trade goods than neighboring chiefs had done.[14]

Refugees continued to enter the hardveld, and many now came as large groups including the Kgatla and Tlokwa chiefdoms, which settled east of the Kwena, and the Malete chiefdom, which settled east of the Ngwaketse. When Britain declared the Protectorate in 1885, the Ngwato, Kwena, and Ngwaketse chiefs took the opportunity to claim as much territory as possible in return for cooperating with the British, aside from the three strips that they offered for British settlement along the Transvaal border. These 1885 claims served as the basis for the chiefs' demand for reserves when the British government moved to hand over the Protectorate to the BSAC. Khama's Ngwato claim grew substantially over these ten years: In 1885 it was about the same size as the Kwena claim, whereas in 1895, it was some three times larger.[15] The British also awarded reserves to the Tawana and Kgatla chiefdoms. They completed marking out these five reserves with beacons in 1899, the same year that they started collecting a male per capita tax instead of a land rent. As of 1900, then, the Kweneng had become a reserve on the Natal model.[16]

## RANCHES AND RESERVES

Map 3.2 shows the Bechuanaland Protectorate as it stood in the third and fourth decades of the twentieth century. We can see the five reserves defined at the end of the previous century, but there are several other divisions as well. Before turning to the Kweneng, this chapter fills in the rest of the Protectorate map and introduces some of the general features of British rule that affected all reserves in this period.

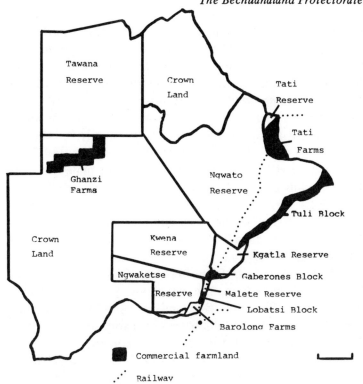

**Map 3.2** The Bechuanaland Protectorate, 1940

From 1880, the Ndebele chief awarded concessions to individual companies in the Tati area, all of which ended up in the hands of the Tati Company. The Shona-speaking inhabitants of the area, plus some recent Tswana refugees, paid rent to the company as tenants. The British confirmed the company's ownership of the land in 1911, on the condition that it set aside a reserve where tenants could claim land, free of charge, if they so desired. The government promised to pay the company £1,000 a year for the loss of this reserve land. Tati Company land and the Tati Reserve are both marked on Map 3.2.[17]

Three other segments of the eastern hardveld became commercial farmland: the Tuli, Gaberones, and Lobatsi Blocks. These were the three strips of land that the Ngwato, Kwena, and Ngwaketse chiefs offered for British settlement in 1885 and which the BSAC demanded in 1895. In 1905 the government formally granted them to the BSAC.[18] The other commercial farmland marked on Map 3.2 is on the Ghanzi limestone ridge, where water lies close to the surface beneath the Kalahari sand. In 1894 the BSAC bought a concession from the Tawana chief and enlisted a party of landless Boers to occupy Ngamiland, but prospecting yielded nothing there and the BSAC lost interest. The land-hungry Boers did not, however, and so the BSAC granted them land titles and an advance party made its own way up to the area, under Protectorate government escort, only to be turned away by the Tawana chief. The government then sent them to Ghanzi instead. The main party, comprising some 55 adult males and their dependants, arrived in 1898.[19]

Although these five areas of commercial land occupied only a small percentage of Bechuanaland, they comprised a much larger proportion of pasture areas accessible to permanent water. Although the hardveld commercial blocks had a number of streams flowing through them, the settlers who took up farms here relied also on wells blasted into the surface rock with dynamite, which also yielded water in the Ghanzi limestone ridge. The sandveld proper was immune to dynamite, except at a few sites where rocklike formations appeared in the sand.

In 1909 the Malete received their own reserve, and in the following year the government declared the Crown Lands shown on Map 3.2. The Tlokwa also received a reserve, but this was so small that it cannot be shown on the map. Arriving in the Kweneng in 1887, the Tlokwa found that the land they occupied was part of that offered for British settlement, which became the Gaberones Block in 1905. The government proposed to move the Tlokwa to the northeast Kweneng sandveld, but they refused to go. Instead, they remained on a small reserve of less than 200 square kilometers, paying their tax to the BSAC, as rent. In the early 1930s the BSAC gave this reserve to the government, which declared it an official reserve in 1933.[20]

The last area on Map 3.2, the Barolong Farms, was a special sort of reserve. The Rolong chief, Montshiwa, had his capital village near Mafeking in the northern Cape just across the Protectorate's southeast border. Pressed by white settlers claiming his chiefdom's land in the Cape, Montshiwa tried to divide his remaining land into private plots, whose boundaries could be clearly marked. That is, he wanted to enclose his own commons, so as to prevent more white settlers from claiming the uncultivated communal pasture between crop fields. After the British annexed the north Cape in 1885, they recognized most of the white land claims but not Montshiwa's enclosure, fearing that the land titles would quickly be sold to white settlers or speculators, leaving the Rolong with no land at all. They made an exception for the less valuable Rolong land in the southeast Protectorate, however, and in 1895 this was divided into 41 plots of 3,000 hectares each. The prominent Rolong who received the leases could not sell them to non-Rolong and paid an annual rent to the chief.[21]

These large Rolong plots were farms only in name, however. Poor market prospects and high capital requirements made large-scale farming beyond the means of their owners. The Barolong Farms remained a reserve. The fully commercial farmlands of the four hardveld blocks and Ghanzi faced similar difficulties, and so they were slow to fill with settlers. The first farm the BSAC rented out was 5,000 hectares in the Lobatsi Block: the settler was to put up £4,000 capital and the BSAC would supply £16,000, for fences and other essential ranching equipment. This was an experiment, to see whether ranching paid.[22]

Later chapters discuss the variety of reasons why Bechuanaland could not sustain such commercial ranches in the pre-World War II era. Those settlers who occupied eastern block farms did so mostly to establish holding grounds for cattle that they bought from the reserves and sold in South Africa. As for the Ghanzi farms, the Kalahari cut them off almost completely from the South African market. Some Boers could not even pay the £5 to £6 annual quitrent on their farms, whereupon the government evicted them.[23] The BSAC also requested transfer of the Crown Lands as commercial ranchland; the government replied that it would only accept applications for specific plots, accompanied by surveys and farm plans and provisions for permanent water supplies. That is, the government refused the request until the BSAC could prove that the land would be fully utilized as commercial ranches.[24]

Because there were not enough commercial opportunities even for the existing commercial farmlands, the Protectorate government postponed the question of extending private tenure into the reserves. The administration did not even contemplate to undertake the great costs of survey and registration until 1940. The effect of commerce on the rural economy was moderated by the system of indirect rule, which left most local administration in the hands of local chiefs who governed through their own laws and customs. Most of the essential features of the rural economy were thus left relatively intact, while the government's administrative costs were greatly reduced.[25] The administration was so poor that its headquarters remained in Mafeking,

Bechuanaland's railhead in the Cape, where transport and other costs were much lower than if it tried to build a new town somewhere in the Protectorate.[26]

Bechuanaland's chiefs thus collected the tax, at first keeping a percentage and later receiving salaries, and tried civil and criminal cases by local law. A British official was always available for appeal, however, and in 1934 the government curbed some of the powers of the chiefs, who is some areas had exceeded their precolonial powers. Nevertheless, the most important laws for our purposes, especially those involving land tenure and cattle ownership, remained essentially the same as they were in the nineteenth century, although we shall note a number of changes as well.[27]

## THE KWENENG

As Map 3.3 shows, the Kweneng displays the typical sandveld-hardveld pattern of Botswana's southeastern quarter, where the Tswana population is concentrated. According to Isaac Schapera, the Kwena chiefdom has operated on essentially the same principles as neighboring Botswana chiefdoms have done. Although Schapera's work was based on research in the Kgatla and Ngwato chiefdoms, he

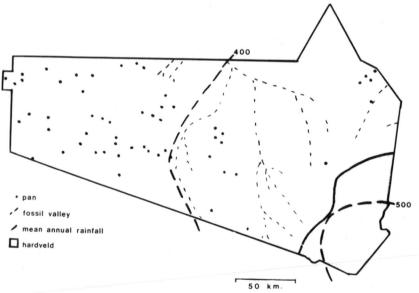

Map 3.3  Kweneng Water

did visit at least briefly all the Tswana chiefdoms of Botswana.[28] His general descriptions apply to the Kweneng as well. Indeed, the most important points to emerge from this discussion of the rural economy can be applied to some degree to most of Southern Africa.

Map 3.3 shows the geography of the Kweneng in greater detail. The total area is some 38,000 square kilometers, a bit less than Switzerland's. Almost all of this is Kalahari sandveld. Although there is no permanent surface water in the sandveld, the Kalahari's level but undulating surface creates a patchwork of small drainage systems, a series of very shallow basins, each of which collects a pool of water during the summer rains from October to March. These pools can be one square meter or several square kilometers, depending on the size of the basins they drain and the depth of the sand. The largest of these pools are called pans, and the largest in the country are the Makgadikgadi salt lakes shown in Map 3.1. Map 3.3 shows only the Kweneng's largest pans. During the rainless winter, from April to September, the water evaporates from a pan, sometimes leaving a layer of salt on its surface. Sometimes too the water reacts with the sand to form a rocky crust of bone-white calcrete. The recurrent flooding and the salt keep some pans free of vegetation, so that when they are dry the soil is completely bare. The winter wind then blows this dry soil away, deepening the pan. Although the smallest pools dry up within a week, an unusually good summer rain might pour enough water into the largest pans to last through the dry winter until the next rain. All dry up eventually, however. Shallow wells in some pans yield water throughout the year, although their water is often too salty to drink.[29] The major watering pan of the western Kweneng is Dutlwe, which a traveler reported in 1910 to support a cattle population of 3,000.[30]

Other places in the Kweneng sandveld where one would look for pools in the summer and dig pits in winter are the beds of fossil rivers, also marked on Map 3.3. These were probably cut in an ancient era when the area received more rain. Nowadays their shallow valley slopes collect rain water that trickles down to accumulate in the river bed, in much the same way as in a pan. Salt accumulation, the formation of calcrete, and shallow water pits are also similar in dry valleys and pans. The Letlhakeng Valley mentioned in Chapter 1 is the most important of these water sources in the Kweneng sandveld, and Letlhakeng itself has long been the Kalahari's largest village.

Map 3.4 shows the Kweneng hardveld. There are two major divisions here, the southern hardveld and the northern transitional hardveld, separated by a broken range of hills. The southern hardveld has

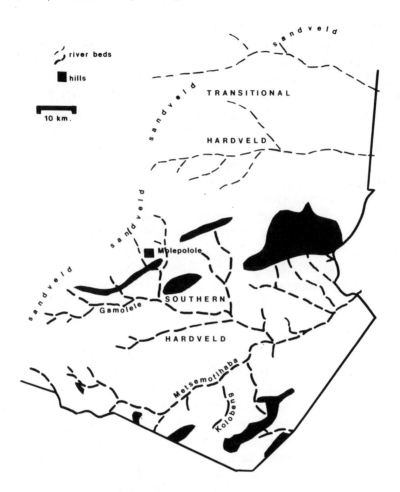

**Map 3.4** Kweneng Hardveld

a bedrock of granite, along which the Metsemotlhaba River and its tributaries flow eastward into the Limpopo. The Metsemotlhaba and its Gamolele and Kolobeng tributaries usually contain pools of water throughout the dry winter, and pits dug at other spots along their beds yield water as well. The northern hardveld has a bedrock of quartzite and sandstone, above which no rivers flow. There are broad shallow valleys here, however, so that water trickles east toward the Limpopo, and some pits in these valleys yield water throughout the year. This northern hardveld is very much like the Letlhakeng Valley, a transitional zone between the southern hardveld and the sandveld.[31]

Returning to Map 3.3, we can see that the southern hardveld receives a bit more rain than the transitional hardveld, and the western sandveld receives less than 400 mm. per year. In both rainfall and surface water, then, the eastern sandveld is more favored than the western sandveld, the hardveld is more favored than the sandveld, and the southern hardveld is more favored than the transitional hardveld. The sandveld has no proper soil, except where pools of water have hardened the sand to a salty crust, and the hardveld soils tend to be sandy as well, especially in the north. The vegetation of the Kweneng is exclusively savanna, in both the hardveld and sandveld.

In a variety of ways, the Kweneng's physical character guided how its residents made a living from it. For example, the dominance of grass made hunting, herding, and sorghum cultivation the most important sources of livelihood in the early nineteenth century. A wide variety of large, hardy antelope thrive on savanna grass, as do cattle, sheep, and goats; and sorghum itself is a drought-resistant grass. As elsewhere in eastern Botswana, the nomadic Sarwa hunters and gatherers occupied most of the Kweneng in the early nineteenth century, and the Kgalagari herded at a few sand wells in the desert. The Kwena occupied the southern hardveld and herded some of their cattle in parts of the transitional hardveld and the eastern sandveld. Hunting and gathering were common to all three of these groups and concern us little here, beyond noting that both inevitably decline as cattle and human populations expand into the hunting and gathering grounds. The Sarwa were most affected by this expansion, because they had no other independent means of livelihood. This study follows only Kwena agriculture, however, whose tools and techniques were similar for Kgalagari agriculture as well. The Kwena are also the most numerous, and have gradually incorporated the Kgalagari.[32]

There is one more important geographical feature that affected economic life in the early nineteenth century Kweneng: the extreme temporal and spatial variability of rainfall. Throughout most of Botswana, rainfall in one place will vary greatly from year to year, month to month, and even day to day. A few inches of rain might fall in a day, followed by several rainless weeks, or one good rainy season might be followed by years of drought. Moreover, a few square kilometers might receive a torrent of rain while adjacent areas receive none.[33] Average evaporation exceeds average rainfall in every month of the year, so that cultivators and herders had to rely on above-average days for crops and pasture to grow, as well as for drinking water.[34]

Water was not only scarce, but its availability was unpredictable. As the next chapter shows, the rural economy was organized to address this very problem.

## NOTES

1. See I. Schapera, *The Tswana*, London, 1953; Sansom, "Traditional economic systems"; Wilson, "The Nguni peoples," and "The Sotho, Venda and Tsonga"; D. Beach, "The Shona economy," in Palmer and Parsons, *Roots*; V. Sheddick, *Land Tenure in Basutoland*, London, 1954; F. Vivelo, *The Herero of Western Botswana*, St. Paul, 1977.

2. Leppan, *Agricultural Development*, pp. 114-15. See also B. Thomas, "The African savanna climate and problems of development," in D. Brokensha, *Ecology and Economic Development in Tropical Africa*, Berkeley, 1965.

3. See C. Boocock and O. van Straten, "Notes on the geology, and hydrogeology of the central Kalahari region," *TGSSA*, 65, 1962; A. Rains and A. MacKay, *The Northern State Lands*, Botswana, Surrey, 1968; A. Rains and A. Yalala, *The Central and Southern State Lands*, Botswana, Surrey, 1972; B. Wilson, "A mini-guide to the water resources," in M. Hinchey, *Symposium on Drought in Botswana*, Botswana Society, 1979.

4. For the Kalahari beyond Botswana, see W. Talbot, "Land utilization in the arid regions of South Africa," in Stamp, *History*, Paris, 1961.

5. As in P. Gillmore, *The Great Thirstland*, London, 1879.

6. M. Bawden and A. Stobbs, *The Land Resources of Eastern Bechuanaland*, Surrey, 1963, pp. 48, 62; A. Mitchell, *The Irrigation Potential Along the Main Rivers of Eastern Botswana*, Surrey, 1976.

7. Estimates of arable land in Botswana follow Bawden and Stobbs in excluding the sandveld. For example, BP, DoA, *Annual Report*, 1965, reports 6 percent of Botswana's area as cultivable hardveld, and one-sixth of this actually cultivated. Yet the DoA knew that the sandveld was also cultivated. As we shall see, it was aiming for a certain standard of farming that only the hardveld could sustain.

8. Hance, *Geography*, pp. 50-51; Leppan, *Agricultural Development*, pp. 63-72.

9. H. Walter, *Ecology of Tropical and Sub-Tropical Vegetation*, New York, 1971, argues that savanna is the natural vegetation of African areas with 200 to 600 mm. annual rainfall. Wetter areas often have savanna vegetation as well because human fire and agriculture cut back the trees. See also H. Bartlett, "Fire, primitive agriculture and grazing in the tropics," in W. Thomas, *Man's Role in Changing the Face of the Earth*, Chicago, 1956. Average annual rainfall, meanwhile, is only the most approximate measure of rainfall utilization: see, for example, S. Nieuwolt, "The influence of rainfall in rural population distribution in Tanzania," *JTG*, 44, 1977.

10. Walter, *Ecology*, pp. 40-55; P. Weare, "Vegetation of the Kalahari," in Botswana Society, *Sustained Production From Semi-Arid Areas*, Gaborone, 1971.

11. See Schapera, *Native Land*, pp. 7-8; G. Okihiro, "Hunters, herders, cultivators and traders: interaction and change in the Kalahari, 19th century,"

Ph.D., UCLA, 1976, ch. 4; M. Legassick, "The Sotho-Tswana peoples before 1800," in L. Thompson, *African Societies of Southern Africa*, New York, 1969.

12. Wilson, "Sotho, Venda and Tsonga," pp. 137-67.

13. For a twentieth century survey, see I. Schapera, *The Ethnic Composition of Tswana Tribes*, London, 1952.

14. See N. Parsons, "Khama III, the Bamangwato and the British," Ph.D., Edinburgh, 1973; Dachs, *Road*.

15. The chiefs claimed the same territory in some cases. Khama offered concessions in territory that he and the Ndebele both claimed, in return for guarantees of Ngwato water and grazing rights there. An 1855 map, in BNA HC 117, shows the territories claimed and offered for settlement: the Kwena chief, Sechele, offered all the Kalahari west of Dutlwe and the territory between the Notwana and Marico-Crocodile rivers. See also BP RC Correspondence, 21 Sept. 1893, BNA AC 2/1/6; 22 May 1894, BNA HC 108; GB, CO, *ASD*, 461, 1895, 27, GB, CO, *ASD*, 441, 1893, 114.

16. Schapera, *Native Land*, pp. 9-10.

17. Schapera, *Native Land*, pp. 11-12.

18. Schapera, *Native Land*, pp. 10-11.

19. L. Truschel, "The Tawana and the Ngamiland trek," *BNR*, 6, 1974; GB, CO, *ASD*, 899, 1908, 18.

20. Schapera, *Native Land*, p. 12.

21. Schapera, *Native Land*, pp. 12-13.

22. GB, CO, *ASD*, 717, 1903, 94, 114.

23. GB, CO, *ASD*, 969, 1910, 71.

24. GB, CO, *ASD*, 969, 1911, 17, 45. See also B. Clifford, "Habitability of the Kalahari," *GJ*, 77, 1931.

25. The British used this system first in India and in Natal. See especially, L. Lugard, *The Dual Mandate in British Tropical Africa*, London, 1922.

26. Great Britain, *Financial and Economic Position of the Bechuanaland Protectorate*, 1933, p. 148, estimated that moving from Mafeking would cost £70,000, more than two-thirds of the previous year's total budget. Protectorate officials were also paid less than elsewhere in the Colonial Service, according to Resident Commissioner, "Progress and development in the Bechuanaland Protectorate, 1929-37," BNA S 382/14.

27. See Schapera, *Handbook*, pp. 41-44.

28. I. Schapera, *Handbook*, p. xii; *Native Land*, p. vi.

29. Boocock and van Straten, "Notes"; I. Lancaster, "The pans of the southern Kalahari," *GJ*, 1978; L. Hyde, "Groundwater supplies in the Kalahari area," in Botswana Society, *Sustained Production*. See also F. Debenham, *Kalahari Sand*, London, 1953.

30. S. Townshend, "Development of the British Bechuanaland Protectorate (Southern Block) by a light railway," GB, CO, *ASD*, 969, 1910, 98.

31. Bawden and Stobbs, *Land Resources*, pp. 48, 62.

32. For the Sarwa, see R. Lee and I. deVore, *Kalahari Hunter-Gatherers*, Cambridge, 1976. The best historical source for the Kgalagari is Okihiro, "Hunters," ch. 4. See also I. Schapera and D. van der Merwe, "Notes on the tribal groupings, history and customs of the BaKgalagari," University of Cape Town,

School of African Studies, n.s. 13, 1945; A. Kuper, "The Kgalagari in the 19th century," *BNR*, 2, 1969; A. Kuper, *Kalahari Village Politics*, Cambridge, 1970; J. Solway, "Report on Dutlwe village," MoA, 1979; P. Devitt, "Man and his environment in the western Kalahari," and H. Fosbrooke, "Man in the Kalahari tribal areas," in Botswana Society, *Sustained Production*.

33. F. Debenham, *Report on the Water Resources of the Bechuanaland Protectorate, Tanganyika Territory, Kenya and Uganda Protectorate*, London, 1948, p. 33; Schapera, *Native Land*, ch. 7.

34. J. Pike, "Rainfall and evaporation in Botswana," UNDP, Gaborone, 1971. More generally, see W. Thompson, *Moisture and Farming in South Africa*, Pretoria, 1936.

# 4

# The Hoe, the Pit, and the Pack Ox, 1800–1900

This chapter presents the Kwena rural economy in the nineteenth century, before the new commercial economy changed greatly its tools, techniques, and organization. This periodization is only approximate, for there were important changes before the nineteenth century, and the commercial economy made its first entrance in the middle of the century. This chapter's purpose, however, is only to outline the organization of the rural economy before the new commercial economy made its full impact. The first part of this chapter describes the tools and techniques of Kwena cultivation and cattle herding, and the second part describes how the Kwena interacted with each other in order to employ these tools and techniques.

## CULTIVATION

Cultivation depended on the rain, yet as we noted at the end of the last chapter, the rain was never dependable. Figure 4.1 shows the pattern of rainfall in Molepolole and Letlhakeng during the major summer planting months of November, December, and January over two ten-year periods. October rains were often also sufficient for planting, but grain sown in February risked dessication before ripening by the dry winds of May. The first thing to note from Figure 4.1 is the great difference between the two ten-year periods: The first was very dry and the second was wet. If we look at individual months, the variety is just as great. Sometimes only November (year 15), sometimes only December (10), and sometimes only January (6) had sufficient

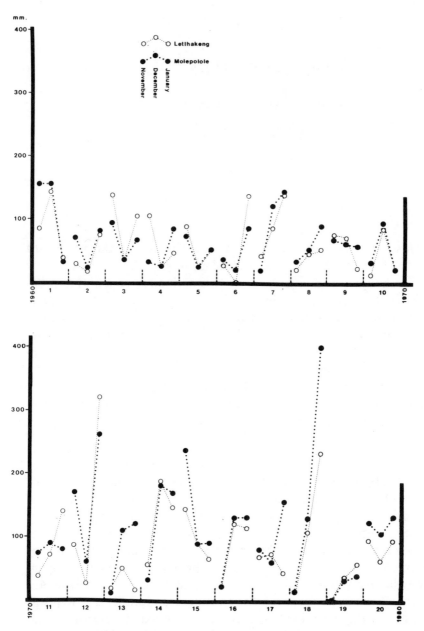

**Fig. 4.1.** Letlhakeng-Molepolole Plow Rains (From RB, Department of Meteorological Services, records for Molepolole and Letlhakeng.)

rain for planting. Sometimes two months did (18); sometimes all three had enough rain (20); and sometimes none had enough (19). Moreover, Letlhakeng received more rain than Molepolole in thirty percent of these months. Over a fifty-year period in Molepolole, if we take 250 mm. as the minimum required for a good crop, more than four-fifths of the years fall below this level.

Because it was so difficult to time planting in such uncertainty, cultivators simply planted whenever it rained during these three months, and sometimes in October. Sometimes they planted in dry earth, hoping for rain to follow. Areas planted on different days thus received different amounts of rain at different times. The result was a patchwork of plants growing and ripening at various rates. This staggered planting increased the chances of at least one area receiving the right amount of rain.[1]

Planting entailed broadcasting the seed over a small area and then turning it under with a hand-held hoe. A cultivator tried to cover a large area quickly rather than a small area carefully, so that some part of the field might catch some rain. An adult could plant ten square meters or so in a morning or an afternoon: more if clouds shaded the field, less if the sun beat down on the hoer's back.[2]

Cultivators hoed standing up. Their wide iron hoe blades were imported from Tswana smiths in the eastern Transvaal, and to them cultivators attached their own long wooden handles.[3] Weeding with the same hoe followed a month or so after planting, when the grain stood about a foot high. The removal of weeds left the grain as the highest plants in the field, and this headstart had to suffice. There were no subsequent weedings. When the sorghum rose above a meter and its head began to form, usually in March or April, its large exposed grains became the target of seed-eating birds. Bird-scaring now consumed most of the worktime.[4]

Because different parts of a field were planted at different times, their plants ripened at different times as well. In May and June, the bird-scarers began to harvest the dry ripe heads one by one, selecting each at its prime. At some point the cultivator decided that all the heads were sufficiently ripe for a clean sweep of the field. Only the head was taken, cut from atop its two-meter stalk with a small metal knife. At the end of each work day, the harvesters piled up the grain on wooden racks on the nearby threshing floor.[5]

Threshing floors were made of mud mixed with a bit of cow dung. Every year during bird-scaring someone had to clear it of last year's weeds and resmear it to smooth the surface. The harvesters now assembled piles of grain heads perhaps a meter square and beat them with long thick wooden poles. They swept away the refuse and winnowed the grains from the husks by dropping them from a basket held to the wind. Sorghum was easier to thresh than the less important bulrush millet, whose smaller grains adhere more tightly to its head. Millet is even more drought-resistant than sorghum and was once the major crop of the Kgalagari. The Kwena planted only a small amount of it among their sorghum as further insurance against drought.[6]

Out in the field and then on the threshing floor, the reapers made three separate piles of pure, rusted, and degenerate sorghum. They threshed this sorghum separately and threw it in with the pure grain. The degenerate grain, pollinated with wild grasses from the surrounding countryside, was handled and finally stored separately. Threshing pure grain yielded three distinct products, because imperfectly formed grains were lighter than the others and fell in with the chaff, which then had to be resifted. Repeated siftings of pure grain produced "clean" grain, *ditshane* and *dithoka*, in descending value. If a typical field of half a hectare yielded 125 kilograms of clean sorghum, or about 150 liters, there were also some 15 liters of *ditshane* and 3 of *dithoka*.[7]

Because of the general aridity of the country, grain storage was an uncomplicated affair. Sorghum kept well for two years and was still edible thereafter.[8] Large grain baskets in ordinary mud houses sufficed as grain bins, although mud bins were also used. Cooking sorghum into porridge required first pounding it into flour in a large wooden mortar with a large wooden pestle more than a meter in length. Cooks used earthen pots and wood fires and made beer by sprouting some of the grain and grinding it on a stone with a smooth rock. They brewed this malt powder along with unmalted grain and then sieved the beer in gourds. *Ditshane, dithoka*, and all degenerate sorghum products were used for beer, although *ditshane* also made a passable porridge.[9]

Melons were the most important secondary crop, because they could be substituted for water in cooking porridge. They ripened earlier than grains, and so contributed to the diet just when last year's grain was often running low. Beans too made an early-season contribution, although they were harder to harvest—by bending and hunting—and also required threshing to separate the pods. Both melons and beans grew large leaves close to the ground, and so interfered with weeding. Squashes and maize were only minor crops in the nineteenth century, although both ripened early and could be planted late.[10] Maize yields were probably higher per hectare than sorghum's, and its closed cob required no bird-scaring. Today maize planted among sorghum still feeds bird-scarers until the sorghum is ripe. Maize is not as drought-resistant as sorghum, however, and it is more difficult to remove from the cob and to pound into flour. Still today, most home-grown maize is eaten roasted on the cob.[11]

Aside from these activities, cultivation required a host of other tasks to sustain the cultivators through the year. We must be careful to include such nonagricultural tasks because their neglect has led some economists to misjudge the efficiency of many rural economies. That is, they estimated the amount of time needed to work the land that agricultural surveys reported being utilized; when this time amounted to much less than a full year of full days of work for the adult population, they concluded that labor was under-or unemployed. They forgot that nonindustrial rural citizens must provide most of the essentials of life themselves, not only food. Although extremely difficult to measure, the hours that cultivators spent off the field were not idle ones: They had to fetch water and firewood, grind grain, cook, make or mend clothing, build and repair their dwellings and tools, as well as negotiate with their neighbors for loans, field help, or other assistance. It is extremely difficult even to estimate, especially for the past, the amount of labor employed or unemployed in agrarian economies.[12]

In the nineteenth century Kweneng, the technology of these non-agricultural activities was as simple as that of cultivation. Dead fire-wood, abundant in the dry savanna, was carried by headload to the fire, which simply rested in the open on a flat patch of ground. Water was also carried by headload in gourds and earthen pots. Houses were circular walls of branches or mud, with conical roofs of grass-covered poles. Clothing was made from the skins of domestic and wild animals. The latter were hunted with iron-tipped spears and brush lair traps. Grain itself was transported in baskets and skins. Small loads of less than 20 liters were carried on the head in grass baskets and larger loads were carried in bags stitched of single or double goat or harte-beest antelope skins. An adult could carry two 20-liter single goatskin sacks across the shoulders, whereas a pack ox could carry two double hartebeest skins of 150 liters each. These skin sacks included the ani-mals' legs, stuffed stiff with grain. The pack ox could also be ridden like a donkey.[13]

We can see that all these tools and techniques attending nine-teenth century cultivation were simple but appropriate. The only im-ported items were hoe blades, knives, and spear tips. Output remained low because of the poverty of the natural resources available and be-cause the technology was so simple. A low technology means low pro-ductivity, defined as output per hour worked. More or better tools or techniques allow the same amount of human labor to produce a larger output in the same natural environment.[14]

Why Kwena cultivators did not develop a more advanced technology should be obvious: The harsh climate hardly encouraged the stable population with steady surpluses over centuries necessary for technological development. When drought struck and harvest after harvest failed, simply surviving was a great accomplishment. The technology was also so simple as to be accessible to all members of the community. Yet if everyone employed the same low technology, how do we explain the differences in wealth? Could two persons end up with different incomes only by one working harder, by luck, or by one taking something from the other?

This certainly seems to be the case in cultivation, but Kweneng producers also owned cattle. Cattle are an unusual item of technology: With enough rain and land, they simply grow. In this way they are very much like the crops, yet in the dry Kweneng savanna, they require far less human labor and yield a much greater return than sorghum. In this way, the dynamics of productivity and surplus are somewhat different for cattle, and it is here that we must look for the origins of differences in wealth in the nineteenth century Kweneng.

## CATTLE

There are two distinct elements of herding technology to consider here: the tools and techniques that herders employed; and the dynamics of cattle reproduction. As for the first, herding tools were as simple as those used in the activities attending cultivation. A knife was needed for castrating bulls; water pits in the soil and sand were dug with handleless wooden spades; clay pots and gourds lifted the water out; brush fires killed ticks and removed woody plants from above the grass; circular cattle pens were made of brush; and herders carried sticks to hit cattle on the rump.[15] The techniques of herding appeared just as simple as these tools but actually required great precision and careful judgment. This apparent simplicity derived from the minimal needs of the cattle: As we have noted, with enough water and grass, they matured and reproduced. Although grass covered the Kweneng, water was scarce, and thus herding entailed a constant pursuit of water.

Unlike humans, who could survive on only the water from melons, cattle needed some 30 liters per full-grown animal per day to grow properly.[16] In summer, they could wander the range, drinking from pools of rain water as they grazed. These pools dried as the summer waned. Herders sometimes dug them deeper to postpone the move away from the surrounding pasture, and some of these pits even kept water through the winter. Pits in sand had to be redug every year, for a hole in sand does not keep its shape. Pits dug in proper soil could be deeper and thus more permanent. By mid-winter, however, there were very few water supplies left in the Kweneng.[17]

The most important winter water supplies were the pools and pits in the Metsemotlhaba River and its tributaries, the Gamolele and the Kolobeng. Secondary sources were the pits in the valleys and pans of the northern hardveld and the Kalahari. Yet even the Metsemotlhaba pits were barely perennial, for its banks are everywhere less than 20 meters apart, its sandy bed is a mere 3 meters or so below the banks, and the water level seldom rises to a meter. In bad years the pools dried up quickly and herders dug the pits deeper and deeper. After a number of bad years the pits began to dry up as well. Humans relied when they could on a few springs in the few hills in the southern hardveld, but elsewhere they drank the same water as cattle did.[18]

A herder maintained a permanent pen at one permanent water source but kept the cattle away from it as long as possible in search of other water and pasture. In dry years they could not range far, because there was little water beyond the few perennial sites and most years of course were dry. Thus there were small clusters of cattle at a handful of the sandveld pans and valleys, most notably Dutlwe and Letlhakeng, and a few more in the transitional hardveld. The vast majority spent their winters in the Metsemotlhaba Basin.[19]

Drought in this situation was relative. Every winter was a drought of sorts, with cattle retreating to permanent water. If the summer rain was especially poor, some of these normally perennial sources dried up. Several years of poor summer rain saw more and more of them dry, until only a few or even none remained. At a permanent water source, herders usually let cattle graze in the morning, drove them to water at midday, and then let them graze back to pasture in the afternoon. As winter approached and more cattle came to this permanent water, the area around the water point was progressively stripped of grass. This meant that every morning herders had to drive their cattle farther out to graze, walk them a longer way to water and a longer way back to pasture. In dry years, when other normally permanent water sources dried up and more and more cattle came to drink at this one water point, the overgrazed area around the water grew larger and larger. As more months passed without rain and more water points dried up, so many cattle would come to water at this one point that it now took an entire day to walk to water from the distant pasture. Since they now had to travel so far over ground stripped of edible grass, the cattle grew weak and slow. The herders now abandoned their daily schedule and let cattle graze for two waterless days in the distant pasture, where they grew fatter but thirsty. The herders then drove them to the water point, where they might have to wait in line a day or two to drink. The cattle grew weaker and weaker from walking farther and farther from water to grass, which also lost nutritional value as it grew drier and drier. This was how drought killed cattle.[20]

The relentless pursuit of water and grass required intimate knowledge of the countryside and the condition of the cattle. In addition to this spatial strategy of moving cattle from water to water and grass to grass, herding required managing the biological lives of the stock themselves. Here small stock were first of all distinguished from cattle. Goats were valuable for meat, milk, hides, and their hardiness and fertility. They survived droughts on only the moisture in the vegetation they ate, and they reproduced quickly, sometimes bearing twice a year and sometimes bearing twins. Sheep, on the other hand, were no hardier than cattle and bore twins twice a year more rarely than goats did. Sheep yielded meat and, more important, warm pelts.[21] Only July and August are cold, but frost in these months is common.

Cattle were more valuable than small stock because the volume of their milk and meat was far greater. Tswana cattle are very large by African standards, averaging in maturity some 400 kilograms. Their maximum reproductive rate was one calf per cow per year for twelve years of the cow's life. Water and grass deficiencies and disease weakened cows and bulls, thereby reducing the birth rate, and weakened and killed young calves. Spared the strain of reproduction, castrated oxen were far hardier than cows, bulls, or calves.[22]

October was the best time for calves to be born. A cow grazed from September to December on new grass sprouted by the summer rains and so was in good condition for conception in January. The critical early months of pregnancy were spent grazing on the plentiful summer grass. The dry season occupied its later pregnancy, but the first showers in September and October brought it back up to good condition for calving. A calf born in October survived on only its mother's milk until December or January, when it began supplementing its diet with grass still sweet from summer rain. A calf born earlier than October was born of a cow still weak from the dry season, whereas a calf born later than October was still too small and weak when the rains stopped and the grass lost most of its moisture and nutrition.[23]

Weaning was a natural process in which the calf came to rely more on grass and less on its mother's milk. It stopped sucking altogether at about one year of age, and this step was a sudden one if a new calf was born. Herders did not wean calves forcibly because they could never guess what the next season would bring. If the summer rains were poor, a calf might need milk beyond a year. Herders did separate calves for milking, but only for half the day. By January calves were strong enough to be deprived of some milk and so were kept in a separate pen at night and not let out to graze with the other cattle in the morning. At midday, the cows were led one by one into the calf pen. The calf sucked once or twice to start the milk flowing and then the herder chased it away to take a liter or so from the cow. The calf was then allowed back to drink and afterward accompanied its mother out to pasture. By April, the abating rains reduced the cow's milk and so milking ceased. Milk was drunk immediately or stored in clay, leather, or gourd pots to thicken and sour.[24]

Good rains not only added beef to growing cattle but also improved the rate of reproduction by producing healthy cows. This reduced miscarriages and still births and increased the rate of conception and the amount of milk available to young calves. Healthy bulls were also important. Bulls posed the further problem of which young males should be castrated. All males would have been castrated to make them hardier, except for the need to reproduce. The first two years of the cattle's lives were perilous, so that castration within the first year would have raised the survival rate. Herders castrated at the end of two years, however, so as to insure that they left intact the best survivor. If they castrated at one year all but one male, they could not know whether this was the strongest of the crop. After a second year it became clearer which uncastrated male was strongest, and so the genetic lives of all the rest were ended.[25]

There was one more vital technical decision facing herders: when to remove an animal from the herd. This required looking into the herd and assessing each animal's condition. Herders distinguished one animal from another by a variety of physical features, such as the shape of their horns and the markings on their bodies. They knew their own cattle from those of their neighbors in much the same way: that is, a stray cow claimed by two different persons went to whomever could describe its features in more intimate detail. There was also a general system of branding by marks cut into the cattle's ears, but as large groups of herders shared a common mark only positive identification counted.[26]

Deciding when to cull a certain animal depended on an owner's economic circumstances. One herder could handle up to fifty cattle on the range and four could handle several hundred. Having too many cattle was seldom a problem. More often, herders had too few. Owners tried to hold on to cows as long as possible in the hope of gaining more calves. Although fertility declined with advancing age, even a cow ten years old or more could grow fat in a very good year and bear a calf. Yet some cattle had to be culled to meet various economic obligations and especially to be exchanged for food when the owner's crops failed. A herder did not cull only oxen, because a herd of cows and calves would disappear in a drought. A balance of oxen and cows insured that if drought did strike, some oxen would remain to be traded for food and young cows to rebuild the herd. This means that an owner culled both cows and oxen. Moreover, an owner wanted to use cattle for economic obligations before they died out in the pasture, where their meat had to be eaten immediately by anyone who happened to be there at the time, or else dried in strips.[27]

If an owner's herd was small, cattle might have to be culled for economic obligations faster than the herd produced them. In this case, the herd grew only smaller. If a herder was able to meet pressing economic needs without dipping into the herd at all, its growth could be rapid indeed. This was the strategy of the Kweneng's agriculturalists: break even in the activities attending cultivation and leave the growing herd alone.

We can catch a glimpse of this herd growth in the simple model in Table 4.1, which charts the history of a two-year-old female and its offspring over a twenty-year period.[28] Despite the statistical inelegance of this model, here we need only note the size of the herd after twenty years. Calves are assumed to alternate male and female: a female first results in 73 head and a male first results in a herd of 36. Actual calving does not alternate like this, of course, so that a string of many calves of one sex is a common occurrence. We can see from this model that a run of female calves will result in a tremendous growth rate, whereas a run of males will slow the herd's growth. Luck is therefore a significant factor in cattle accumulation. Nevertheless, we can conclude from the rough approximation in Table 4.1 that a herder could expect one young cow to produce about fifty cattle in twenty years.

Imagine a man inheriting a dozen cattle from his father, breaking even in the activites attending cultivation, and passing an untouched and thus greatly enlarged herd on to his eldest son. If this son did the same, and his son after that, generations of inheritance would produce a herd of tremendous size. We now have a hint of what led to differences in wealth in the Kweneng, for its chief, like chiefs throughout Southern Africa, claimed to be the senior son of a senior son of a senior son. The rest of this chapter discusses how men accumulated more cattle than women, and chiefs accumulated more cattle than other men, through the activities of cultivation and herding described above.

**Table 4.1** The Growing Herd

| | | | Herd A: First Calf Female | | | | | |
|---|---|---|---|---|---|---|---|---|
| Year | Heifers | Cows | Calves | Tollies | Oxen | Culls | Increase | Total |
| 1 | 1 | | | | | | | 1 |
| 2 | | 1 | 1 | | | | 1 | 2 |
| 3 | 1 | 1 | 1 | | | | 1 | 3 |
| 4 | 1 | 1 | | 1 | | | | 3 |
| 5 | | 2 | 2 | 1 | | | 2 | 5 |
| 6 | 1 | 2 | 1 | 1 | 1 | | 1 | 6 |
| 7 | 2 | 2 | 1 | 1 | 1 | | 1 | 7 |
| 8 | 1 | 3 | 2 | 1 | 2 | | 2 | 9 |
| 9 | 1 | 4 | 3 | 2 | 2 | | 3 | 12 |
| 10 | 3 | 3 | 2 | 2 | 3 | 1c* | 1 | 13 |
| 11 | 3 | 4 | 2 | 2 | 4 | | 2 | 15 |
| 12 | 2 | 6 | 5 | 2 | 5 | 1c | 5 | 20 |
| 13 | 3 | 6 | 4 | 4 | 6 | | 3 | 23 |
| 14 | 4 | 7 | 4 | 5 | 7 | | 4 | 27 |
| 15 | 4 | 9 | 6 | 4 | 10 | | 6 | 33 |
| 16 | 5 | 10 | 7 | 5 | 12 | 1x | 6 | 39 |
| 17 | 7 | 11 | 7 | 6 | 13 | 1c, 1x | 5 | 44 |
| 18 | 7 | 14 | 9 | 7 | 16 | | 9 | 53 |
| 19 | 8 | 17 | 12 | 8 | 18 | 1c, 1x | 10 | 63 |
| 20 | 11 | 18 | 12 | 10 | 22 | 2c | 10 | 73 |
| | | | Herd B: First Calf Male | | | | | |
| 1 | 1 | | | | | | | 1 |
| 2 | | 1 | 1 | | | | 1 | 2 |
| 3 | | 1 | 1 | 1 | | | 1 | 3 |
| 4 | 1 | 1 | | 1 | | | | 3 |
| 5 | 1 | 1 | 1 | | 1 | | 1 | 4 |
| 6 | | 2 | 1 | 1 | 1 | | 1 | 5 |
| 7 | 1 | 2 | 2 | 1 | 1 | | 1 | 7 |
| 8 | 2 | 2 | | 1 | 2 | | | 7 |
| 9 | 1 | 3 | 2 | 1 | 2 | | 2 | 9 |
| 10 | 1 | 3 | 1 | 1 | 3 | 1c | | 9 |
| 11 | 1 | 3 | 2 | 2 | 3 | | 2 | 11 |
| 12 | 1 | 4 | 1 | 2 | 4 | | 1 | 12 |
| 13 | 2 | 4 | 3 | 1 | 5 | | 3 | 15 |
| 14 | 2 | 4 | 1 | 2 | 6 | 1c | | 15 |
| 15 | 2 | 5 | 4 | 2 | 6 | | 4 | 19 |
| 16 | 3 | 6 | 2 | 2 | 7 | 1x | 1 | 20 |
| 17 | 3 | 6 | 5 | 3 | 7 | 1c | 4 | 24 |
| 18 | 3 | 7 | 4 | 4 | 9 | 1c | 3 | 27 |
| 19 | 4 | 8 | 6 | 5 | 9 | 1x | 5 | 32 |
| 20 | 5 | 9 | 5 | 5 | 12 | 1c | 4 | 36 |

* c = cow, x = ox

## WOMEN[29]

Cultivation was mostly a woman's preserve, and herding was mostly a man's. Investigating the economic relations involved in each activity will give us some notion of one level of differences in economic opportunity, those between men and women. Let us begin by tracing the working life of a model female producer, from childhood through old age, assessing her economic position and the choices she faces at each stage.

A girl was usually born into her father's compound in the village, in the same circle of compounds as his own father's and married brothers'. That is, when a son married, he built a compound near his father's, so that over the generations these male descendants formed their own circle of compounds in the village. Such circles are called *makgotla*, the singular of which is *kgotla*. A wife left her parents' *kgotla* and moved into her husband's.[30]

Once the girl could walk, carry, and follow directions, she began participating in small household tasks in whichever compound she found herself. At any time she could be shifted among other relatives' compounds, especially those in the *kgotla* from which her mother had come. She was fed wherever she worked, and learned all the domestic tasks along the way. She could also be sent more formally for a longer period to a childless or other compound that needed her services. This was usually recompensed with a gift to her parents when she returned. Or she could stay at her new home until she married.[31]

Most girls stayed with their mothers, however, beside whom they began working in the fields as soon as they could hold a hoe. Here they learned all the tasks attending cultivation. All the grain a girl helped to produce remained mixed up with her mother's, but she did receive more than daily food as a reward. Her mother allocated to her a young female goat or sheep or even cow if she was able. This animal remained in the herd that her father oversaw, but whoever tended it, usually her brother, remembered which were its offspring and so kept track of the girl's growing herd. If the small stock remained in the village, the girl herself herded them.[32]

Upon marriage, the girl, now a woman, moved out of her parents' compound and into her new husband's new compound in his father's *kgotla*. If her new husband had not been able to build a new house by the time of the marriage, the couple stayed in a house in either parent's compound.[33] Any stock she had accumulated as a child could now be transferred from her father's herd to her husband's. This decision was sometimes a difficult one, for if the husband's herd was small he of course wanted them to come over. If the father's herd was small, he of course wanted them to stay. Her father had the final say, yet if he sent over no cattle his daughter would have a hard time calling on her new husband's family for help in the future. If the cattle stayed in her father's herd, they remained her property jointly with him. That is, he usually asked her permission, and she needed his, to dispose of them. If some or all of them went over to her husband's herd, they became the couple's joint property, known together with their offspring as *ketleetso*.[34]

A woman's marriage was also marked by a transfer of cattle in the opposite direction, from her husband's family to her father's. This bridewealth payment sealed her transfer to her husband's family. Yet she remained very much in the economic orbit of her parents' family as well. Indeed, from this relationship came a large measure of the interdependence that insured the entire village against hunger. Figure 4.2 and the following paragraphs explain how this was so.

Once married, a woman helped her husband clear a field, if he had not cleared one already. This field was nearby his father's and his married brothers' fields. That is, the village *kgotla* formation was reproduced in the surrounding countryside: When a man married, he cleared a field near his father's, so that over the generations these male descendants formed their own circle of fields.[35] A wife left her parents' circle of fields and cultivated the field of her husband. She and her husband formed a team alongside the teams of his parents and his married brothers and their wives. Her husband was responsible for providing her with skins to buy two hoes, one skin per hoe. She now owned these hoes, but one she allocated to him to help her. During planting season they left their house in the village every morning to work in their field, a short walk away.[36] He was also responsible for herding their cattle, and so usually drove them from the permanent water, usually at the village, to distant summer pastures during or even before planting season. He carried his hoe on his shoulder, so that if he found himself in one place long enough with enough rain, he could scratch out a small field and plant.[37]

The woman might help her nearby in-laws plant, and they might even work together, moving from field to field so as to plant quickly each one precisely at its prime. Her first responsibility was always her own field, however, and her second responsibility was none of her in-laws' fields at all. It was her mother's. She and her married sisters, that is, all her mother's married daughters, left their own disparate

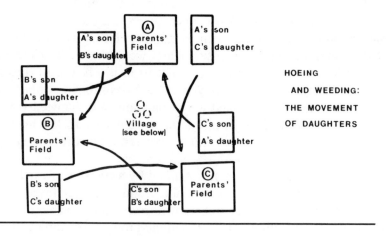

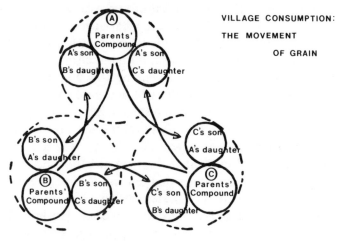

**Fig. 4.2.** Grain Production and Distribution (Nineteenth Century)

fields to converge on the field they had worked as children. Here they helped their mother and unmarried sisters plant. The same sequence applied at weeding, the daughters weeding their mother's field after their own. Harvesting was hoeless and thus easier work, and casual helpers could be compensated with the final product, so that daughters were not needed as much as for planting and weeding.[38]

This mother-daughter tie was reproduced again in the village. A woman stored her clean sorghum, not in the village compound that she shared with her husband, but in her mother's. Each married daughter had her own grain bin in her mother's storage house and every day she walked there to fetch a basket of grain for the day's meal. A woman did not take from only her own bin, however. After the harvest, her mother called her married daughters together to grade the grain in each bin for quality, after which they opened the worst bin first and all took from it until it was empty. Then they moved to the next worst and then to the next, until the following harvest. The best grain, in the last bin, was thus saved as seed for planting.[39]

If we turn now to Figure 4.2, we can see that Mother A stored grain from fields north, west, and southeast of the village. If rain fell on at least one of these areas, at least one bin in her storehouse contained some grain. Even if the other two bins were empty, their owners ate from the one that was not. In this way, each woman was insured against the failure of her own crop. At the same time, the collection of grain from different areas and the reservation of the best grain for planting served as a long-term process of seed collection and improvement. We can also see that a daughter of A would tend to help and be helped by her in-laws in the field, because her field bordered theirs and she was now a member of their family. Back in the village, she would again tend to serve food to and be served by these same in-laws, in the adjacent compounds in her husband's *kgotla*.[40] Even if only one of the fields in Figure 4.2 yielded grain one year, everyone would have some access to this harvest.

Figure 4.2 shows only three sets of parents and their married children: In Molepolole in the late 1870s, there were 2,600 dwellings, housing some 10,000 persons, so that an actual network comprised not three but hundreds of such sets, uniting all individuals and all fields, keeping food circulating throughout the rural economy, insuring every woman against the failure of her own field.[41] Despite this interdependence, however, a woman acted in her own self-interest. She had to judge how much time to spend on her own field versus her mother's versus her in-laws' fields. If her in-laws were wealthy, her reward for working with them might exceed the grain she could call on from her poorer sisters and mother. Or if her in-laws were the poor ones, feeding them back in the village might not yield her much return. At all times, however, a woman balanced such considerations against the knowledge that wealthy could become poor very quickly in the harsh savanna. Moreover, it was in her self-interest to sustain others, especially those with the closest economic ties to her, in order to keep as many cultivators in production as possible, thereby scattering more fields across the countryside to catch the rain. Whomever she helped helped her, and everyone at some time needed help.

Labor and grain circulated far more widelt than even suggested in Figure 4.2. Kin far beyond those shown and nonkin as well contracted to work with and for each other according to their respective needs and capabilities. A woman might give beer and meat to several persons over a few months in return for them all assembling on a certain day to clear a new field. Or if a mother was short of seed for herself and her daughters, one of them might work for a day planting someone else's field in return for a basket of seedgrain. Working on someone else's field like this was known as *majako*. Someone unable to attract anyone to work with her might offer to work instead on someone else's field from planting to harvest. This was also *majako*. And someone whose field failed could acquire grain directly rather than rely on mother or sister or being fed from someone else's pot, by helping at harvest in return for some of the grain. This was *majako* too. A woman stored only the first-grade clean sorghum in her mother's house: she paid second-grade *ditshane* to her *majako* helpers at harvest, usually adding some clean grain as well. The small quantity of third-grade *dithoka* she gave as a gift to her mother's mother, for years of kindnesses and because great-grandmothers tended to be too old to work well in their own fields.[42]

We can see how women distributed work and grain, but did they do so equally? If one daughter consistently filled her bin to overflowing, was this excess grain simply eaten by her sisters and her next-door in-laws? No, this was not necessarily so. If her sisters and their husbands, her mother, father, and husband all agreed that there was enough grain in the other bins, the successful woman could exchange this extra grain for livestock.[43] If they refused, she could stop storing grain in her mother's house and accumulate it herself. Withdrawing from the reciprocal network was extremely dangerous, however. If her field failed later, where could she turn for help?

If there was enough grain for exchange, our successful woman's husband went out into the open market to trade one hartebeest skinful of grain, about three 90-kilogram bags of today, for three goats. If there was even more grain to spare, she could exchange a double hartebeest skinful for a cow.[44] This ability to accumulate livestock gave Kwena women an economic position perhaps better than that of most women in precolonial Africa. The cow that a woman acquired from grain, plus its future offspring, were remembered as "grain cattle." She allocated one of the female calves to each of her daughters, who were remembered as the owners of the subsequent offspring as well.[45]

In this way women were able to remove cattle from the sphere of men and pass their accumulation down to other women. They could also acquire cattle in smaller increments by trading grain for goats, letting the goats multiply, and then trading six or seven for a cow. Two things always worked against an accumulating woman, however. First, poor rainfall kept excess grain harvests few and far between. Second, women did not herd their own cattle. For this they depended on men, who always took their cut.

## MEN

We can comprehend what prevented women from herding and why this reduced their economic position by investigating what herding actually entailed. A male herder, like his cultivating sister, was usually born into his father's compound. He helped with household tasks, but as soon as he was able, at about five years of age, he began helping out at the nearby family cattle post. A cattle post comprised a herd, a cattle pen and, if it was too far from the village to walk home every night, a makeshift hut. Within a few years he joined his male elders in their annual exodus beyond the southern hardveld to fresh summer pastures. As soon as he began herding, usually the small stock and the immature cattle, his father allocated to him one of the female calves as his own. Thus the boy learned the skills of herding as he accumulated cattle of his own on which to practice them.[46]

If his cattle were numerous enough by the time he married, the young man established his own cattle post alongside his father's. The advantage of having two cattle posts was having two sets of herders, who could cover twice as much pasture as one. A set of herders usually comprised one man or older boy, plus one younger boy. One set of herders could handle up to a hundred animals in one post. Yet few fathers had enough cattle by the time their eldest son married to divide the post in two. Most sons thus left their cattle in their father's post even after marrying.[47]

Even if he did establish his own post, a young man's cattle remained under his father's control. He could not dispose of them without his father's consent, and if father and son disagreed, the father had the last word. The allocation of a cow and hence its future offspring did not transfer full ownership to a son, but rather defined which cattle he would inherit when his father died. If upon a father's death all the family cattle were still in one post, the married sons had to decide whether or not they should remain so. Each son became the full owner of his allocated cattle, and the unallocated ones were distributed among all the children and the widow. The senior son tried to convince them all to remain a close family, to look to him as their father's successor as head, and to keep all the cattle in one post under his control. Younger sons tended to want their own posts. For small herds, however, there was seldom any question of splitting the cattle.[48]

A herder growing up in the pastures also spent his time making connections. These were necessary first of all to fill gaps in the herding force. If cattle multiplied faster than sons, or if a boy fell sick, a man might borrow someone else's son to help herd for a while. Or if many of his cattle suddenly died or had to be traded away, a man and his sons need not lay idle: They could help out on someone else's cattle post. A man kept constant watch on the labor market, slowly building up a network of fellow cattle owners to whom he could turn when he needed such help. Through acts of reciprocity he strove to establish a good reputation as both a generous returner of favors and a successful accumulator of cattle.[49] As for assessing the creditworthiness of prospective lenders or borrowers, the kinship system allowed even strangers to trace people who could report on both a man's reliability and his whereabouts if something went wrong.[50] Moreover, simply knowing who his closest relatives were gave some indication of how much wealth he might possess and how much he might be able to call on in a pinch.

A herder made connections not only to shift labor. More important was shifting cattle; this was done by two means. The first was dealing in the open exchange market. A man with too many male or female calves in a row exchanged with other owners to restore balance. Or if disease struck a man's cattle post, he might want to trade a surviving ox for two immature females with someone looking for an ox for slaughter. This exchange market thrived on calculations herders made in different situations and stages of herd growth. Without it, our ambitious herder would have had much less flexibility in managing the composition of his herd.[51]

The second method of shifting cattle among herds was lending them, usually as *mafisa*. Here the credit-referral function of kinship found its fullest expression. When his herd grew faster than his son grew, the cattle owner preferred farming out cattle to taking in more herders. This was because he wanted to scatter his cattle widely rather than concentrate them in his one post. This maximized his access to the erratic rainfall and reduced the risk of losing all his cattle if disease swept one cattle post. A man would approach another to say, *Ke kopa lefisa*"; that is, "I am asking for a *lefisa* cow." This was always an immature female. Usually the herd owner would already know the asker, but if not, he would trace him back to his relatives and friends in order to find out how responsible, skilled, and wealthy a herder he was. If the asker checked out to be a good risk, the herd owner would give him one *lefisa* or even two *mafisa*, which the borrower herded at his own cattle post. These cattle and all their offspring remained the property of the owner, except for the second female calf of the original *mafisa*. This and all their offspring were payment to the borrower for his herding services. After ten years or so, the borrower returned all the owner's cattle and kept his own. Even a small herd owner might give out *mafisa* and take in someone else's in order to spread his risks without changing the number of cattle at his post.[52]

One of the system's most important functions was to enable a man suffering sudden cattle losses or just beginning his own cattle post to start a herd.[53] This kept more cattle posts in production, thereby increasing the number of productive units spread across the countryside to catch the rain. Table 4.2, a modification of Table 4.1, suggests the benefits of *mafisa* to both lender and borrower. Here we follow the two herds together rather than separately, by starting with two immature females, which now represent the initial *mafisa* loan. We then follow their offspring for ten years, noting the award of the second female calf to the *mafisa* borrower. Calves again alternate male and female, and again we take two cases.

Table 4.2 shows that nearly a quarter of the herd accrued to the borrower. This was why a man preferred depending on his sons to herd cattle: although a son received the same calf allocation as in *mafisa*, he did not collect his reward until his father died. *Mafisa* herders collected immediately, and for the duration of the contract the cattle were out of the owner's control. Reclaiming the *mafisa* cattle early was to the owner's disadvantage: If he suddenly withdrew them after the third year, for example, he would have given the borrower a female calf in return for three years of herding instead of ten.[54]

We can now see that a woman's inability to herd her own cattle or to have her daughters do so deprived her of a sizable portion of their increase. All herders demanded a calf allocation, and the only way she could avoid paying this directly was to keep her cattle in the herd of her father, her husband, or if these two died, her son. Even these men took a calf, although indirectly, by using it to reward their own sons or other herders tending the larger herd in which the woman's cattle were kept. A man therefore met his obligation to allocate

**Table 4.2** Mafisa

| | Heifers | Cows | Calves | Tollies | Oxen | Culls | Increase | Total |
|---|---|---|---|---|---|---|---|---|
| Year | O–H* | O–H | O–H | O–H | O–H | O–H | O–H | O–H |
| **Herd A: First Calf Female (Total Herd and Mafisa Herd)** | | | | | | | | |
| 1 | 2– | | | | | | | 2– |
| 2 | | 2– | 2– | | | | 2– | 4– |
| 3 | 1– | 2– | 1–1 | 1– | | | 1–1 | 5–1 |
| 4 | 1–1 | 2– | | 2– | | | | 5–1 |
| 5 | –1 | 3– | 2–1 | 1– | 1– | | 2–1 | 7–2 |
| 6 | 2– | 3–1 | 1–1 | 1– | 2– | | 2– | 9–2 |
| 7 | 2–1 | 3–1 | 2–1 | 2– | 2– | | 2–1 | 11–3 |
| 8 | 1–1 | 5–1 | 3– | 2–1 | 3– | | 3– | 14–3 |
| 9 | 3– | 5–1 | 4–2 | 1–1 | 5– | | 4–2 | 18–5 |
| 10 | 4–1 | 4–2 | 2–1 | 3–1 | 5–1 | 2– | –1 | 18–6 |
| **Herd B: First Calf Male (Total Herd and Mafisa Herd)** | | | | | | | | |
| 1 | 2– | | | | | | | 2– |
| 2 | | 2– | 2– | | | | 2– | 4– |
| 3 | 1– | 2– | 1–1 | 1– | | | 1–1 | 5–1 |
| 4 | 1–1 | 2– | | 2– | | | | 5–1 |
| 5 | –1 | 3– | 3– | 1– | 1– | | 3– | 8–1 |
| 6 | 1– | 3–1 | 1–1 | 2– | 2– | | 1–1 | 9–2 |
| 7 | 2– | 3–1 | 2–1 | 2–1 | 2– | | 2–1. | 11–3 |
| 8 | 2–1 | 4–1 | 2– | 1–1 | 4–1 | | 2– | 13–3 |
| 9 | 2–1 | 5–1 | 4–1 | 2– | 4–1 | | 4–1 | 17–4 |
| 10 | 3– | 4–2 | 3–1 | 3–1 | 5–1 | 2– | 1–1 | 18–5 |

*O = Owner (lender), H = Herder (borrower)

a calf to his herdboy with a woman's cattle, either his daughter's, his wife's, or his mother's. This was the man's reward for managing her cattle.[55]

And so although a woman was able to remove cattle from the sphere of men, she was able to pass on only a portion of that increase to her daughters. But what prevented a woman from setting up her own cattle post tended by her daughters, who inherited their cattle allocation only when the mother died? These female herders would have had a hard time finding cooperative men in the pastures, however, to lend and borrow labor and cattle. Herding was a monopoly that men did not want to give up. A woman refusing to give up a calf to a male herder faced the unhappy prospect of herding them alone, without a network of mutual assistance in the pastures, with no wife to supply grain while she herded. And so women gave up the calf.

## NEWCOMERS AND CHIEFS

Now that we can see what separated women from men, what made some men richer than others? The surplus generated by cultivation and herding flowed from women to men, who accumulated cattle. Within one lifetime, however, the wealth derived from past production, in the form of cattle, yielded more income than the surplus derived from the labor of women. That is, a small surplus of grain turned into cattle this year yielded its full return only in later generations, when the cattle had grown into a large herd. If the original surplus came from women, its increase came from the rain, the grass, the cow's own biology, and the labor of men, plus the small additional surplus that the present generation of men derived from women in the form of food.

Some men were richer than others, therefore, not because they extracted more surplus from the present generation of women, but because they inherited more cattle from the last generation of men. As suggested earlier in this chapter, men tried to break even in the activities attending cultivation so that they would not have to exchange cattle for food. That is, they tried to leave their inherited herd intact, to let it reproduce. But who inherited the most? Just as sons inherited more from their fathers than daughters inherited from their mothers, among sons the senior son usually inherited the most cattle.[56] This was because the eldest was the first to begin herding and thus receive a calf allocation, giving him a headstart on his brothers in accumulating cattle.

But did not each family have a senior son? Yes, but some senior sone were more senior than others, and the most senior of all was the chief. This was only the theory, however; the facts tended to more variety.[57] Picture a chief's senior son managing his cattle poorly or suffering a run of luck much worse than a younger brother's. He might pass on to his senior son fewer cattle than his younger brother passes on to his own senior son. If the same pattern repeats, that is, the chief's line of cattle grows more slowly than does a junior's line, eventually the chief will no longer be the wealthiest cattle owner. At this point, or even sooner, the wealthy junior might claim the chiefship or strike out on his own to form a new chiefdom. In the latter case, if the new chief's cattle continue to thrive, more and more followers might leave the old chief to join the new one. Eventually the old chiefdom might disappear completely. Which son inherits the most cattle and becomes chief is a question of which line of sons can keep their inherited cattle multiplying faster than the rest.[58]

A wealthy man tried to insure rapid cattle accumulation by reducing his dependence on *mafisa*, which lost a quarter of the herd growth every decade. The best alternative was having sons herd instead, for, as we noted above, sons took their calves only when their father died. A wealthy man thus married more than one wife, so as to produce sons faster.[59] Boys took years to grow up, however, and could not be chosen: If a son proved to be irresponsible, a man might have to wait several years before another one grew old enough to take over. Even this next son's reliability could not be guaranteed in advance. A wealthy man thus looked beyond his sons to the wider market to choose his herders. These he contracted by giving not *mafisa*, but *moraka* (pl., *meraka*).[60]

The word *moraka* has three related meanings. First of all, it means "cattle post," that is, pen plus hut plus cattle.[61] If we turn to Figure 4.3, we can see the variety of relationships that a cattle post can comprise. Two married sons, A and B, both keep their herds in their father's post. If we look within the herd of married son A, we can see the cattle he inherited from his father, plus more of his own, plus *mafisa*, plus the *ketleetso* and grain cattle from his wife. We can also see the cattle allocated to his sons, from within his own cattle, and to his daughters, from within the grain cattle.

A second meaning of the word *moraka* is any group of cattle herded by a close relative: We thus say that married son A kept a *moraka* for each of his two daughters. A third meaning of *moraka*, and this is the one that concerns us here, is more than two cattle loaned out to someone else. This was a number only the wealthy could afford to give. As with *mafisa*, the herder of a *moraka* received a calf allocation. Unlike *mafisa*, however, the herder never gave the *moraka* back to its owner, although he was always free to do so. The relationship was permanent, inherited by the senior sons of both owner and herder, so that the line of owners received lifetimes of herding labor for only one female calf. Furthermore, the owner added and subtracted at will, so that his *moraka* remained in his control.[62]

Who would accept such herding terms? The name *moraka* provides two clues. When a wealthy man gave a *moraka*, the recipient took these cattle out into the countryside and established a new cattle

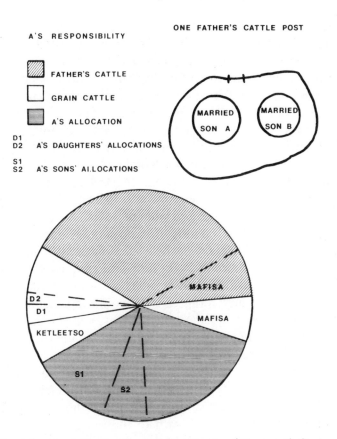

**Fig. 4.3.** Cattle Production and Distribution (Nineteenth Century)

post, the first meaning of *moraka*. The second meaning connotes a close family relationship. The recipient of the third kind of *moraka*, then, was a new recruit to the society who had no cattle post or family of his own. In giving him a *moraka*, the wealthy man adopted him as a sort of son.[63] Throughout the Southern African savanna, the cattle barons of one chiefdom always tried to recruit followers away from the cattle barons of other chiefdoms.[64]

We can now understand how the Kwena chiefdom and its neighbors absorbed refugees from the Zulu and Boer wars through the nineteenth century. Let us take a closer look at the Kwena chiefdom during this period, by following the career of Sechele I, their chief from 1829 to 1892. When Sechele was born around 1810, the Kwena numbered fewer than a thousand in a village along the Molepolole hills. He was the senior son of Chief Motswasele, whom a wealthy junior line, Tshosa, assassinated in 1822. The men of Tshosa took over Molepolole and chased away the boy Sechele and his royal uncles and followers. Refugees had already begun arriving from the east, but only after this coup did raiders reach the Kweneng in force. Sechele's people fared worse than the Tshosa people encamped at Molepolole, although all the Kwena and the refugees joining them spent a large part of the next twenty years scattering, wandering, regrouping, and running for their lives through much of present-day Botswana.[65]

Sechele himself ended up along the Kolobeng River, shown in Map 3.4. The ox-wagon trade arrived there in the 1840s, as did David Livingstone, who set up his Kolobeng mission in 1845. Dr. Livingstone seems to have helped channel guns from these traders to Sechele, who in 1848 became this most famous of African missionaries' only convert in all his years in Africa.[66] Sechele's Kwena used these guns to kill game and traded their products for more guns and goods, such as Sechele's full wardrobe of European dress. They also used the guns to protect themselves and any refugees who would join them. The Tshosa people were farther from the traders, guns, and refugees, although their position on the edge of the sandveld enabled them to keep their cattle safely at Letlhakeng and shoot game in the teeming, hitherto gunless Kalahari. Sechele won out and the Tshosa people capitulated in 1846. A major defeat by Boer raiders followed in 1852, but after this Sechele moved his headquarters back to the Molepolole hills, and the rural economy settled down to the general pattern described above.[67]

Refugees from the Transvaal continued to arrive, however, well into the twentieth century. The Kwena assimilated them as always, through the *moraka* system. Singly or in groups, refugees arriving in the village were brought to the chief, who either gave them a *moraka* himself or sent them to someone else wealthy enough to do so. Unattached women refugees, unable to herd, were taken in by Kwena women to help cultivate. The *moraka*-giver also allocated to the male newcomer a grain field near his own field and a compound site behind his own. A *kgotla* of village compounds thus comprised men linked by cattle descended from one cattle post owned now by the kgotla head. They were either his sons, as in Figure 4.3, or his younger brothers, or sons of his father's younger brothers, or sons of his grandfather's younger brothers, and so on. Or else the members of his *kgotla* were newcomers or their sons, each holding a *moraka* from him or one of the other *kgotla* members.[68]

We can see this process of *kgotla* formation and newcomer assimilation, plus the competition between brother herders, in the Mokgalo ward, which was the newest of the five major divisions of Molepolole at the turn of the century (see Map 8.1, p. 205). The founder of Mokgalo was Kgosidintsi, Sechele's junior brother and chief advisor. Their father, Chief Motswasele, had sons by five wives, whose senior sons are shown below. Of these five brothers, at first only the first two led *makgotla*, although as a senior son of one of Motswasele's wives, each was expected to do so eventually. Sekweni joined Sechele, while Basiamang and Tebele joined the *kgotla* of Kgosidintsi, who grew wealthier and wealthier as the years went by.[6 9]

*Mokgalo Genealogy*

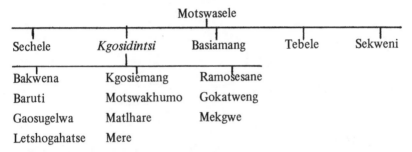

Kgosidintsi himself had three wives, whose sons are also shown above. He had so many cattle that he divided his one cattle post into several. The division of a *kgotla* head's cattle post entailed a parallel division of his *kgotla* in the village. This is because the *moraka* he gave to a newcomer remained attached to the herd from which it was taken. That is, if Kgosidintsi gave a *moraka* from the cattle herded by one son, let's say Baruti, and if Baruti's herd grew so large that he needed a separate cattle post, Baruti formed a new *kgotla* and the *moraka*-holder joined it. Tracing *kgotla* formation, then, traces the cattle fortunes of their heads.[7 0]

As senior sons of one of Kgosidintsi's wives, Bakwena, Kgosiemang and Ramosesane each expected to establish his own *kgotla* and cattle post, with his younger brothers beneath him. Such a herding scheme would have looked like Figure 4.4A. The fortunes of Kgosidintsi's sons turned out differently, however. Motswakhumo ended up the wealthiest by far and so established his own cattle post and *kgotla*. Baruti and Gaosugelwa were wealthy enough to do the same. Letshogahatse joined Gaosugelwa. Kgosiemang did set up a post and *kgotla*, as expected, but Ramosesane did not. He joined Motswakhumo instead, as did all the remaining sons of the second and third wives. The cattle posts would have looked like Figure 4.4B.

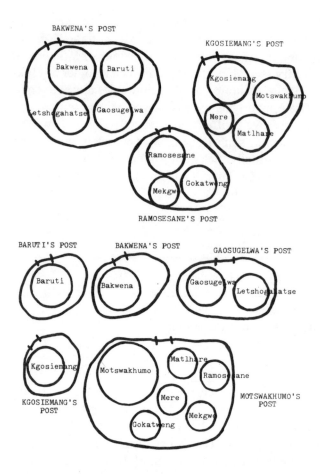

**Fig. 4.4.** The Cattle Posts of Kgosidintsi's Sons

Attached to each cattle post were *meraka*, scattered in cattle posts across the countryside. The holders of these *meraka* were the followers of each respective *kgotla* to which the *moraka* was attached. Motswakhumo of course attracted far more newcomers than his brothers, and we can see from Map 4.1 that he clearly dominated his ward. This map was drawn in 1976, forty years after the center of Molepolole moved from a hilltop site to the plain below. Although the cartographer did not pick up all the compounds from the aerial photographs, there is enough detail to make out the *kgotla* circles, whose locations I checked by foot in 1981. Note first of all the *kgotla* of Bakwena, the senior son of Kgosidintsi's first wife. This is Kgosidintsi's original *kgotla*. Note next the *makgotla* of Basiamang and Tebele, the brothers of

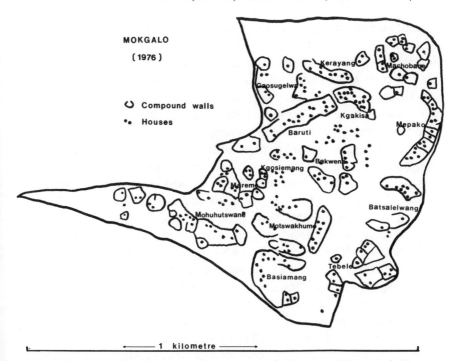

**Map 4.1.** Mokgalo. Based on Department of Town and Regional Planning, Molepolole Map, 1976. For better detail of ward houses and compounds, see Schapera, *Native Land*, Diagram II.

Kgosidintsi who joined his *kgotla* at the beginning. Their sons did not do as well as Kgosidintsi's. Then note the *kgotla* of Kgosiemang, the senior son of Kgosidintsi's second wife. As for the senior son of Kgosidintsi's third wife, Ramosesane built his house in the *kgotla* of his junior brother, Motswakhumo. Note too the *makgotla* of Baruti and Gaosugelwa, the younger sons who, like Motswakhumo, grew wealthy and set out on their own.[71]

As for the other *makgotla*, Batselelwang derived from Sechele, not from Kgosidintsi. As Mokgalo grew to great proportions, Sechele established this *kgotla* with its head as his voice in the ward's affairs, and with newcomers beneath him.[72] The rest of Mokgalo's *makgotla* were founded entirely by newcomers, and so these are the most junior in the ward. Kgosidintsi gave a newcomer a large *moraka* and distributed subsidiary *meraka* among others, with the first newcomer as *kgotla* head. The Kgakisa *kgotla* is the purest example of this. Kgosidintsi founded the other *makgotla* by taking cattle from the herds of his sons. The Kerayang *kgotla*'s cattle came from Kgosiemang's herd.

Its people were refugees of the same Malete who received one of the eight Bechuanaland reserves. The three *makgotla* of Machobane, Mareme, and Mohuhutswana were established with cattle from the vast herds of Motswakhumo. The first claim to be Shangaans, that is, non-Tswana speakers from the distant eastern Transvaal. The other two claim to descend from Kalaka refugees, that is, Shona-speakers from the northern tip of the Bechuanaland hardveld.

The last *kgotla*, Mepako, provides a good illustration of newcomer assimilation. It can be traced to two refugees, Kokgorwe and Motsomi, who arrived independently in Mokgalo's midst. Kgosidintsi gave them each a *moraka* from the herd of his senior son. This was now Baruti, for Bakwena had already died. Instead of each forming a tiny independent cattle post, Kgosidintsi instructed them to pool their resources into one post, called Mepako. In the village itself, these refugees fell under Baruti's *kgotla*. When Molepolole moved downhill in 1936, its occupants took the opportunity to make a few adjustments, one of which was the establishment of Mepako as a separate *kgotla*. Its herders had done so well that their cattle post was large enough to accommodate a full complement of followers.[73]

We can imagine in days gone by a *kgotla* like Mepako continuing to prosper until it produced a fabulously wealthy junior son like Motswakhumo, who might ultimately claim the chiefship or set out on his own. This was how the descendants of newcomers once aspired to become chiefs.

## BRIDEWEALTH

We can now see how herding relations contributed to the production and circulation of wealth in the nineteenth century Kweneng. Still we have not discussed bridewealth, a cattle transaction that missionaries attacked all over Southern Africa. From the beginning of British rule, British missionaries led the fight for freely contracted wage labor, inveighing against the various other labor relations found in Boer and African societies. They suspected that bridewealth was a form of forced labor, or slavery, involving the sale of a woman to a man.[74]

Our own understanding of bridewealth in the Kweneng must take account of the newcomers in the economy. In 1975, Okihiro found that Molepolole had 37 major newcomer *makgotla* of more than 10 compounds each: 10 of these *makgotla* were formed before Sechele's time; 19 were formed during his time; 5 were formed during the rule of his senior son Sebele I (1892-1911); and 2 were formed later. Alongside these were only 24 major Kwena *makgotla*, that is, those whose first head was not a newcomer. And most of the members of these Kwena *makgotla* were newcomers as well.[75] A large percentage of marriages in the second half of the nineteenth century thus involved newcomers. Yet a refugee man almost always arrived cattleless. How did he manage to pay for a wife?

First of all, a husband himself paid bridewealth only in the last resort. In the case of nonnewcomers, ordinarily a young man's father organized his bridewealth for him. The minimum was four immature stock: two cattle and two sheep, one of each sex. More could be paid and cattle could replace the sheep, but always in immature male-female pairs. The father handed over four animals from his own herd to the bride's family. He then sought replacements from relatives and friends. His wife's eldest brother and his own brother and sister were each expected to contribute one, although anyone could give more. All animals went first to the father's pen for him to decide how many should go to the bride's family. He himself was expected to end up giving at least two from his own herd, but it was possible for him to take in more contributions than he gave over as bridewealth and thus make a profit from the arrangement.[76]

On the bride's side, the cattle went first to her father, who passed them on as follows: The first two went to his wife's eldest brother, the next two went to his own sister and brother, and the fifth went to his wife's sister. Any others he kept for himself. Generosity from the husband's family was strongly encouraged for two reasons. First, a payment of fewer than six left none for the bride's parents. Second, the recipients of the first four bridewealth animals supplied four slaughter cattle to the marriage feast. A payment of eight was thus recommended in order to leave a net gain of four, three of which the bride's father kept.[77]

The marriage could even take place without any payment at all. The four feast animals were still provided by the bride's maternal and paternal uncles and paternal aunt from their own herds, and the bridegroom's father was obliged to replace them later. Until he did so the husband, or rather his family, could not receive any bridewealth for the daughters born of the unpaid marriage. When the first of these daughters married, her bridewealth went not to her father but to the patient in-laws who long ago gave four cattle for slaughter.[78]

Certainly bridewealth amounted to more than a meal, yet it was a loose arrangement and even seemed somewhat redundant. The maternal uncle of one bridegroom, that is, a cattle-giver, was also the maternal uncle of some other bride, that is, a cattle-taker. He was also a paternal uncle, and a father, and once he had been a bridegroom himself. This redundancy disappears when we consider a newcomer with no relatives at all. Who gave bridewealth in the case of a bridegroom, and who received it in the case of a newcomer bride? To begin with, someone offered to adopt the newcomer upon his or her arrival. A man was given a *moraka* by a foster father, who also organized his bridewealth. A woman newcomer helped in the fields but moved away from her foster parents when she married. In return for this adoption, the new daughter stored the grain from her new field in her foster mother's house, she helped her plant and weed, and her foster parents received her bridewealth. The bridegroom's new father canvassed his own relatives and friends for bridewealth contributions, while the bride's new father canvassed his own relatives and friends for animals to be slaughtered at the marriage feast. Thus whoever had an expanding herd, and so was looking for an extra reciprocal relationship to initiate, was given this chance to do so. The foster father of the newcomer bridegroom had a tougher time, of course, because the givers gained nothing directly until the next generation, when a daughter of the newcomer marriage brought in bridewealth to them. This was why there was no time limit for payment.[79]

Consider the position of a newcomer man's son. Because he inherited only one generation of accumulated cattle, his position was particularly precarious. What if he lost all his cattle? As with any man, the same individuals who gave him bridewealth came together to contribute replacements for his herd. Again, the wide range of relatives involved increased his chances of receiving at least something.[80] We can see, then, that bridewealth was much more than the purchase of a woman. It sped the incorporation of newcomers by quickly involving them in a wide network of cattle transfers that in the end delivered no man an automatic advantage but helped all men stay in production.

## NOTES

1. Okihiro, "Hunters," p. 71; Interviews 7, 9.
2. Okihiro, "Hunters," pp. 71-72; Interviews 7, 9, 40, 41, 43. C. Lightfoot, "Broadcast planting in perspective," MoA, 1981, explains the agronomic logic of broadcasting.
3. Okihiro, "Hunters," p. 73; Interview 12.
4. Okihiro, "Hunters," p. 75; Interview 6.

5. Interviews 6, 7.
6. Interviews 33, 37, 55.
7. Interviews 9, 37. Average yields is a difficult question with such erratic rainfall. Whether average yields in average conditions rose or fell with the plow is virtually impossible to ascertain. My informants reported no significant change. Throughout, I use a constant average of one bag per acre, the national rule of thumb established by the government's first crop survey in 1948, and I consider variations of yields according to the time of planting. That is, better timing equals above average yields. E. Parish, "Crop survey of the Bechuanaland Protectorate," DoA, 1948.
8. Okihiro, "Hunters," p. 76. See also A. Hamilton, "A review of post-harvest technology in Botswana," MoA, 1975.
9. Interview 7.
10. Okihiro, "Hunters," p. 65; Interviews 19, 33.
11. Interview 37. In 1926-27, the Kweneng District Commissioner reported the Kwena still sowing very little maize, which they ate on the cob. Kweneng District, *Annual Report*, 1927-27, BNA, DC Molepolole, Box 2, File M 22.
12. The best known statement of this view of "traditional" agriculture is W. Lewis, "Economic development with unlimited supplies of labour," *MSESS*, 1954. The problem of incomplete counting of rural activities is discussed in C. Kao, "Disguised unemployment in agriculture: a survey," in C. Eicher and L. Witt, *Agriculture in Economic Development*, New York, 1964; S. Brush, "The myth of the idle peasant," in R. Halperin and J. Dow, *Peasant Livelihood*, New York, 1977; G. Helleiner, "Smallholder decision-making: tropical African evidence," in L. Reynolds, *Agriculture in Development Theory*, New Haven, 1974; S. Hymer and S. Resnick, "A model of an agrarian economy with non-agricultural activities," *AER*, 59, 1969; J. Tosh, "The cash crop revolution in tropical Africa," *AfA*, 79, 1980. For a recent example of incomplete counting in Botswana, see M. Lipton, "Employment and labour use in Botswana," MFDP, 1978, vol. 1, ch. 1.
13. Interviews 6, 43.
14. For a brief explanation of productivity in African agriculture, see M. Upton, *Farm Management in Africa*, Oxford, 1973, pp. 145-46.
15. Interview 33.
16. RB, MoA, APRU, "Beef production and range management in Botswana," 1980, pp. 11-12, 128. Horses need some 90 liters, and so remain rare in the Kweneng to this day. See also S. Curl and J. Schuster, "Ecological and physiological constraints," in Botswana Society, *Sustained Production*.
17. Interview 33.
18. Interview 14.
19. Interview 14. Townshend, "Development," GB, CO, *ASD*, 1910, estimated 2,000 cattle at Letlhakeng, 3,000 at Dutlwe, and 17,000 at Molepolole.
20. A 1910 eyewitness account reported this scene in May-June at a Kweneng water point, presumably Letlhakeng, with cattle grazing two days and watering one out of every three. Townshend, "Development," GB, CO, *ASD*, 1910.
21. Interviews 15, 17. These were fat-tailed sheep with pelts much thinner than the imported merino wool sheep mentioned in Chapter 2.

22. Interviews 3, 22.
23. APRU, "Beef," pp. 11-12, 40-41. Grass in Botswana is some 70 percent water in the early wet season, but only 10 percent in the dry winter.
24. Okihiro, "Hunters," pp. 169-71; Interview 18.
25. Interview 5.
26. Schapera, *Handbook*, p. 221; Interviews 2, 28, 29.
27. Interviews 3, 22.
28. Calves are 12 months old or younger; tollies and heifers are 13 to 35 months; cows and oxen are 36 months or older. Interviews and APRU suggest long-run effective calving rates of 50 percent, so cows calf in their fourth, fifth, seventh, ninth, and eleventh years. They are culled in the twelfth year, and oxen in their fifteenth. See APRU, "Beef Production"; G. Dahl and A. Hjort, *Having Herds*, Stockholm, 1976; A. Hjort and W. Ostberg, *Farming and Herding in Botswana*, Uppsala, 1978.
29. The social position of women is a major theme of Schapera's *Married Life in an African Tribe*, London, 1940.
30. See I. Schapera, "The social structure of the Tswana ward," *BS*, 9, 1935; Okihiro, "Hunters," ch. 1.
31. Schapera, *Handbook*, pp. 173-75; Interviews 1, 2.
32. Schapera, *Handbook*, p. 216; Interview 16.
33. Schapera, *Native Land*, p. 81; Interview 8.
34. See Schapera, *Handbook*, pp. 177, 220; Interviews 5, 28, 36, 37.
35. Schapera, *Handbook*, p. 149.
36. Okihiro, "Hunters," p. 68; Interviews 1, 2, 12, 40.
37. Interview 11.
38. Interviews 7, 36.
39. Schapera, *Handbook*, p. 225; *Native Land*, pp. 199-200; Okihiro, "Hunters," p. 77; Interviews 7, 37.
40. Schapera, *Handbook*, p. 149.
41. J. S. Moffat made these counts during his residence in Molepolole from 1877 to 1879. High Commission Correspondence, BNA HC 192/2, 24 June 1885. An 1885 estimate put the Kwena population at 30,000. C. Conder, "The present condition of the native tribes in Bechuanaland," *JAI*, 16, 1886. Earlier Molepolole estimates were 300 in 1843 and 20,000 in 1857, both by David Livingstone. Okihiro, "Hunters," pp. 23-24. W. Baldwin reported 20,000 in 1857, in *African Hunting and Adventure*, New York, 1863, p. 162.
42. Schapera, *Native Land*, p. 201; Interviews 7, 9, 37, 38.
43. Schapera, *Native Land*, pp. 200-1.
44. These prices from Interview 12 are consistent with those Okihiro reported for the turn of the century. "Hunters," p. 82.
45. Okihiro, "Hunters," p. 89; Interviews 29, 36, 39, 40.
46. Schapera, *Handbook*, p. 177; Interviews 4, 11.
47. Schapera, *Native Land*, p. 218; Interview 13.
48. Schapera, *Handbook*, pp. 177, 240; Interviews 13, 24.
49. Interview 24.
50. Schapera, *Handbook*, pp. 17-19.
51. Schapera, *Handbook*, pp. 241-42.
52. Schapera, *Handbook*, pp. 246-48; Interviews 3, 5.

53. Interviews 5, 18.
54. Interviews 14, 35.
55. Interviews 5, 16, 35, 42.
56. Schapera, *Handbook*, pp. 230-34.
57. Schapera, *Handbook*, pp. 53-57.
58. The family disputes that scattered chiefdoms across Southern Africa thus reflected solidly economic concerns: Legassick, "Sotho-Tswana," follows the trail of fission involving the Kwena before the nineteenth century.
59. Schapera, *Handbook*, p. 13.
60. Schapera, *Handbook*, pp. 248-50, outlines a variant of this system among the Ngwato and Tawana.
61. Interview 16.
62. Interviews 32, 35. There was a third system, *madisa*, which involved the Kgalagari, whose history this study does not pursue. *Madisa* was similar to *moraka* except that a herder received no calf allocation; the Kgalagari knew the Kalahari pastures intimately, however, and they spirited away so many calves that many grew rich. There was a decidedly feudal element to the relationship as well, at least until the turn of the century when Sebele I pacified the administration and perhaps also hurt his rival brother, Kgari, by declaring the Kgalagari free. Thereafter, they were much like the most disadvantaged newcomers. That their relationship with the Kwena did not alter significantly the organization of production and the circulation of wealth is indicated by the situation of non-Kalahari chiefdoms such as the Kgatla, on which Schapera's work is most directly based. See Schapera, *Tribal Innovators*, London, 1970, p. 90; Okihiro, "Hunters," ch. 4; BP, RC Correspondence, 3 August 1900, BNA RC 5/12; Interviews 14, 33. The Sarwa too fell under feudalistic control: see BNA DC Molepolole, Box 5, File M 341, 1929, and E. Tagart, *Report on the Conditions Existing Among the Masarwa of the Bamangwato Reserve of the Bechuanaland Protectorate*, Pretoria, 1933; G. Silberbauer and A. Kuper, "Kgalagadi masters and Bushmen serfs," *AS*, 25, 1966; T. Tlou, "Servility and political control: *Botlhanka* among the Batawana of northwestern Botswana," in S. Miers and I. Kopytoff, *Slavery in Africa*, Madison, 1977.
63. Interviews 8, 10, 35.
64. See Wilson, "The hunters and herders," p. 63; "The Nguni people," pp. 120-21; "The Sotho, Venda and Tsonga," p. 155; J. Holleman, *Shona Customary Law*, London, 1952, p. 319, n. 1.
65. This account follows F. Nangati, "Constraints on a pre-colonial economy: the Bakwena state, 1820-1885," *P*, 1, 1980; G. Okihiro, "Resistance and accommodation: BaKwena bagaSechele, 1842-1852," *BNR*, 5, 1973; A. Sillery, *Sechele*, Oxford, 1954. Throughout this study, "Molepolole" refers to a number of adjacent sites in the Molepolole hills. See Schapera, *Native Land*, pp. 59-60. For other areas in this era, see T. Tlou, "A political history of northwestern Botswana to 1906," Ph.D., Wisconsin, 1973; L. Ngcongco,' "Aspects of the history of the Bangwaketse to 1910," Ph.D., Dalhousie, 1975; N. Parsons, "The economic history of Khama's country in Botswana, 1844-1930," in Palmer and Parsons, *Roots*; J. Chirenje, *A History of Northern Botswana*, Cranbury, 1977.
66. See I. Schapera, "Livingstone and the Boers," *AfA*, 59, 1960.

67. Okihiro, "Hunters," p. 205; Interviews 8, 10.
68. Schapera, "Social structure."
69. This example follows Okihiro's genealogical outline of Mokgalo in "Hunters," pp. 11-12.
70. Interviews 10, 25.
71. Okihiro, "Hunters," pp. 11-21; Interviews 53, 54.
72. Interviews 53, 54. Okihiro, "Hunters," reports this post as *ntona*, from the Nguni word *induna*.
73. Interviews 53, 54.
74. See South African Native Affairs Commission, *Report*, 1905, vol. 1, p. 60.
75. Okihiro, "Hunters," pp. 22-24, 222-24. For other chiefdoms, see Schapera, *Ethnic Composition*.
76. Schapera, *Handbook*, pp. 138-41; Interviews 15, 40.
77. Schapera, *Handbook*, pp. 134, 142-43; Interviews 15, 40.
78. Schapera, *Handbook*, pp. 139-41, 143-45; Interview 44.
79. Interviews 27, 28.
80. Interviews 27, 28. This group of relatives is called *bareri*. Their meeting is a *morero*.

# 5

# The Plow, the Well, and the Wagon, 1900–1940

Whereas the last chapter explained how the Kweneng rural economy met the demands of its natural environment, this chapter discusses how it met the new demands of the commercial economy that absorbed it. Because the Protectorate government was so poor, its agricultural development policy remained minimal until after World War II. For the most part, the agricultural changes in the Kweneng from 1900 to 1940 resulted from the meeting of the commercial and rural economies, with a minimum of state mediation.

During these first four decades of the twentieth century, the Kweneng rural economy flourished as never before. It appeared at this time, though certainly not thereafter, that the rural economy made the commercial economy conform to its demands, rather than the reverse. Producers sold grain and cattle on the new South African markets and adopted the imported technology of plows, wells, and wagons to increase production. Even with these new tools and market connections, however, agriculture in the Kweneng appeared as "traditional" as ever. Although there were important changes as well, they did not become conspicuous until after World War II. Nevertheless, we must watch for the new rural order rising slowly out of the old.

## TECHNOLOGY IN THE KWENENG

The most conspicuous changes in Kweneng agriculture during this period were in the dominant tools of the trade. Although of dubious accuracy, the 1911 census gives us at least some picture of the new technology. Table 5.1 presents some of these census figures. The

103

Table 5.1   Census, 1911

|  | African Reserves | | | |
|  | Kwena | Ngwato | Other | Total |
| --- | --- | --- | --- | --- |
| Population | 13,103 | 34,886 | 75,314 | 123,303 |
| Wagons | 242 | 618 | 1,336 | 2,196 |
| per capita (A) | .02 | .02 | – | .02 |
| Plows | 767 | 3,072 | 5,330 | 9,169 |
| per capita (B) | .06 | .09 | – | .07 |
| Cattle | 39,591 | 97,166 | 187,154 | 323,911 |
| per capita (C) | 3.02 | 2.79 | – | 2.63 |
| Horses, Mules, Donkeys | 142 | 500 | 3,580 | 4,222 |
| per capita (D) | .01 | .01 | – | .03 |
| Sheep, Goats | 33,407 | 150,245 | 174,684 | 358,336 |
| per capita (E) | 2.55 | 4.31 | – | 2.91 |

Ngwato of Chief Khama are included here to show that this one chief-dom comprised from a quarter to a third of the Bechuanaland population and economy. The Kweneng accounted for about one-tenth. Per capita figures are similar for both and for the total Protectorate as well.

Overall, there was one wagon for every fifty persons (row A), and more plows than wagons: one plow for every seventeen Kweneng residents and one for every eleven residents of the Ngwato reserve (B). Did producers share wagons and plows or did some go without? As we shall see, both these things happened. Rural producers used cattle (C), rather than horses, mules, or donkeys (D), to pull their wagons and plows. This was because keeping cattle had other economic benefits, such as meat, milk, and an attractive exchange value, increasingly in the commercial market. Besides, horses needed more water and were more susceptible to disease.

There were about as many sheep and goats (E) as cattle, whereas cattle numbers were overwhelmingly greater in later decades. This partly reflects better counting, but there was definitely a shift in favor of cattle during the twentieth century. In 1980, for example, the national ratio of cattle to small stock in Botswana was 3.7 to 1.[1] Drought-resistant goats were still a herding necessity in 1911; as modern, reliable water supplies spread through Bechuanaland's pastures, the insurance of goats became less necessary.

The plow appeared in the Kweneng in the late nineteenth century, brought on the wagons of white traders who set up stores in the major hardveld villages. There were 40 plows reported in Ngwato territory as early as 1878.[2] The Kweneng was not booming, however, and so Sechele's people could not afford as many plows as Khama's.[3] Molepolole's handful of traders—there were 6 in 1877—sold plows in exchange for livestock and game skins.[4] Two types of plows were available: an English plow with an iron frame, and a cheaper American plow with a wooden frame.[5] Cultivators at first preferred the cheaper wooden plow because they could fix it themselves. Although a metal plow was much more durable, if it did break, only a blacksmith could fix it, for a price.[6] As a result, a few Boer blacksmiths settled in Molepolole.[7]

The iron plow soon won out, once plowing's advantage proved clear: A hoe could till 10 square meters in one morning, while a plow could till 2,500. Yet a hoe required only two hands, and cost far less than a plow from the trader's shop. A plow cost one ox, required at least four hands to use it, several cattle to pull it, nearby water for these draught cattle, constant repair, and part replacement.[8] These things were hard to come by all at once, so that the number of plows per capita in Table 5.1 is not surprising.

The most popular plow was fairly large and heavy, and teams of six or eight draft cattle became the rule.[9] Such large teams enabled cultivators to plow very quickly and so take most advantage of the few weeks or sometimes days when rain wet the fields. Hard work weakens cattle, so that plowers preferred to use oxen. They used weaker cows and immatures when oxen were few, so the quality of a draft team could vary tremendously. Plowers tried to place at least one well-trained ox in the front to lead the team in a straight line and two strong mature cattle at the back to bear the full weight of the plow. Cows weakened by plowing produced fewer healthy calves less often and so slowed the growth of the herd.[10]

Cattle yokes were hand-made wooden bars across the shoulders of a pair of animals, lashed around the neck with leather thongs. An iron chain from the trader's shop connected the yokes and led to the plow behind. Yoking untrained cattle could take several hours, for Tswana cattle have long sharp horns. Once they learned the routine well, they took only a few minutes to yoke. Yoking always went faster the more hands to help: One per animal was best, but one person could do the whole job alone if forced to do so.

During plowing season, the cattle were penned near the field and let out to graze at night. At first light the plowers yoked them, and let up to a quarter hectare or so until midday, unyoked them, and let them graze to water and back. After another quarter hectare of plowing in the afternoon, they unhitched the cattle and let them graze again. A few cultivators exceeded this rate by using two teams and two plows at once, but most fell far below it. Sick, old, or untrained animals, cows or immatures instead of oxen, distant water, poor grazing—all these reduced plowing speed.[11]

The human input could vary greatly as well. One person with a perfectly trained team could possibly have planted alone by first broadcasting the seed, then yoking the team, and then guiding the plow with two hands on the plow handles and letting the team follow the furrow. It is doubtful that anyone in Bechuanaland ever tried this. Realistically, plowing required at least two workers, one to hold the plow and one to drive the oxen with a whip. The plow-holder's strategy was to cut as wide a furrow as possible in each pass across the field, so as to increase the area plowed in one morning or afternoon, thereby plowing as large an area as possible during the brief rains. A driver's strategy was to keep the oxen moving in a straight line at a fast, even pace.[12]

If there were only two persons to plow, one yoked the team while the other broadcast the seed; then one held the plow while the other drove; then one drove the cattle to water at midday while the other cooked a meal; then in the afternoon again one held the plow while the other drove. This was an exhausting schedule, and fatigue slowed the pace. More workers saved time. The most efficient number was five: All helped to yoke and unyoke the team; two plowed, alternating driving and holding the plow; one broadcast; one cooked and carried firewood and water; and one ranged the field with a small axe to weed out the bushes grown up since last year.[13]

Only with access to sufficient draft cattle, pasture, water, and labor could a field owner take full advantage of the plow. Even the majority who had to borrow at least some of these things, including the plow itself, were able to cultivate vastly larger fields than with the hoe. At first field owners merely expanded their tiny hoe fields, which were clustered in choice spots around Molepolole.[14] From the second half of the nineteenth century, the Kwena gave some groups of Tswana newcomers separate village sites in the southern half of the Metsemotlhaba basin: Gabane in 1860, Mankgodi in 1863, Kopong in 1881, Mogoditshane in the early 1900s, and Thamaga in

1934. Molepolole still housed more than half the southern hardveld population throughout the period to 1940, however.[15] The southern hardveld now grew congested with large plow fields and plow teams, moving Sechele's son and successor, Chief Sebele I, to urge the Kwena to expand into the transitional hardveld to the north. From the beginning of Sebele's rule in the 1890s throughout our period to 1940, the Kwena did precisely this.[16]

How was this expansion possible, without perennial surface water in the transitional hardveld? Some plowers became totally transhumant, moving north with their cattle at the beginning of the summer rains, plowing, harvesting, and returning to Molepolole in the dry winter. This was a risky venture, however, because one could never be sure that there would be enough rain water to sustain the draft team through the plowing season. Those who could afford to do so blasted wells to create their own perennial water supplies, where they now kept their cattle throughout the year. This allowed them to plow near the well at any time, which they did at just the right time. Well-owners thus gained access to as much virgin pasture and soil as their herds and draft teams could utilize.[17]

At first a well cost five cattle.[18] The best sites were in the rock beds of the transitional hardveld's riverless valleys, where water collected just below the surface. The dynamite cost two oxen at the trader's store, and the well-blaster demanded one ox to start the job plus one young cow if he struck water. Blasting was a specialized skill, at first possessed by only a few traders but quickly learned by a few Kwena. The blaster cased the rock hole with wood and the owner bought a windlass, bucket, and chain from the trader for an ox, or a blacksmith would make these items for the same price of one ox.[19] Herdboys often preferred hoisting water without the windlass, however, by bending over the hole with only a rope and bucket.[20]

The Kwena blasted a few wells in the calcrete crusts of the Letlhakeng and Lephepe sandveld valleys, yet empty thirsts still separated these valleys from Molepolole. The transitional hardveld was much more accessible, beginning right at the northern edge of the village. Wells were so expensive that their numbers grew slowly even here. In 1932, Chief Tshekedi of the Ngwato told the Protectorate government that a man needed to own at least 40 cattle to be able to afford one.[21] Some people who could not afford blasted wells dug new sand pits, some of which proved perennial, which they now used as their permanent water supplies for the new cattle posts and plowlands. This slowly filled up the spaces between the blasted wells. A cattle owner would rather have a well because anyone was free to dig a sand pit anywhere; if someone discovered a good pit site, others came to dig pits nearby and so filled the surrounding pasture with their cattle.[22]

Pit technology was ancient and simple: Why did the Kwena suddenly dig so many more of them from 1900 to 1940? The plow increased the demand for new water sources, and the scattered wells now provided emergency water supplies in bad years when even the deepest pits ran dry. There was another contributing factor: the wagon. Wagons carried plows, plowers, seed, food, cooking utensils, tools, and even water out to any spot a field owner chose to plow, and they carried the harvest back to the village. Wagons thus connected the scattered water points of the transitional hardveld with the southern hardveld, allowing the Kwena to move much more quickly and thus efficiently to catch the rain that fell there. This aided the development of wells and pits and thus permanent cattle posts and plow fields in an area that had previously served mainly as a summer pasture.[23]

Molepolole traders procured South African wagons on special order. The cost was very high, about one ox per foot for wagons of 12, 14, or 18 feet in length. A wagon also required about one ox per foot to pull it. The smallest wagon thus required an investment of some 24 oxen, and the largest required 36. No wonder Table 5.1 reports only one wagon per fifty Kweneng residents as of 1911. As we shall see, however, most had some access to a wagon. The 18-foot wagon could carry 35 bags of grain weighing well over 3,000 kilograms. Like a plow, a wagon required occasional repair by a blacksmith.[24]

The plow, the well, and the wagon changed the scale of agriculture in the Kweneng, expanding the area of cultivation and permanent pasture, and allowing the Kwena to produce more than before. Yet we must also note what remained the same. The new tools did not greatly alter the techniques that the Kwena used to produce. Turning the soil was the only cropping activity that the plow revised. Broadcasting, hoe weeding, bird-scaring, harvesting, and threshing remained as described in the previous chapter, except that larger fields required more time to work. As for herding techniques, blasted wells were used exactly as the well-known perennial pits were. And the wagon was essentially a team of pack oxen hitched together. In turn, some things changed and some remained the same in how the Kwena were organized to use their agricultural technology.

## A NEW AGRICULTURAL TRADITION

One of the most important of these organizational changes was a revision of the production unit. The circulation of daughters in the nineteenth century kept all cultivators and homesteads united in a network of reciprocal exchanges. The plow now interrupted this circulation. With the hoe, there had been one small field per nuclear family, overseen largely by the wife. The plow greatly enlarged this field to three or four hectares or so.[25] Hitherto, the husband had left some time during the hoeing season to take the cattle out to the distant summer pastures and occasionally hoed a small plot alongside his temporary herding shelter, but now he planted this field, greatly enlarged by the plow, alongside his wife's. And now when a daughter grew old enough to help farm, she established a separate field as an extension of her mother's. The precedent for this was that a daughter who failed to marry immediately upon maturity was given her own field to hoe for herself alongside the one family field. As for a son, as soon as he grew old enough to help, he too started a separate field as an extension of his father's. He would have eventually cleared such a field for his bride. Now he simply established this field when he was still a boy.[26]

Instead of one hoe field for the whole family, there was now one plow field for each worker. The reason for expanding the area tilled is obvious: A plow covered far more ground than a hoe. But why not plow one big field rather than several smaller ones? The latter made climatic sense, for scattered fields spread the chance of catching at least some rain. Yet these family fields were usually contiguous and so did not spread this chance very far. The real reason involved the circulation of grain. We recall that formerly the wife stored the grain from her hoe field in her mother's house in the village. With the plow, this was suddenly a very much larger amount of grain. The husband and wife were now wary that her mother and father might misuse such large quantities of grain. It was not that they mistrusted her parents. There was simply no longer a need to trust them. With the plow, one husband-wife-children team could now produce enough grain in good years to tide them over in bad years. They no longer needed as much insurance from the wife's mother and married sisters' fields. There was no longer a need to store grain in her mother's house.[27]

Such family matters are delicate, however. A wife and husband could not suddenly stop delivering grain to her parents, at least not until they were absolutely sure that they could consistently produce enough on their own. Instead, they took a large part of the harvest out of consideration in the first place. We can see this by comparing Figure 5.1 with Figure 4.2 above. In the case of a daughter's plow field, a girl or woman always stored her grain in her mother's house, and so this daughter's crop stayed right in the wife's storehouse. The man's field enlarged and gained an extension, the son's field. The man's field had never sent grain to his wife's mother, so grain from these two fields went into the wife's storehouse.[28]

Yet the previous circulation of daughters and grain did not end altogether. The wife's field was still the largest and its grain still went to her mother's storehouse. She and her sisters still helped out in her mother's field. But now that each wife had enough grain from her nuclear family fields to feed her household, she no longer walked to her mother's house to fetch the daily food. She now cooked grain from her own storehouse. Whereas before, a mother's married daughters stored all their grain in her house and took out only what they needed for cooking, now these daughters stored all their grain in their own houses and gave to their mother only what she needed for cooking.[29]

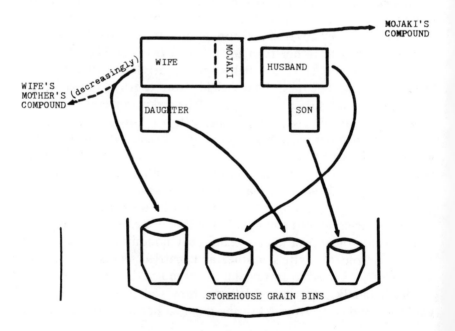

**Fig. 5.1.** Plow Fields and Grain Distribution. (See Schapera, *Native Land*, Diagram III, for a map of multiple fields.)

This picture of the new family plow fields is an ideal one. Very few nuclear families could muster enough oxen, water, pasture, and labor to be so self-sufficient. Here the *majako* system flourished as never before. With the hoe, someone lacking seed, or too sick to plant, or whose field failed, worked on a neighbor's field for a small quantity of seed or grain. The hoe was cheap, abundant, readily loaned, and required only two hands to use, making it unusual for poverty to prevent someone from planting. The plow, in contrast, required so much more than two hands that in any one season most cultivators were unable to meet their plowing needs alone. Either they borrowed some of the essentials, or, if they reckoned that they could not cheaply assemble enough of them to plow a large enough field in time to produce a decent crop, they worked *majako* on someone else's field.[30]

A *majako* helper might help an oxen owner plow in return for the loan of the team to plow the helper's field later, with or without the assistance of the oxen owner. After plowing, prospective *majako* helpers might roam the fields looking for someone who managed to plant a large field at the right time. In this case the helpers might offer their services for the rest of the season to help with the large amount of weeding, bird-scaring, and harvesting ahead, in return for a portion of the harvest. Or a *majako* helper might help only to plow, weed, or harvest in return for food and a small amount of grain.[31]

We can see that *majako* stood somewhere between reciprocal assistance and wage labor. Indeed, a *majako* helper looked to work on a relative's field first, so as perhaps to be considered not a *majako* helper at all, but rather a family helper. Because some past or future reciprocity returned the favor, family helpers received more grain than ordinary *majako* helpers. For example, a married daughter was not a *majako* helper when she helped to weed her mother's field, nor if she helped on the fields of her husband's family adjacent to her own fields. If she helped other relatives, however, they might consider it *majako*, depending on how much reciprocity she and they had hitherto established.[32] Whether as *majako* or as family helpers, all who worked from planting to harvest were accommodated within the wife's large field. That is, a certain part of the field was set out that season as the helper's, in much the same way a daughter or son received their own plots. Although the helpers and family worked together on all the fields, each person received the pure grain from his or her allocated plot: wife, husband, daughter, son, helper. The *ditshane* was shared among the women who harvested it, especially the wife herself.[33]

In the wife's storehouse stood grain bins for each family member, including sometimes the helper's, if she had no other storage space (see Figure 5.1). The disbursement of excess grain followed much the same procedure as in the time of the hoe. If any family member's bin overflowed, this grain could be exchanged for livestock by the bin's owner.[34] Communal seed selection seems to have stopped, however, for the family did not open the worst grain bin first, but rather ate mostly from the wife's and left the husband's last, to accumulate a surplus for livestock.[35]

The *majako* system generally operated without legal sanction, although in theory a breach of contract could be taken to the *kgotla* courts composed of the men of each compound. In practice, poor workers acquired bad reputations and so had difficulty finding field owners willing to take them on, whereas stingy field owners had trouble attracting helpers. *Majako* benefited field owners by allowing them to borrow labor quickly and cheaply, without cash, and it benefited *majako* helpers by allowing them to reap some harvest from someone else's field. All tried to avoid working *majako*, however, and struggled first of all to plow their own fields even if they had to borrow to do so. Yet it was not always possible to borrow, especially for those with few or no cattle. A team owner was reluctant to lend six or eight cattle to someone unable to return an equivalent favor in the forseeable future. The cattle-poor might have to wait until others finished plowing to borrow two animals here and two animals there and two more somewhere else. Late planting meant only a small area planted.[36]

Those with many cattle were able to begin plowing early each year and to plant large fields, but they were also able to borrow in a pinch. This had not been so with the hoe, which required only two hands. Women especially were disadvantaged in plowing, not only because they owned fewer cattle than men, but also because as *majako* helpers they were prevented from handling cattle. That is, men extended their cattle herding monopoly to the plow field. The most popular *majako* arrangement involved a helper pitching in to plow the field of a draft-team owner in return for the entire work-team plowing the helper's field afterward. The field owner's wife usually broadcast the fields because this was the most important task to do carefully. A male helper then worked in the field, holding the plow and driving the cattle, in return for the work-team later plowing a field of the same size for him. A female helper did not handle the cattle and the plow but only cooked and carried water. In return the work-team plowed a field of only one-third the size for her. A woman was free to handle her own cattle, of course, and two women plowing alone is not an uncommon sight today in the Kweneng. Yet among the cattle-less and cattle-poor, a man was more able than a woman to plow a field with someone else's cattle. So it was overwhelmingly women who roamed the fields after planting, their children in tow to help work, seeking engagement for *majako*.[3][7]

We can see that the plow delivered harvests in proportion to how many cattle a cultivator could call on. Women had great difficulty plowing alone, and so relied on fathers, husbands, brothers, and sons for draft cattle and plowing labor. When these men were all to poor to help adequately, they and their female dependents might work *majako* or join another household altogether. Or a man would leave to work in South Africa, primarily in the Rand gold mines. The flexible rural economy allowed men to leave their fields and herds in the hands of others, work for wages in South Africa, and return to invest this cash in cattle, plows, wells, and wagons. Women were less able to follow suit, for three reasons: First, they did not have wives to work on their fields in their absence; second, their labor was in much less demand in South Africa, and so they could not earn much cash there; and third, they could not reap as high a return on wages invested in agriculture, because men herded and handled cattle. Plows, wells, and wagons were thus the preserve of men as well.[3][8]

South African wages were the chief source of cash in the Kweneng. Molepolole's traders—there were 12 as of 1937—sold large items like plows and small items like blankets less for cash than for "good-for" receipts, good for a certain value of items from their stores.[3][9] A trader did this not only because he wanted a customer to buy only at his store but because he often operated without much cash himself. Many Protectorate traders, especially north of the Kweneng, enlisted a Rand cattle dealer to pay for his trade goods in Johannesburg. The trader then exchanged these goods for cattle in Bechuanaland, sending the cattle to the Rand to repay the Rand dealer.[4][0] On their side, the Kwena cattle sellers operated as they had always done. Someone with an ox to sell took it from trader to trader for offers. He either took the best offer or decided that none of the prices was high enough for his ox.[4][1]

Cash penetrated deepest into the rural economy during this period in the hiring of draft-teams for plowing. A man working in South Africa sent back money, or arranged in person on journeys home, to pay a draft-team owner to plow a field supervised by his relatives, usually his wife, or if he was still unmarried, his mother, father, or sister.[4][2] This payment from the cattle-poor to the cattle-rich was less like capitalist wage labor, which is usually meant to mean that those without access to the means of production are forced to sell their labor, than the more universal payment of precious cash to a specialist or artisan, whose superior skills or tools, in this case cattle, fetched a high price.[43]

Most transactions remained cashless, however, and there appeared now to be many more transactions than before. Plows, wells, and wagons were so much more productive than the earlier technology that everyone wanted to use them. Because they cost so much more, most were unable to buy them. Even those who could afford these things were not so wealthy as no longer to need the insurance provided by the fields and herds of others, so that there was more borrowing and lending than ever before. Thus the inconspicuous reciprocity of circulating daughters and grain gave way to the more visible reciprocity of lending plows, wells, and wagons.[44]

This new agricultural tradition was most apparent in the transitional hardveld. As population growth filled up the southern hardveld, herding became more difficult there. Herders could no longer simply let their cattle wander in the summer; they now required a herder to lead them carefully from one patch of grass to another, seeking to avoid the most overgrazed spots. Also, the proliferation of large plow fields not only reduced summer pasture in the southern hardveld, but also forced herders to pay even closer attention to their cattle, lest they trample a field. Whereas out in the open range, two herders could handle a hundred cattle, each tiny herd in the crowded southern hardveld was tended by its own herder driving it constantly from spot to spot.[45]

And so everyone tried to escape from the southern hardveld. A few had done so in the nineteenth century, establishing permanent cattle posts at Letlhakeng, Lephepe, or the few perennial sand pits in the transitional hardveld. This required either that a husband live there year round and so never help his wife plant, or that the cattle post be entrusted to someone else by the *moraka* system. Only the wealthiest could afford to allocate so many cattle permanently as *moraka*, and so only they reaped year-round benefit from the pastures beyond the southern hardveld. We can now understand why the Kwena were so eager to follow Sebele I's advice at the turn of the century to expand into the transitional hardveld. Those able to afford wells and wagons led the way, but they did not leave everyone else behind. Because the senior head of a *kgotla* was usually the largest cattle owner, he was the first to buy a wagon, which he used to set up a distant cattle post and fields. On his trips, he carried fellow *kgotla* members as well, and whenever his wagon lay idle, they merely asked to borrow it. They always repaid the kindness with beer or a goat or some other gift; for example, they might return a borrowed wagon full of firewood for the owner.[46] Thus the wagon was constantly earning income for its owner, but others had access to it as well. As for a well, its owner loaned its use to relatives and friends for a fee, at first one calf per year. He could rescind this access in bad years, but such unfriendly behavior threatened his own ability to borrow. Moreover, wells and wagons were so expensive that often family members grouped together to make the purchase, usually brothers whose cattle grew up in the same father's herd. Each had his own network of lending, so that many others gained access to these wagons and wells.[47]

Because borrowing a wagon required a team of cattle to pull it, cattle owners benefited more than the cattleless did, who hoped merely to hitch a ride.[48] Those with few cattle were less able to pay a calf a year for access to a well. The cattle-poor were less able to repay favors in general, and so it was mostly they who remained confined to the increasingly overgrazed southern hardveld.[49]

We can catch a glimpse of the dilemma of the cattle-poor in Table 5.2, which is a further amendment of Table 4.1 above. Table 5.2 follows two immature cows over 10 years with a female calf first, which, as Table 4.2 shows, produces only one more animal in 10 years than a male first does. Table 5.2 also reports draft potential and the value of the crops and meat it could obtain on the open market in 1935. The prices used are export prices, and so are overestimates because of trader profits. The value of the herd is thus overestimated as well. Because the South African cattle market was sometimes officially closed to Bechuanaland cattle, a smuggling trade also developed, especially in the 1930s, so that many cattle exports evaded the official reports from which the prices in Table 5.2 are derived. Smuggler cattle prices are assumed to be half the officially reported prices. Figure 5.2 shows how these prices compare with those of other years.

Ten years of herding resulted in a herd worth only £30. The future value of this herd was great, however, for the herder could expect the herd to reach 100 head after another 10 years. These first 10 years were thus crucial, with the herder always torn between selling animals to cover immediate consumption needs and holding on to them so as to hasten the herd's growth. Throughout the twentieth century, most Kweneng residents probably never made it past the level depicted in Table 5.2. In 1936, for example, the Protectorate

**Table 5.2.** A Growing Herd's Income, 1935

| | | | Herd Growth | | | | |
|---|---|---|---|---|---|---|---|
| Years | Heifers | Cows | Calves | Tollies | Oxen | Cull | Total |
| 1 | 2 | | | | | | 2 |
| 2 | | 2 | 2 | | | | 4 |
| 3 | 1 | 2 | 2 | 1 | | | 6 |
| 4 | 2 | 2 | | 2 | | | 6 |
| 5 | 1 | 3 | 3 | 1 | 1 | | 9 |
| 6 | 2 | 4 | 2 | 1 | 2 | | 11 |
| 7 | 3 | 4 | 3 | 2 | 2 | | 14 |
| 8 | 2 | 6 | 3 | 3 | 3 | | 17 |
| 9 | 3 | 7 | 6 | 1 | 5 | | 23 |
| 10 | 5 | 6 | 3 | 4 | 6 | 2[c] | 24 |

| | | | Herd Income | |
|---|---|---|---|---|
| Year | Draft Animals[a] | Grain[b] (bags) | Grain Value[c] (£) | Value of Mature Cattle[d] (£) |
| 1 | — | — | — | — |
| 2 | 1.0 | 2.5 | 1.3 | 4 |
| 3 | 1.5 | 3.8 | 1.9 | 4 |
| 4 | 2.0 | 5.0 | 2.5 | 4 |
| 5 | 3.0 | 7.5 | 3.8 | 9 |
| 6 | 4.5 | 11.3 | 5.6 | 14 |
| 7 | 5.0 | 12.5 | 6.3 | 14 |
| 8 | 7.5 | 18.8 | 9.4 | 21 |
| 9 | 9.0 | 22.5 | 11.3 | 29 |
| 10 | 11.0 | 27.5 | 13.8 | 30 |

[a] ox = 1, cow = .5, tolly = .5
[b] 6 draft animals = 6 hectares; 1 hectare = 2.5 bags of 200 lbs. each.
[c] at £.5 per bag
[d] at £2.5 per head: cow = £2, ox = £3

census reported 2.1 cattle for each of the Kweneng's 24,639 residents: an estimate of 7 persons per household gives us about 14 or 15 cattle per household, or year 7 in Table 5.2.[50] The amount of grain such a household needed to consume per year was perhaps 10 bags, leaving 2.5 bags for sale for the pittance of £1.25. The temptation for this average household to sell their cattle was thus great. Yet if they held on to them for just two or three more years their value would double.

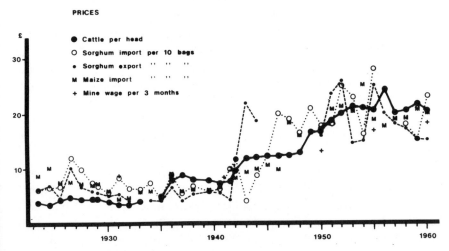

PRICES

● Cattle per head
○ Sorghum import per 10 bags
• Sorghum export  "   "   "
M Maize import  "   "   "
+ Mine wage per 3 months

**Fig. 5.2.** Bechuanaland Prices. (Figs. 5.2-8.2 are from BP, *Annual Report*, 1902-1965, and RB, *Statistical Abstract*, 1966-80. There is no adjustment for "real" prices. South Africa converted from pounds to Rands in 1960 at a rate of 2 to 1; Botswana converted from Rands to Pula in 1976, at a rate of 1 to 1. These ratios are maintained throughout, following Q. Hermans, "A review of Botswana's financial history," *BNR*, 6, 1974.)

So they sold grain, sometimes their entire harvest, hoping to borrow or to be fed by others for the rest of the year. Yet the entire harvest in year 7 of Table 5.2 amounted to only £6.30. So they also sold cattle. Cash wages mitigated the crisis somewhat, but mine wages were very low, and some men had to remain to herd their cattle. As of 1936, there were 1,820 Kweneng residents working in South Africa. Our estimate of 7 persons per household yields 3,777 households, so that if we assume one absent worker per household, half the households had no wage earner.[51]

Moreover, drought and disease hurt small owners more than large because it pushed them further down the scale. An owner of 100 cattle who lost three quarters of them in a drought still stood at year 10 in Table 5.2, whereas an owner of 24 who lost three quarters was sent back to the poverty of year 3 or 4. The worst disease outbreak in the period covered by this study seems to have been the 1896-97 rinderpest that forced the BSAC to build the railway to Rhodesia through the Bechuanaland hardveld.[52] Before World War II, the worst drought came in 1933, drying up most water sources that were usually perennial, including the new pits in the transitional hardveld. The cattle that had recently entered this zone to thrive and multiply now fell back on the southern hardveld, especially to its northernmost perennial water at Molepolole. The hordes of cattle quickly ate up the surrounding grass and then they began to die. Because the official South African market was completely closed at the time, smuggling was the only export channel, so that traders offered only rock-bottom prices for these cattle.[53]

Although the rains and the market improved in subsequent years, many producers never recovered. We have no survey data from this era, but we do have some indirect indications of impoverishment. The heaviest border smuggling took place in the late 1930s, when official prices and exports had recovered. South Africa kept a limit on the weight and numbers of Bechuanaland cattle it accepted, so that most cattle sales in this period yielded low smuggler prices. Cattle owners were desperate to sell, because the 1933 drought had destroyed their cattle reserves, presenting them with the grim accounting sheet suggested by Table 5.2. Every year they were forced to sell off their surviving cattle to make ends meet, including their precious cows. They were on a perpetual treadmill, struggling to accumulate enough cattle to allow them to meet their consumption needs plus continue building their herds.

Kweneng residents also tried to sell grain, in order to avoid selling cattle.[54] Although the grain price remained stable, Bechuanaland grain exports rose to significant levels only during this postdrought period.[55] In the Kweneng, so many people sold so much grain that the chief prohibited exports from the district, fearing a food shortage. Smuggling rendered this order meaningless. Some women were so desperate that they sold their grain for money immediately after the harvest, only to buy food back from the traders later in the year.[56]

We can see that the rural economy scored both successes and failures in the new commercial economy. It quickly absorbed the new technology of plows, wells, and wagons; it sold produce to South Africa, yet it still maintained much of its flexibility and reciprocity. Its participants adjusted accordingly their strategies of accumulating wealth; men especially widened their opportunities, drawing income from the distant Rand back into rural production. Yet the technology and income available from the new commercial economy were not adequate to prevent overgrazing from slowly overtaking the hardveld.[57]

The effects of overgrazing take decades to peak. Overgrazing means that livestock removes grass faster than it grows back, so that overgrazed pasture is deteriorating pasture. This deterioration can be fast or slow. If the rains are good, cattle can thrive on extremely poor pasture. Good pasture can endure one or several poor years, but poor pasture dries up and blows away in only a very short drought.[58] Before 1940, the Kweneng had not yet suffered the effects of overcrowding, largely because of the expansion into the transitional hardveld that the plow, well, and the wagon made possible. The same was true of the other reserves adjoining the Kalahari, that is, the Ngwato, Ngwaketse, Kgatla, and Tawana. The Malete, Tati, and Tlokwa reserves had no such new land into which to expand. By 1940 these areas were overgrazed. The Barolong Farms were in an area of transitional hardveld, so they were still being occupied during this period.[59]

Not all the Kwena could afford to leap out of the crowded southern hardveld. Although there was considerable lending of plows, wells, and wagons, those least able to repay such loans were at least able to escape. Differences in wealth grew more conspicuous, although the process of its accumulation remained much the same as before. Plows, wells, and wagons were very much like cattle in that increases in output required little additional labor input.

The wealthy, then, were owners of capital, not hirers of labor. Although *majako, mafisa,* and *moraka* were unequal relationships, the same person might enter them from both sides at different times. That is, someone whose oxen are herded at a distant cattle post might work *majako* one year, bring in the oxen and hire *majako* the next year, and give out *mafisa* at the same time as taking them in. Herding *moraka* was a privilege, for this meant plowing with a wealthy man's cattle, drinking their milk, eating their meat, and watching one's own herd grow alongside them, usually in the wide pastures beyond the southern hardveld.[60] A *moraka* holder also might give out *mafisa* and hire *majako* workers.

Although the poor had the same legal rights to arable land and to pasture as everyone else, they were too poor to use them. How did they become poor? First of all they might suffer some misfortune: a string of male calves; a son hurt in the South African mines; a husband failing to send back money from South Africa. These things in sequence could leave a household destitute. Individual misfortune had always occurred, of course, but the key differences between the nineteenth and twentieth centuries is the decline of collective self-interest in putting victims back on their feet. Formerly, those unable to produce on their own were loaned tools, cattle, grain, and labor, or were accepted into someone else's production unit. Everyone wanted everyone else producing, so as to increase the number of fields and herds scattered across the countryside to catch the rain. Now in the twentieth century, a segment of the population was depending less and less on the production of their neighbors and more and more on the commercial market and new technology. Those suddenly unable to produce on their own found fewer neighbors willing to help them out. This was a gradual but unmistakable process: Those Kwena women selling their grain to traders only to buy it back later in the year surely had nowhere else to turn.

## CHIEFLY WEALTH[61]

Among those vaulting into new pastures, the chief was certainly the most conspicuous. Throughout the Protectorate, especially in the sprawling Ngwato territory, he seemed much more than just the largest cattle owner, acquiring his wealth in the same way as others, only in larger volume. The chief did have a more privileged economic position than this; yet there were only eight chiefs in all Bechuanaland, and explaining what separated the chief from everyone else helps very little to explain the differentiation among the other members of his chiefdom. Although the chief did receive tribute, this did not amount to a regular system of surplus extraction. Moreover, new forms of chiefly wealth arose in the new commercial era that did not derive from local production.

Chiefly tribute took several forms, and these changed during the twentieth century. The most important agricultural tribute was the *lesotla*. In the early nineteenth century every member of the chiefdom shared the responsibility of plowing a large field for the chief, in addition to their own individual fields. This *lesotla* was planted in one full day by all the adults in the chief's village. They used their own hoes, and later they weeded and harvested it at their convenience. During the early nineteenth century, grain from the *lesotla* was supposed to stand as a reserve for the chief to distribute in time of famine, although in a series of good years the chief was free to dispose of it as he pleased.[62]

As refugees poured into the Kweneng, Sechele contracted a few to be special *moraka* holders, to plant fields as well as herd his cattle. Those who accepted were called *makata*, and when the plow arrived these *makata* used the chief's *moraka* cattle to plow the chief's fields. They received their *moraka* calf and used the chief's cattle to plow large fields of their own as well. As for the rest of the Kwena, they no longer worked a *lesotla* nor needed the chief's famine grain as often.[63] Another agricultural tribute was *dikgafela*, a postharvest thanksgiving ceremony that in good years entailed each household taking a basketful of grain to the chief's *kgotla*, most of which they brewed as beer on the spot. Most years were poor, however, and in these they gave nothing.[64]

The chief's only other intrusion into the agricultural activities of his subjects was a regulatory one. A man received a field adjacent to his father's, but if there was no more suitable land nearby, the father asked the head of his *kgotla* to ask other *kgotla* members for a plot. If they had none the *kgotla* head asked the ward head, and so on up to the chief. The chief then did not actually allocate land; he was rather the apex of a pyramid of authority that did so. The allocation itself was never a question of whether or not to grant an applicant land, but rather which plot an applicant would receive. If an applicant asked for a particular piece of land, it was the responsibility of the *kgotla* and ward heads and then the chief to check whether someone else had already claimed it, and if so, to find the applicant another plot. An unmarried woman had the same rights to land as a man, again going through her father.[65]

The regulation of grazing land operated on different principles, because all pasture was communal. Anyone could graze any animal anywhere, except in someone else's unharvested field. Although *kgotla* heads had responsibility for specific pastures, their function was only to serve as a primary court for disputes over cattle ownership. Toward this end, everyone setting up a permanent cattle post had to inform the appropriate overseer, who had no right to refuse access to any area. Again, the chief was the final court of appeal.[66]

The system of land rights presented a minimum of barriers to production, but rather helped speed the movement of resources across the countryside to catch the rain. Producers struggled instead to acquire other requirements of production, most especially cattle. The land system allowed the wealthy to claim as much land as their ox teams could plow, while guaranteeing the poor the bare minimum of productive assets. A well owner was able to control somewhat the use of land around his well by denying water to the cattle of others, but this was also true of pit owners in the nineteenth century. A well was better than a pit, however, because it cost more to dig. If someone found a new pit site, others would rush to dig pits a few dozen meters away and thus immediately crowd the pasture with cattle. A well owner was more confident that few others could afford to dig a well nearby. Someone who could afford a well thus sought a new site not alongside existing wells but several kilometers away in new pasture. Other cattle remained free to graze there in summer, however, drinking from rain pools.[67]

A wealthy cattle owner moving into new pastures to plow and to water his cattle might also claim that he had allocated the surrounding land to his children and their future children and so insist that this land was not available to others applying for plow lands. Schapera reported that chiefs denied these claims, supporting the applicants instead.[68] There was also a report in the 1930s that chiefs themselves tried to control the movement of plow teams out to the distant fields at the beginning of the rains, declaring that no one was allowed to begin plowing before they gave the word. Although the chiefs did indeed tell the administration that they had this power, they were constantly trying to impress upon the government how wide their powers were. This one report of a chief delaying the movement of plow teams was this brief statement, which Schapera quoted, in the Kweneng District Commissioner's 1936 *Annual Report*:

> The pernicious custom of waiting for an order from the Chief before going out to plough must be abolished. . . . The early and copious rains which fell in October prepared the ground for early ploughing, but owing to delay on the part of the Chief, no ploughing took place in October. In November, when the order was eventually given, rains failed, and very little ploughing was done during November and December.[69]

But did the Chief really hold up the plowing? The government always urged cultivators to plow early in October, so as to take advantage of every drop of rain, whereas the oxen needed several weeks of good rains to eat enough sweet grass to regain strength from the dry winter. Once the oxen gained strength, the vast majority of cultivators who did not own sells had to wait for rains to fill the temporary pools from which their cattle drank during plowing. This was clearly understood by the Kweneng District Commissioner in 1940, whose statement Schapera also quoted:

> At present cultivators, most of whom live in Molepolole, have to depend on accumulations of surface water in small ponds and dams for their draught oxen and for their own needs. They are therefore unable to plough until they know that these ponds and dams are full. The alternative is ruinous: it entails the transport of water by waggon for human needs from Molepolole. In other words, oxen must go to Molepolole, drink there, haul out a waggon, and then plough. It is hardly necessary to stress the strain that is imposed on these beasts, which inevitably lose condition, and the temptation to the people to hasten their cultivation.

This season provides ample evidence of the difficulties facing the tribe, which, with supplies available from last season, is unwilling to tackle them. The lands were in a fit condition for ploughing, but the water was insufficient for human and animal needs. The spectre of hunger has not offered an incentive. Recently good light rain has fallen over a period of days and has soaked into the ground, including the fields; it has not run off to accumulate in the surface reservoirs. Ploughing is therefore not practicable, even though theoretically there is time for crops to be planted and to mature.[70]

My own informants did not remember the chief giving the order to move out too late, and there is no reason for him to have done so.[71] In the time of the hoe, he might have wanted to make sure that his *lesotla* was finished before others could go to their fields, but in those days everyone slept in the village and the *lesotla* took only one day to hoe.[72] With the plow, the chief's own *makata* plowed his tribute fields, not the chiefdom at large. There is no report of a chief ever fining someone for plowing before he gave the word, nor would the government have condoned such a fine. Was the DC in 1936 indulging in a common mistake of colonial officials, to see barriers to progress in "pernicious customs" rather than in the concrete economic difficulties facing producers?

The chief also received nonagricultural tribute in the form of fines and hunting spoils. Each *kgotla* had its own court, as did each ward, and the ultimate court of appeal was the chief's. If the chief ruled that a convicted defendant must pay a plaintiff two cattle as restitution, the chief might demand another beast for himself as punishment. We have no way of knowing the size of the chief's court income. After 1934 the courts kept official records, but few of these survive.[73] A 1935-36 list of 51 cases in the eight official courts of Molepolole's five wards and Gabane, Kopong, and Thamaga reports 22 fines totaling 45 cattle, £7 and 1 goat. This is some 2 cattle per court per year.[74] We know very little about the chiefs' courts in the nineteenth century, before the British guaranteed their authority.[75]

As for hunting spoils, the chief claimed a portion of any game slain in his territory. This was known as *sehuba*, or "breast." In the case of game skins, the chief claimed not the breast but a percentage of the skins sold, and in the days of the elephant, he claimed one tusk of every two. Again, we do not know how much *sehuba* added to chiefly income. For Khama during the late nineteenth century wagon-trade boom, it certainly totaled a large sum, for the volume of ivory and skins sold in his village under his watchful eyes was immense.[76]

Nevertheless, the value of this wealth came not from the labor of his subjects but from the world economy suddenly offering a far higher price for game products than the local market had previously commanded. In the Kweneng, the Kwena tried to avoid *sehuba* by selling their treasures in other villages, as far south as Mafeking.[77] Schapera reporting hunting *sehuba* virtually extinct by World War II, thanks to game extermination and the low prices for skins.[78]

The new commercial economy brought chiefs other forms of income as well. The chief became a civil servant as of 1899, when he began collecting the government tax and keeping one-tenth of it as personal income.[79] He also collected store rents from traders and had sold concessions in the late nineteenth century. We have noted that prospecting yielded nothing after the 1867 Tati gold find, but the BSAC bought up all the extant concessions in the Protectorate after an 1893 government commission disallowed the specious ones. In this way the BSAC secured its position, at very little cost, in case minerals were found in the future. A small amount of money to the BSAC, however, was a large amount of money in the Kweneng. From 1896, the BSAC gave Chief Sebele I, son of Sechele, an annual payment of £405.[80]

Meanwhile, in 1902 two South African contractors agreed to pay Sebele a royalty on timber that they collected on the site of present-day Gaborone. This amounted to £1,187, which the Kwena insisted Sebele should not keep as personal income. The Protectorate administration intervened and removed two-thirds of the sum from Sebele's pocket, putting it instead into a Kwena Tribal Fund.[81] Sebele died in 1911 and his successor, Sechele II, died in 1918. The next chief, Sebele II, in 1919 drew from the BSAC and the tax a cash income totaling £700. Store rents went directly to him, but this payment was obscured in the sizable debts he owed to the traders.[82] In 1919 the Protectorate administration established a Native Fund in each chiefdom from a 5s levy on each taxpayer, and in 1928 the major Kwena *kgotla* heads asked the government to remove the store rents and BSAC payment from Sebele's irresponsible hands. This was done in 1929. Henceforth, Sebele received only a monthly salary of £20. The store rent and BSAC payment went into the Kwena Fund.[83]

In 1931 the government deposed Sebele altogether. His successor, Kgari Sechele, drew in 1932 the same monthly salary of £20 plus some £400 in tax, while the Fund collected £189 in store rents and £405 from the BSAC.[84] In 1938 the government at last took the tax from all Protectorate chiefs, marking all Tribal revenue for a Tribal

Treasury and paying each chief only a salary. Long before 1938, however, other chiefs had seen the writing on the wall and kept tribal income separate from their own.[85]

The chiefly wealth of this period, then, appears to have begun in the nineteenth century as cattle accumulated in the same way as the cattle of other citizens; then control of trade gave some chiefs enlarged incomes; and finally their interactions with traders, the BSAC, and the government earned them the most income of all. A chief's wealth thus derived more from the new commercial economy than from the labor of his subjects. When turned into cattle and multiplied by his heirs, this wealth was considerable: Sebele I's annual £405 BSAC payment amounted to 81 oxen at £5 each, which could purchase five plows, four wells, and four 14-foot wagons every year.

## NOTES

1. RB, MoA, *Agricultural Statistics*, 1980, Table 2.
2. Parsons, "Economic history," p. 123; Schapera, *Native Land*, p. 133.
3. Okihiro, "Hunters," pp. 80-81, dates the era of the plow in the Kweneng from 1885. The plow must have been dominant by 1896, because the loss of cattle in the rinderpest epidemic of that year moved the Molepolole missionary to report that women had "reverted" to using hoes. Molepolole Mission, *Annual Report*, 1896, LMSA, ASR, Box 2.
4. A. Anderson, *Twenty-Five Years in a Waggon*, London, 1888, p. 133.
5. S. Ransome, *The Engineer in South Africa*, London, 1903, pp. 151-52.
6. Okihiro, "Hunters," p. 81.
7. The 1904 census reported 46 "whites" and 13 "others" in the Kweneng. *BNA* S 295/2. Molepolole gained a small South African Coloured community in 1912. BNA S 467/5. There were 14 Boer blacksmiths as of 1937. BNA DC Molepolole, Box 4, File M 299, 1937.
8. Interviews 20, 22. The price of one ox per plow is confirmed for Molepolole in Resident Commissioner Correspondence, 10 October 1895, BNA HC 115.
9. In 1924 the Molepolole missionary reported a plow team of four cattle. J. Burns, Correspondence, 4 December 1924, ZNA BU 5/1/1/1.
10. Schapera did not discuss the plow, and in *Native Land*, p. 125, he declared that a detailed discussion of agricultural methods was beyond the scope of his study. Okihiro kept to the time of the hoe.
11. Interviews 20, 22.
12. Thobo Lesatlhe explained this strategy as he taught me to plow.
13. Interviews 20, 21.
14. Interview 24.
15. R. Silitshena, "Notes on the origins of some settlements in the Kweneng District," *BNR*, 8, 1976; Schapera, *Native Land*, p. 64. Schapera reports Hurutshe founding Gabane in 1860, while Silitshena reports Lete arriving there in 1891.
16. Interview 21.

17. In 1915, the Molepolole missionary reported the Kwena spending more time at their distant fields and cattle posts, building houses there like those in the village: "The town season becomes shorter each year." Molepolole Mission, *Annual Report* 1915, LMSA, ASR, Box 5.
18. Interview 21.
19. Interview 21.
20. Interview 47.
21. Schapera, *Native Land*, p. 241. Interview 21 reported that 60 to 70 cattle were required. Schapera reports here some 774 blasted wells in Ngwato pastures at this time (1942). His report of only 17 in the Kweneng in 1938 comes from a District Commissioner's report that included only village wells and the unusual concentration of wells at Suping. Chapter 8 below provides further information on the location of Kweneng wells. Kweneng DC, Report, 1939-40, BNA S 378/3/1.
22. Interviews 14, 16.
23. Interview 21.
24. Interview 22.
25. Interview 19.
26. Schapera, *Native Land*, p. 136.
27. Schapera, *Native Land*, pp. 199-200; Interviews 19, 36, 41.
28. Interviews 19, 21, 36, 41.
29. Okihiro, "Hunters," p. 77. Schapera, *Native Land*, p. 200, offers this small survey table showing where grain was stored:

| Chiefdom | Number of Fields Surveyed | Place of Storage (%) | |
|---|---|---|---|
| | | Wife's | Mother's |
| Malete | 71 | 94 | 6 |
| Kgatla | 302 | 89 | 11 |
| Tlokwa | 57 | 88 | 12 |
| Ngwato | 764 | 70 | 30 |
| Kwena | 174 | 64 | 36 |
| Ngwaketse | 857 | 55 | 45 |

30. Interview 11.
31. Interviews 37, 41.
32. Interviews 12, 28.
33. Interview 37.
34. Schapera, *Native Land*, pp. 200-1.
35. Interviews 36, 37.
36. Interviews 36, 37, 43.
37. Interviews 37, 41.
38. See I. Schapera, *Migrant Labour and Tribal Life*, London, 1947.
39. BNA, DC Molepolole, Box 4, File M 299. During the 1922 depression, Kweneng traders gave only good-fors, and no cash. Kweneng District, *Annual Report*, 1922/3, BNA, DC Molepolole, Box 2, File M 22.
40. Resident Commissioner Correspondence, 1950, BNA S 518/3. This system was more prevalent in the north of the country, because of its greater distance from the Rand.

41. A description of this process can be found in Kweneng VO, *Annual Report*, 1956, BNA V 10/3.
42. Schapera, *Migrant Labour*, p. 180.
43. Nonagricultural wage labor spread quickly to the Kweneng. In 1903 the resident Molepolole missionary had to pay cash for firewood and fence-building labor. R. Lewis, Correspondence, 27 February 1903, LMSA, ASC, Box 62. The earliest reference I could find for women selling beer was 1913. Molepolole Mission, *Annual Report*, 1913, LMSA, ASR, Box 5.
44. Schapera, *Native Land*, p. 244; Interview 43.
45. Schapera, *Native Land*, pp. 136-37, 215; Interviews 47-52.
46. Okihiro, "Hunters," p. 165, reports a similar arrangement among the Kgalagadi.
47. Interview 22.
48. Interview 22.
49. A shift of village site in 1900 showed that not all Molepolole residents had access to a wagon: some carried their belongings on their heads. Molepolole Mission, *Annual Report*, 1900, LMSA, ASR, Box 3.
50. BP, "1936 Census," BNA S 86/17.
51. BP, "1936 Census."
52. See GB CO, *ASD*, 522, 1897, 22, 65, 192.
53. See BP, *Annual Report*, 1933; Kweneng District, *Annual Report*, 1933, BNA S 360/15.
54. Interview 30.
55. See Figure 8.1.
56. The Kweneng DC reported of the 1936 harvest: "The crop was generally not good. In spite of this, the Bakwena women proceeded to sell their grain." BNA S 468/4. He further estimated that three-fifths of this 1936 harvest was sold. Kweneng District, *Annual Report*, 1936, BNA S 471/1. That cow sellers were poor and that grain sellers were women was well known. See BNA NAC, March 1939. See also Schapera, *Native Land*, pp. 203-4.
57. There was a way to do this through modern ranching techniques, which later chapters discuss.
58. See D. Field, "A handbook of basic ecology for range management in Botswana," MoA, 1978. For general discussions of overgrazing, see G. Hardin, "The tragedy of the commons," *Sc*, 162, 1968; R. Dasmann et al., *Ecological Principles for Economic Development*, London, 1973, pp. 76-110; C. Runge, "Common property externalities," *AJAE*, 63, 1981.
59. Schapera, *Native Land*, pp. 215-17.
60. Schapera, *Handbook*, pp. 248-50, stresses the privileged position of a herder of a wealthy man's cattle.
61. See Schapera, *Handbook*, ch. 3.
62. Schapera, *Native Land*, pp. 43, 155-57; Interview 4.
63. Okihiro, "Hunters," pp. 92-93; Interview 34.
64. Schapera, *Native Land*, pp. 196-98; Interview 8.
65. Schapera, *Native Land*, pp. 150-51; Interviews 31, 32, 41.
66. Schapera, *Native Land*, ch. 12. On p. 224, Schapera reports that an overseer could refuse access to a new post if the area was already fully stocked. My own informants (Interviews 2, 32) and subsequent developments dispute this statement. Rather, it appears that the chiefs told Schapera that they had mechanisms for preventing overgrazing, in order to dissuade the govern-

ment from altering the land tenure system. This issue is discussed further in Chapter 9.

67. Schapera, *Native Land*, pp. 245-46; Interview 14.
68. Schapera, *Native Land*, pp. 137, 181-82; *Tribal Innovators*, p. 98.
69. Schapera, *Native Land*, p. 186; Kweneng District, *Annual Report*, 1936, BNA S 471/1.
70. Schapera, *Native Land*, p. 131; Kweneng DC, 1939-40, Report, BNA S 378/3/1.
71. Interview 9.
72. Schapera, *Native Land*, pp. 156-57.
73. See Schapera, *Tribal Legislation Among the Tswana of the Bechuanaland Protectorate*, London, 1943, and D. van Niekerk, "Notes on the administration of justice among the Kwena," *AS*, 25, 1966.
74. BNA DC Molepolole, Box 3, File M 158.
75. Schapera catalogued the changing power of the chiefs in *Tribal Innovators*, London, 1970.
76. Parsons, "Economic history," p. 120 reports Khama owning seven to eight thousand cattle in 1878 and earning £2,000 the year before, although it is unclear whether this sum includes herd growth and cattle sales. See also N. Parsons, *The Word of Khama*, Lusaka, 1972, p. 3.
77. Kweneng DC Correspondence, BNA S 433/9. Molepolole was the Protectorate's leading skin and sewn-fur export center. BP, *Annual Report*, 1927/8.
78. Schapera, *Native Land*, p. 43.
79. Eventually the Kwena chief's collectors pursued men as far as the Rand to collect the tax. Kweneng DC, *Annual Report*, 1924/5, BNA DC Molepolole, Box 2, File M 22. A licensed cattle buyer accompanied the tax collector into the Kalahari to turn cattle into cash. BNA DC Molepolole, Box 5, File M 367, 1928.
80. Details of these payments are found in BNA S 113/1, and GB CO, *ASD*, 702, 1902, 320.
81. GB CO, *ASD*, 702, 1902, 379; 802, 1906, 131.
82. Kweneng District, *Annual Report*, 1919, BNA DC Molepolole, Box 2, File M 22. Wealthier Kwena were in debt to traders early on, attracting official attention in the 1890s. BNA HC 154/5. In 1920, Sebele II was in debt £1,782 to Molepolole and Mafeking traders. In 1932, the government ruled that traders would no longer be supported in court for the collection of debts above £25. Kweneng DC Correspondence, 1932, BNA DC Molepolole, Box 2, Files M 27, M 92.
83. BNA DC Molepolole, Box 6, File M 416.
84. BNA S 313/11, 1933.
85. Schapera, *Tribal Innovators*, pp. 74-81.

# 6

# Southern African Agriculture, 1900–1940

This chapter has two purposes: first, to show the problems that African commercial agriculture posed for its further transformation into an agricultural industry; and second, to examine the government policies designed to solve these problems in the first four decades of the twentieth century. Although some of the features of Kweneng agriculture were peculiar to the area, the general pattern of its commercialization was common throughout most of Southern Africa.

## THE PROBLEM OF AFRICAN AGRICULTURE

At the end of the Anglo-Boer War, the British ruled all of Southern Africa except for Namibia and Mozambique. The British High Commissioner, Lord Milner, brought a team of administrators to plan the region's development into a modern industrial economy.[1] Milner's planners informed their judgments with a full range of reports and studies; perhaps the most important of these was the five-volume report of the 1903-5 South African Natives Affairs Commission (SANAC), whose mandate was to advise on "the state and condition of the Natives" and "the lines on which their advancement should proceed."[2] This report presents a richer portrait of Southern African agriculture than any other published source, and its recommendations formed the basis of a wide range of government policies through the period with which this chapter concerns itself.

The SANAC's jurisdiction extended to all the British colonies south of the Zambezi, whose 1904 populations are reported in Table 6.1.

**Table 6.1.** British South Africa: Population, 1904.

|  | European | Coloured | Asian | African |
|---|---|---|---|---|
| Cape | 579,741 | 395,369 | 9,907 | 1,424,787 |
| Natal | 97,109 | 6,686 | 100,918 | 904,041 |
| Transvaal[a] | 300,225 | 23,946 | b | 1,030,029[c] |
| Orange River Colony | 143,419 | 6,160 | b | 235,466 |
| S. Rhodesia | 12,623 | 1,944 | b | 591,197[c] |
| Basutoland | 895 | 163 | 59 | 347,731 |
| Bechuanaland | 1,004 | 361 | b | 119,411 |
| Total | 1,135,016 | 434,629 | 100,884 | 4,652,662 |

| African Population | Private Farms | In Town | Crown Land | In Reserves | Private Locations |
|---|---|---|---|---|---|
| Cape | 213,843 | 113,828 |  | 1,057,610 | 39,506 [d] |
| Natal | 426,674 |  | 13,985[e] | 463,382 |  |
| Transvaal | 479,753 | 28,264 | 180,427[f] | 207,840 |  |
| Orange River Colony | 195,494 | 22,972 |  | 17,000 |  |
| S. Rhodesia | 82,023 | 9,959 | 151,503[g] | 264,618 | 62,727 [d] |
| Basutoland |  |  |  | 347,731 |  |
| Bechuanaland | 1,000 |  | 18,311[g] | 100,100 |  |
| Total | 1,398,782 | 175,023 | 364,226 | 2,458,281 | 102,233 |

[a]Includes Swaziland.
[b]Included as Coloured.
[c]Includes laborers temporarily present: Transvaal, 133,745; Rhodesia, 20,367.
[d]As recognized under 1899 Location Act (Cape), and High Commission proclamation, 1896 (Rhodesia).
[e]£2/hut/year rent.
[f]£1/year rent.
[g]rent-free.

Let us take each African category in turn. More than half the African population was in reserves, where the legal base of African agriculture remained largely undisturbed, although overcrowding had already taken its toll in some areas, such as the Ciskei. The SANAC found that the plow had already replaced the hoe in most places, thereby increasing the demand for hardy oxen. Africans sold grain and cattle, and also yoked their oxen to wagons and carts.[3] Many in the east Cape, Free State, and Basutoland had merino sheep as well. Yet, the tenure system remained largely unchanged: Individuals were still entitled to as much land as they could cultivate; everyone had a right to communal pasture; and men could depart to work for wages, leaving their fields and herds in the care of relatives and friends, and invest their wages back into agriculture by buying cattle, plows, and wagons.[4] The same was true of Africans on Crown Land, that is, areas that the government intended to sell as commercial farmland.[5]

The second largest African category in Table 6.1 is Africans on commercial land, who outnumbered all the whites in Southern Africa. The 1904 census also showed that most whites were in town, so that the ratio of blacks to whites on commercial land was nearly 3 to 1.[6] Moreover, this was only two years after the Anglo-Boer War, during which Africans had retreated into the reserves. As of 1904, they were still returning to commercial land. Only Cape and Natal farms were actually surveyed yet, and the British had no means of discerning accurately how many Africans fell into each of the five categories by which they occupied commercial land in any of the territories: ownership, rental, share-cropping, labor tenancy, and wage employment.

The SANAC provided valuable details, however, if not numbers, on all these categories. As for ownership, Africans were permitted by law to buy land in the Cape, Transvaal, Natal, and Rhodesia, although very few were able to do so. Almost all purchases were effected jointly, usually by chiefdoms or subchiefdoms, so that the system of agriculture resembled that of the reserves.[7] The same was true of rentals, by which Africans made regular payments to an absentee landowner. Renting was found mostly in Natal, where speculators began to buy up land soon after British annexation; in the Transvaal and Rhodesia, where individual and company prospectors bought up land in the hope of finding minerals beneath it; and in the Ciskei, where the government converted most of the land to commercial tenure after the 1857 cattle-killing decimated the Xhosa there.[8]

Sharecropping differed from renting in two respects: first, the landlord lived on the land; and second, tenants paid a share of their produce rather than fixed rents. This system was most prevalent in the Free State, and again, African agricultural techniques remained substantially intact.[9] The fourth method of African occupation was labor tenancy, which differed from sharecropping in only one respect: instead of produce, the tenant paid the resident landowner with a certain number of days labor in his field. This system was most prevalent in the Free State and Transvaal. In most cases, the owner simply called upon the tenant when needed, so that Africans maintained their own fields and herds as well.[10]

The fifth method by which Africans occupied commercial land was outright wage employment, without fields and herds of their own. This method was almost exclusive to the winter rainfall zone, where Africans formed a minority of the population on commercial land, and to the sugar estates of Natal, where most workers were still Indian.[11] Almost all Africans on summer zone commercial land maintained their own fields and herds, keeping African agriculture substantially intact despite the legal change to private tenure. The nineteenth century conquests by Boers and the BSAC had thus enclosed the commons only on paper. Africans continued to move and exchange cattle over the legal boundaries of white farms, to cultivate as much land as their cattle could plow, and to send family members out to work for cash.[12] Whereas they paid tax in the reserve, on commercial land they made their payments to a white landowner.

But why did white landowners permit African agriculture to occupy their land? Here absentee landlords differed from resident landowners. The former were usually speculators with enough cash to buy land, but who did not want to invest more capital in their holdings. As we shall see, there were a number of reasons why men of means were reluctant to invest in agricultural production at this time. Absentee landlords expected land values to rise in the future and agricultural prospects to improve. Meanwhile, they collected rents from Africans, or rented the land to a Boer, who engaged African sharecroppers or labor tenants.[13]

Resident Boer farmers, either owners or renters, had little money to invest in agriculture but also lacked literacy in English or other commercial skills. Thus they remained in the countryside. They depended on African agriculture because it was so well adapted to the dry grassland environment. When the Boers arrived in the summer rainfall zone, the only important new technology they brought was horses and guns, neither of which helped them farm. These military items did allow Boers to enforce their land claims, however. Although each Boer family lived alone on its farm, there were local agreements of mutual armed assistance, by which Boers would grab their horses and guns and rush to help a neighbor. This "commando" network proved useful in raiding African cattle, and in fighting the British.[14]

In time of peace each Boer was left alone on his private farm without the constant cooperation of a wider rural economy. He staked his claim by locating a permanent water source and riding in a circle around it to mark out one to three thousand hectares or so. He negotiated an agreement with the land's former owners or other Africans for them to pay some form of rent in return for their occupation of his farm. In this way, a Boer drew off wealth from African agriculture, while leaving it essentially intact. Like most Africans, most Boers tried to accumulate large herds with many hardy oxen to insure against drought and to pull plows.[15] Labor tenancy was much like the Tswana *lesotla* system, by which every member of the chiefdom was once obliged to work on the chief's fields a few days of the year. A Boer was like a small African chief, or an African well-owner, conforming to the pattern of agriculture that he found already on the land.

In conclusion, the SANAC found that African agriculture had adapted smoothly and successfully to the new commercial order of the nineteenth century and remained essentially intact throughout the summer rainfall zone. To the SANAC's dismay, however, the commons was not yet enclosed. Their report begins as follows:

> The first item of reference, and perhaps the most important, is Land Tenure. From it there is a common origin of many serious Native problems. It dominates and pervades every other question, it is the bedrock of the Native's present economic position, and largely affects his social system.[16]

They deemed that African "communal" tenure was "admirably suited to the needs and habits of the aboriginal races":

> The Native population as a whole instinctively cling to it and cherish the communal system. But there is an increasing number who fret under the conditions of communal life, seeking alike the opportunity to gain independence and assert individualism. . . . The aspiration is healthy and trends in the right direction.[17]

We will remember from Chapter 2 that the first British administration in the summer rainfall zone, in Natal, outlined a gradual change from African to individual tenure. The end result would be a family farm of some twenty-five acres, with the commons completely enclosed and divided. That is, each household would confine its operations to one fixed area, whose boundaries would be clearly marked. This was a drastic step, as Schapera clearly explains for Bechuanaland:

> The local system of farming does not permit a man to concentrate his home, his fields and his cattleposts within a single compact area. His holdings for these various purposes are scattered about in different parts of the country. The Tswana accordingly do not have farms, in the ordinary sense of the word.[18]

Although the British knew that the change they demanded was a dramatic one, they were confident that natural evolution would help the process along. The Cape went furthest in advancing African individual tenure in the nineteenth century, and the SANAC explained its approach as follows:

> The policy followed by the Government of the Cape Colony in respect of Native land tenure has been, to begin by adopting the communal system of occupation observed by tribes in their independent state, and, by gradually adapting it to the changing conditions of life attendant upon the march of civilisation, while at the same time establishing a just and sound administration of their personal as well as tribal affairs, to prepare the way for recognition of the people of the advantages of an individual system tending towards assimilation of European methods.[19]

"Civilisation" here means private property, especially in land, and the pursuit of self-interest in a fully commercial economy. Spreading this gospel was the task of missionaries like Livingstone, who helped promote British commerce. From the first, mission stations offered individual plots to Africans for intensive, irrigated cultivation. The government hoped that all Africans would learn from these examples and stop trying to accumulate livestock on the commons and produce instead a large surplus of marketable grain. In other words, the British wanted Africans to become peasants. They expected that commercial development and Christian education would lead to the development of an African land market and the expansion of cultivation to fill up the pasture. Eventually Africans would enclose their own commons, and confine their agriculture to the twenty-five acre plots that Natal's government planned for them in 1860.[20]

Despite a century of British commerce, however, extensive pastoral agriculture had not given way to intensive cultivation. Yet the Rand boom dated only from 1886, and Boer governments further impeded commercial expansion. Perhaps intensification and individualism had not had enough chance to develop as yet. But African agriculture had always operated on principles of self-interest, as individuals competed to accumulate private property in the form of cattle. The reciprocity system endured not through communal bondage but by a series of contractual agreements, such as *mafisa*, that individuals found it in their self-interest to enter. In the commercial era, African agriculture gave producers the chance to invest in small, easily affordable steps, especially cattle and plows, and to bring in cash from wage employment. Property rights were clearly defined, and individuals reaped full benefits from their investments.

Even if the SANAC did not fully appreciate the logic of African agriculture, however, they understood it well enough to know that they did not like it. Their hope for enclosure, privatization, and intensification sprang from a sober appraisal of Southern Africa's chances on the world market. Despite British experiments with a wide range of products, extensive grain and livestock production still dominated agriculture in the interior summer rainfall zone. The world markets for these crops were extremely competitive, so that the Cape, Natal, and especially the Transvaal were net importers of both meat and grain products from overseas. Only the Free State made a significant net contribution to these two markets.[21] Wheat was the leading agricultural import, and the Transvaal Boer government had levied its highest protective tariff on imported meat, some 100 shillings per pound.[22] Meat imports continued to increase: in 1898 South Africa's first cold storage works were built to hold meat imported from Australia, and meat imports soared to feed imperial troops fighting the Anglo-Boer War.[23] The southwest Cape still exported wine, Natal exported sugar, and wool remained the leading agricultural export. Wool's geographical expansion had largely ended by the time of the SANAC report, however, because merinos were well-suited only to the cooler southern half of the region, that is, the southern Cape, southern Free State, and upland Natal. Most of the summer rainfall zone was better suited for cattle.[24]

The British intended to make Southern Africa self-sufficient and then a net exporter of beef and grains. Both world markets were dominated by North America, Argentina, and Australia. The late-nineteenth-century expansion of the agricultural industries in these other areas met no large indigenous population with large herds of indigenous cattle; soil was more fertile and thus pastures were better; cooler climates supported fewer animal diseases; and wheat could be grown without irrigation. Industrial production methods thus spread more quickly and successfully than in Southern Africa.[25]

There were five essential requirements of successful beef production: fences, permanent water, hybrid bulls, medicines, and fodder. A fence around the farm kept one herd separate from another, preventing diseases from spreading between them, and giving a farmer full control of what happened to his herd. He allowed only a superior bull, which he purchased or bred from another purchased bull, to mingle with his herd to produce calves. Fences within the farm divided it into a number of paddocks, which allowed the cattle to graze leisurely in one spot for a number of weeks. The cattle were then led to the next enclosed paddock, and so on around the farm, so that each patch of grass was grazed and rested in turn, to let it grow back.[26] Fencing had begun only in the 1890s, in a few areas of the east Cape where the cool temperate climate was well suited to dairy farming.[27]

A permanent water source was essential, of course, because the herd never left the confines of the farm. Surface water was often unreliable in dry, flat areas, where there were no sites for large dams that would hold abundant water through even a long drought. In these cases, underground water was better, and in the late nineteenth century steam engines began to be used to drill boreholes. That is, an engine was set up over a potential site and a drill sunk into the surface rock. If water was found then a narrow pipe was inserted and a pump of some sort, usually a windmill, pulled the water to the surface. The steam engine required large volumes of water, however, which was expensive to transport long distances, especially in the dry areas that needed boreholes.[28]

The best method of watering was to pipe water into each paddock, so that the cattle did not have to lose weight walking to drink. One central water source was also possible, though less desirable, with the paddocks radiating out so that each one had a corner close to the water. Farms in wet or irrigated areas could comprise only one paddock if they grew enough fodder for their stock. Usually at least two paddocks were required—one for summer and one for winter.[29]

Medicines were essential not only to reduce deaths, but also to keep bulls and cows in prime condition for reproduction. Young calves were especially prone to disease. Inoculations were the major technique here until the dipping tank reached Southern Africa from Australia at the beginning of the twentieth century.[30] This was a shallow tank containing a medicinal solution into which cattle were immersed to kill disease-bearing organisms clinging to their hides. Fodder was necessary because the dry winters of Southern Africa stripped the natural pasture of most of its nutrition. A farmer thus grew fodder in summer, or bought it from another farmer to feed his herd in winter and in drought.[31]

If a farmer met all these requirements, he produced fat, full-grown cattle in two years. All the two-year-old males were sold, along with any cows that showed signs of impaired reproduction. Because the farmer purchased his bull, or bred it specially from a purchased bull, he castrated all male calves within six months.[32] His herd thus comprised virtually no mature oxen, and only one or two hybrid bulls; almost the entire herd consisted of cows and young cattle less than two years old. If his animals were of especially good quality, they could qualify as chillers; that is, they would not be frozen but only chilled, for rapid shipment to market. Freezing reduced the quality of meat, and so only low-quality cattle were frozen.[33]

The SANAC found that these industrial methods of livestock farming, which apply to merinos as well, had made almost no progress in Southern Africa. The techniques of African herding varied from region to region, but they all resembled the Kweneng's: herds of low-quality, hardy cattle with a high percentage of drought-resistant, mature oxen; castration at the end of two years and maturity at the end of five or six; movement of animals between herds, as in *mafisa*, and over a wide, unfenced commons; a very low capital investment; the retention of old cows in the hope of producing more calves; long walks to water and pasture; and the use of cattle for pulling plows and wagons.[34]

Africans did not adopt the new methods of livestock herding because they could not afford to and because they occupied a commons. Chapter 3 noted that the BSAC's experimental farm in Lobatse cost £20,000, although the above methods could also be pursued in smaller, cheaper steps. Disease and breeding control, however, were very difficult on an unfenced commons. Subsequent chapters provide more details on the difficulties of transforming African herding. Here we need only note that those difficulties were severe.

Efficient grain production was also demanding. Wheat remained the most valuable commercial grain. As we noted in Chapter 2, however, summers in the summer rainfall zone were too hot and wet for wheat to grow. Most wheat still came from the Cape winter rainfall zone, plus a few spots along the highland bordering Basutoland, where rain extended far enough into the cool winter for wheat. Winters in most of the rest of the temperate highlands of South Africa and Rhodesia were cool enough but too dry. Here wheat required irrigation.[35] Missionaries promoted African irrigation in the dry western fringe of the southern rain zone throughout the nineteenth century, and large-scale irrigation works began with the 1876 Irrigation Act in the Cape. This act offered loans and subsidized advice from a government engineer. The loans required farmers to put up their farms as security, however, and few did so. Then came an unusual boom in ostrich farming, which produced feathers for European fashions. The Oudtshoorn area especially, on the dry eastern fringe of the winter rainfall zone, prospered enough for farmers to pay for irrigation without mortgaging their farms. The government engineer helped them build dams and dig channels down to their fields, to grow alfalfa to feed their animals.[36]

In the summer rainfall zone, including Rhodesia, the British wanted irrigation works for winter wheat and for alfalfa and other fodder crops that demanded abundant water. These crops would replace un-irrigated maize, sorghum, and millet. Although they were sensitive to local variations, their general plan for a summer rainfall zone farm was a fenced plot with one or more paddocks and permanent water; an irrigated field growing summer fodder and winter wheat; hybrid dairy, beef, or merino animals; and a dip tank. The end result of these investments would be a more intensive use of the land. Herders would decrease the amount of natural pasture that they used as they increased the amount of fodder. The total number of animals would be reduced, as farmers relied instead on a few high-quality animals. They would produce more wheat and alfalfa and less sorghum and maize. In this way, the same amount of land would produce a much greater output, making Southern Africa self-sufficient in grain and meat, with a surfeit of wool, grain, and beef for export. The 1860 Natal plan aimed at a division of the reserves into just such fully enclosed, one-paddock farms.

British views on evolution and civilization thus sprang from a sober concern for economic efficiency. Southern Africa could compete on the world market only if its agriculture could be transformed. As noted earlier, however, African agriculture had always operated efficiently: why now was it suddenly inefficient? The problem here is to distinguish between the two different meanings of efficiency recognized by economists. Financial efficiency refers to how successfully an individual "firm" judges its costs and benefits; that is, whether a cultivator or herder makes the right decisions about allocating resources so as to make the most gain. There is no reason to doubt the financial efficiency of Southern African producers at any time in their history.[37]

Economic efficiency, on the other hand, refers to a larger unit, usually territorial. The question here is how the individual "firms" within a larger economy, let's say a chiefdom, should allocate their resources so as to take most advantage of the economy's total productive potential. Again, we have seen that the Kweneng rural economy as a whole made efficient use of the natural resources and technology available to it in the nineteenth century. We do not have the data to prove this point. Even with abundant data, questions of financial and economic efficiency are difficult to prove.[38] What we do know is that economic efficiency took on a new scale when the British conquered Southern Africa. The larger unit by which economic efficiency would be judged became a much larger unit, and the technology available changed dramatically as well.

The SANAC was charged with the question of economic efficiency throughout Southern Africa. Africans remained financially efficient as they adapted to the new commercial order; that is, they made their investments and allocated their labor according to how they could take best advantage of the new technology and markets. African agriculture commercialized according to the principles of financial efficiency. The type of commercial agriculture that resulted conflicted directly with the intensive, private, enclosed farming that economic efficiency now demanded.

Indeed, African commercial agriculture suited the financial demands of Boers and white absentee landowners as well. That is, their own profit was best served by keeping African agriculture on the land. Few whites had the capital to make the large investments that the government now demanded. Men of means had better prospects in the booming urban areas, where trading and small factories had already begun to yield good profits. Africans and Boers alike pursued the cheaper investments that their own budgets deemed efficient: cattle, plows, and wagons. They continued to move and exchange cattle across pastures, violating the boundaries that the government wanted secure. Their financial efficiency argued for a preservation of the commons; economic efficiency demanded its enclosure. With the British finallly in control of Southern Africa, there was now little doubt about which agenda would win out.

## THE SOLUTION TO THE PROBLEM

The SANAC recommended a sustained attack on both the commons and the system of agriculture that preserved it. This had begun, of course, with the British endorsing the Boers' private land claims throughout Southern Africa, and although the reserves retained their communal pasture, we have seen that the Natal government immediately planned its enclosure. The Cape first experimented with private African titles to arable land in 1852, and in 1879 its parliament passed a resolution to extend individual tenure to all its reserves. The Rand boom then gave the Cape enough revenue to begin enacting this resolution.[39]

The Glen Grey Act of 1894 empowered the Cape government to grant individual titles to all African reserves, beginning with the Glen

Grey district of the Ciskei. This act was a retreat from the earlier Natal plan, however, which had proposed to enclose each African holding, thereby eliminating the commons completely. This division was a monumental task, and would have resulted in plots too small for each to include a perennial water source. Blasted wells, boreholes, and irrigation works were certainly too expensive to deliver to each small plot. Reserve populations had also increased since 1860: Natal's reserves now held seven times as many Africans as the government first found there.[40]

Although the hope of complete enclosure was not abandoned, Glen Grey took only one step toward that goal. Individuals received quitrent titles to arable plots, but pasture remained communal. To reduce the cost of survey, the government did not grant cultivators the pieces of land that they already cultivated. Rather, surveyors marched through a reserve to delineate uniform plots of a few hectares; they then took a list of qualified landholders and matched names to plots. They allocated land in one valley, left the next valley as communal pasture, and so on through the district. Each plot recipient paid a reduced survey fee and also received a right to graze animals on the commons.[41]

This division of the land was supposed to be final. No one could clear another field, or enlarge an existing field, beyond the boundaries surveyed and marked with beacons. Children who grew to adulthood would have to help their parents on the family field, or else leave the district to find work. Neither could they graze animals on the commons, for this right extended only to plotholders. The act provided for residential sites for the landless to reside on between work contracts, in small villages that the surveyors marked out in each valley. This amounted to a final division between full-time peasants and full-time workers; forcing cultivators to work more intensively on a fixed acreage rather than plowing as large an area as they were able to do; encouraging them to use more labor on their fields rather than to accumulate large herds for plowing, thereby hastening the change from pastoralism to intensive cultivation.[42]

Although the Glen Grey Act had been only partly enforced, with poor results, the SANAC recommended its extension to all the reserves of Southern Africa. Because Rhodesia fell under Cape law, the act already applied there. The SANAC hoped that careful planning in the new industrial era would iron out the difficulties in advancing individual tenure.[43]

The SANAC also endorsed Cape legislation concerning African agriculture on commercial land, most especially an 1899 Squatters Law that restricted the terms by which Africans could occupy commercial land that they did not own. A landowner was required to register the number of African families on his farm as a "private location." A resident landowner was allowed to keep without penalty as many families as were required to labor on his farm. He had to pay a tax on any families over this limit. An absentee landlord who simply collected rent from Africans had to pay tax on all of them. Sharecropping, by which resident farmers collected rent from Africans in the form of a portion of their crop, was illegal.[44]

This law was almost impossible to enforce, because commercial land was so extensive. A landowner was left much to himself, so that evading the law was seldom a problem. He registered the legal limit of African families and then continued to engage as many Africans as he wanted on whatever terms he pleased. The SANAC recommended extending the squatter law to all of Southern Africa, again expecting enforcement to improve in the new industrial era. This would allow Africans to occupy commercial land only as landowners or as employees, thereby forcing farmers to rely on capital investments instead of on African agriculture.[45]

To speed this purge of African agriculture from commercial land, the SANAC further recommended the limitation of African land purchase to certain areas that the government could monitor closely in order to insure that Africans would not simply extend their agricultural system onto land that they purchased. Individuals or small groups of Africans could buy within these areas, but "purchase of land which may lead to tribal, communal or collective possession should not be permitted," in order to prevent the extension of "tribal or communal occupation."[46] On both the reserves and commercial land, the SANAC hoped to eliminate African agriculture as they found it, forcing its transformation into private, intensive farming with cultivation replacing pastoralism as the main pursuit. Africans would be able to own farms in both reserves and commercial areas, but they would farm them on radically different terms than at present.

The SANAC outlined other attacks on African agriculture as well, and again they looked to British experience in the coastal colonies. We saw in Natal that the reserves had a nonagricultural function as well: the government did not put them up for public sale because they feared that Africans would lose all their land and flood into urban unemployment. The British enforced vagrancy laws throughout the nineteenth century, by which residents of their colonies were subject to arrest unless they were gainfully employed. This kept wages low and cleared the streets of unemployed troublemakers. Gainful employment included owning land or a business or working under legal terms of employment. Boers were easy to monitor. Their names were known to relatives and acquaintances and were recorded in official birth, marriage, and landownership records. Africans from beyond the frontier came officially nameless, in search of cattle, which they either stole or worked for on illegal terms. At first the British tried to prevent their entrance, but in 1828 they officially allowed it.[4 7]

The British made entering Africans carry passes, as the Dutch had done for nonwhite residents of the Cape. The British pass recorded the worker's name and his chief, so that the government could find him if he stole cattle or committed some other crime. Once the African found work, his employer's name was written on the pass, so that he could be traced within the colony. This also allowed the government to investigate the terms of contract, so as to prevent illegal arrangements, such as a Xhosa herding Boer cattle in return for a *mafisa* calf. A worker violating a legal contract, usually by deserting, faced imprisonment and a fine, whereas a worker finishing a contract could obtain official permission to look for another. This permission was recorded on the pass, allowing the worker to move about without being accused of being a cattle thief or a deserter.[4 8]

The pass system helped to prevent the mobility of African labor from forcing up wages. Without such a system, Africans could desert a job and return to claim the agricultural rights that African tenure guaranteed them. Rand mine owners complained before the Anglo-Boer War that the Boer government would not or could not enforce its pass system. Africans would come to a border town and buy a pass under one name; take up a mining contract, desert to find a better job, and buy a new pass somewhere else under another name; take up another contract, desert and buy a new pass; and so on.[4 9] Boers did not have this freedom. They could not desert their jobs and take up free land. When they fell into debt or found land prices too high to afford to buy a farm, they left the land for good.

We can see then, that the pass helped to enforce freely contracted wage labor relations, as well as the colonial vagrancy law. The Glen Grey Act extended the vagrancy provisions into the reserves, by imposing an extra tax on all men who did not receive plots, unless they went out to work for wages. Certainly there were abuses of the pass system, and widespread evasion, and the Glen Grey vagrancy law had never been invoked; nevertheless, the SANAC again looked to better enforcement in the twentieth century.[50] They recommended a unified pass system on this original Cape model, and indeed, each territory already had some sort of pass law in effect.[51]

Cape, Rhodesian, and Natal Africans were able to gain exemption from the pass law by proving a certain number of years of continuous gainful employment in the colony without pass violations; all Africans were citizens of British colonies as of 1900, so that all could now aspire to exemption. Most Africans worked for wages for a number of short periods, however, to gain cash for investment in agriculture. Reserve agriculture was not gainful employment according to the law. Exemption only meant that an African could move about without permission written on the pass. Exempted Africans had to carry their exemption papers instead, to prove that they did not need a pass. Only the Cape actually granted a significant number of exemptions.[52]

Beyond exemption, African men in the Cape and Rhodesia fell under the same property and literacy voting restrictions as whites. Women could not vote at all. The SANAC found that Africans numbered 7 percent of the Cape's 114,000 voters and 1 percent of Rhodesia's 5,200 voters. Natal's franchise was also nonracial at first, but its small white population passed a number of laws making African voting more difficult. The SANAC found only two African voters in Natal. The Boer republics had a universal white male franchise, that is, without property or literacy qualifications.[53]

The SANAC knew that its agricultural and pass proposals, and the general British vagrancy laws, would not be acceptable to African voters.[54] It thus recommended a dual franchise that would eliminate the chance of effective African voting strength. A territory would have one parliament and a uniform, qualified franchise, but blacks and whites would vote separately. In districts with large white populations, blacks would vote for separate candidates-at-large that would represent blacks in general, rather than that particular district. Whites in these districts would have direct district representation. By adjusting the number of at-large candidates, African voting strength could be held constant despite a growing number of qualified African voters, and no individual district would fall into African hands. This would be especially important on the Rand, where Africans were most likely to gain the wealth and pass exemptions necessary for voting rights. Black districts, that is, the reserves and African commercial areas, would vote for their own representatives. The Glen Grey Act included provisions for a hierarchy of reserve councils along these lines.[55]

The SANAC drew on the experience of British rule in the nineteenth century to outline a program for economic development in the twentieth. They advanced the British insistence on fully commercial market relations in land and labor and proposed the transformation of African agriculture into private, intensive farming. Note, however, the legal emphasis of all their recommendations. Their agent of change was not a large government budget allocating funds to help individual farmers to make this transition. Rather, they advocated laws that pressed farmers to make these investments themselves. Although it took decades for some of their recommendations to be enacted and enforced, an industrial economy and an attendant agricultural industry eventually took the shape that they proposed.

## AN AGRICULTURAL INDUSTRY

Milner was constrained in the implementation of his plans by the British desire quickly to return the territories of Southern Africa to some local administration. In this spirit of reconciliation the British granted the Boers a conditional surrender. Among the Boer generals were two Cambridge-educated lawyers J. B. M. Hertzog and J. C. Smuts, who led the negotiations and pressed the British most strongly on language and the franchise.[56] Article 5 of the final treaty agreed to the use of the Dutch language in public schools in the two former Boer republics and in courts when the parties involved required it.[57] Article 8 stated that "The question of granting the franchise to natives will not be decided until after the introduction of self-government."[58]

The British expected a rush of British immigrants to take up the new opportunities offered by the Rand. This would give the British a voting majority in the Transvaal government, which would then amend the franchise to a Cape or Natal system. The 1904 census showed Boers in a clear majority in the Transvaal, however. The British immigrants did not appear, and *Het Volk*, a Boer party that Smuts helped organize, won the 1907 Transvaal election. Hertzog helped organize a Free State Boer party, *Orangia Unie*, which also won its 1907 election.[59]

Milner had united all the colonies into a customs union in 1903, from which the Transvaal government now threatened to withdraw. Smuts was one of the first now to propose that the territories whose railways served the Transvaal, namely the Cape, Natal, and the Free State, join together in one government with the Transvaal. The British agreed, hoping to dilute Transvaal protectionism with Cape and Natal voters, who favored open trading borders to the Rand. The Union of South Africa's new constitution followed Smuts's outline, with Hertzog pressing for and winning equality of Dutch and English as official languages. Each province retained its prewar franchise, and the Union became an independent member of the British empire in 1910.[60]

Rhodesia was not considered for this union for two reasons. First, its railway did not serve the Rand. Second, the British and the BSAC wanted to protect its farmland from an influx of poor Boers, who would only entrench African agriculture on the land. They enforced a selective immigration policy, allowing only men with capital to take up farms. In joining the union, Rhodesia would have had to open its borders to the south. Moreover, the BSAC's original charter for Rhodesia had not yet expired.[61]

The constitution of the new Union of South Africa included a provision for the later incorporation of Rhodesia as well as the colonies of Basutoland, Bechuanaland, and Swaziland, which the British had acquired on protective terms that now prevented their joining the Union. The British had expected to hand over these colonies to the self-governing territories that they developed, but the Union of South Africa developed instead. The British declared that they would not turn these three colonies over until the Union improved its racial franchise restrictions.[62]

*Het Volk, Orangia Unie*, and a Cape party joined together in the South African Party to elect General Louis Botha, a wealthy merino farmer, as South Africa's first prime minister. The younger Smuts received three cabinet ministries, while Hertzog received only one. Rivalry between Smuts and Hertzog dominated South African politics until World War II. Yet both accepted the basic formula that the SANAC outlined. Although Hertzog, Smuts, and the British disagreed on many issues, they agreed on many more, especially those involving agriculture, as the rest of this chapter shows.

One of Milner's first agricultural policies was to re-establish Boers back on their farms through generous grants and loans. Although this also kept them out of urban Boer politics, its main purpose was to prevent the further entrenchment of African agriculture on commercial land.[63] The British planned to build large government irrigation schemes to promote intensive wheat and fodder cultivation.[64] Until these projects bore fruit, the government had to find an outlet for the maize that the country now produced. In 1906 the national railway system granted reduced rates to the coast for maize bound for export. The railcars carried imports inland and needed a bulky export for their return trips. Branch rail lines also spread through the country in this period, including only two that explicitly served reserves.[65]

The provincial and then the Union agricultural departments were strengthened and remodeled along modern American lines.[66] The government established a central Land Bank in 1908, which began to offer loans for dip tanks in 1911 and for fences in 1912.[67] The fencing loans were backed by a law that enabled the government to force two adjacent farms to share the cost of a fence between them. The Union's first agricultural census in 1918 reported half the country's 76,000 commercial plots fenced.[68] Yet livestock within the fences continued to walk long distances to and from water and to sleep in pens at night, and cattle were still moved and exchanged between farms, so that landowners were doing little else than staking out their boundaries. Nevertheless, the Union government quickly helped move the commons another step toward effective enclosure. Meanwhile, the colonial and then independent agricultural departments tried to control the movement of stock within the country, allowing no animals to leave any area in which disease broke out. They also inspected stock on the way to market. The city of Johannesburg built its own abattoir and cold storage works in 1912, which slaughtered a constant stream of cattle and stored the meat for bulk purchase. The rationalization of stock movements and processing raised the possibility of exporting meat for the first time.[69]

In 1913 the Union passed a Land Act that embodied two of the SANAC's major proposals. First, it extended the 1899 Cape Squatters Law throughout the country, prohibiting sharecropping and requiring landowners to register the African families on their farms. Absentee landlords paid a tax on all their African tenants, whereas resident landowners, or those employing a manager or renting their land to a white farmer, could register free of charge as many labor tenants as the farm actually required, with each tenant family rendering at least 90 days service per year in return for some sort of wage. Excess labor tenants incurred a penalty tax for the landowner. Second, the 1913 act empowered a land commission to divide commercial land into black and white areas, thereby creating two separate land markets. This commission would also enlarge the existing reserves. Until this commission could be set up, however, the 1913 act temporarily froze the status quo: Any farm owned by a white could only be sold to another white; and a black-owned farm could only be sold to blacks. The British governor-general, who remained the nominal head of state in a British dominion, could grant exemption from this rule.[70]

For the most part, the effects of this act were not immediately apparent. The labor tenancy provisions were almost impossible to enforce, as landowners had every reason to conceal the true number and status of the African families resident on their farms.[71] The 1916 Land Commission that the 1913 act ordained was unable to gather reliable information on how many Africans the act would evict from commercial land, a number that would affect the size of the African commercial areas and reserves that it would delineate. Nevertheless, the 1916 commission recommended adding some 6.7 million hectares to the 8.0 million hectares that the 1913 act listed as African land, making a total of 16 percent of South Africa's area. Disputes over the areas suggested led to local committees in the four provinces making their own recommendations, which amounted to adding 1.1 million hectares less than the 1916 commission recommended.[72]

Neither of these proposals was accepted, however, and so the temporary rules of 1913 remained in force. The governor-general adopted a policy in 1918 to approve black land purchase applications if they were within areas recommended both by the 1916 commission and a local committee. In 1922, the local committee proposals alone became the standard. Africans seeking purchase outside the recommended areas could gain approval only in cases of "hardship," that is, if they had historically occupied the land that they wanted to buy and had nowhere else to go.[73]

The Cape remained exempt from these land purchase provisions, because its nonracial land market allowed Africans to qualify as voting property holders; tampering with the Cape franchise violated the Union constitution. The act's labor tenancy restrictions also had no meaning in the Cape, whose 1899 Squatter Law was already in place. Even in the other provinces, these tenancy provisions were designed to have a somewhat gradual effect. In the Transvaal and Natal, only new sharecropping contracts became illegal: All present sharecropping contracts could be renewed on into the future. In the Free State, where sharecropping was most prevalent, present contracts could run out, but none could be renewed. Upon passage of the act, however, Free State farmers appear to have seized the moment to demand that their tenants give them their livestock, especially their merinos. After this, the countryside returned to its pattern of illegal contracts.[74]

None of these early agricultural policies provoked much disagreement within the colonial or independent governments. Disputes over other policies moved Hertzog to leave the cabinet in 1912 and to form a new National Party in 1914. The Nationalists demanded protection on two levels: Hertzog himself represented men of capital, much of it obtained through government employment, who wanted to invest in manufacturing and trade but faced tough competition from foreign imports, foreign investors, and English-speaking South African businessmen; a poorer but more numerous constituency followed D. F. Malan, a former Dutch Reformed Church minister, in demanding strict protection against nonwhite competition in the labor market.[75] Although Boers made these same protectionist demands in the nineteenth century, poor white voting rights, greater economic prosperity, and a larger labor market gave the National Party considerable political power.

Smuts disagreed most strongly with Hertzog about tariff protection, without which South Africa would produce only what its comparative advantage in the world market dictated. An exception to this rule was the case of "infant industries." A government might find that its natural endowment favored the production of some item, but that the low price of foreign imports prevented the new industry from achieving a running start without some protective barrier. Once the new industry was on its feet, the barriers could be removed. Such judgments were open to abuse by a country claiming protection for products that it could never produce competitively, keeping tariffs permanently high. This was why the British opposed protection.[76]

Smuts favored low tariffs for another reason as well. Britain had annexed its African colonies somewhat reluctantly and looked immediately to turn them back to some local, responsible administration. There were so few local African or white men of means with strong commitments to private property, full commercial relations, and open trading borders, that Smuts offered his government as the best guarantor of British interests in Africa. Britain already anticipated turning over all its territories south of the Zambezi, and Smuts looked far to the north as well. He wanted open trading borders to facilitate the future incorporation of these distant territories.[77]

Hertzog demanded infant industry protection for all sectors, as Britain's European rivals began to enact at the end of the nineteenth century. This tide of protectionism spread quickly to Britain's self-governing dominions. In 1879 Canada declared protective tariffs, which it then began selectively to lower for other members of the empire in 1897. Although Britain itself still adhered to free trade, it reluctantly accepted the Canadian system of protection with imperial preferences for its dominions in 1902. Milner's 1903 customs union followed this scheme, granting mild protection with preferential imperial rates. The Union tariffs of 1914 were also low.[78]

Hertzog was most concerned to protect South Africa's manufacturing sector. With far more coal and iron than any other sub-Saharan territory, South Africa was capable of producing its own steel. A large industrial infrastructure already served the mines. Smuts certainly favored industrial development, but on a fully competitive basis. Malan's Nationalists had far less money to invest, but they too favored protection because it would increase the number of high-paying government, trade, and industrial jobs and thus give them more money to save and invest in small businesses.[79]

Smuts also opposed protection in the labor market. Not only Boers clamored for this protection, for the Kimberley diamond fields and then the Rand mines brought skilled European workers with experience in union organization, thereby giving white protectionism new strength. The Transvaal Boer government promoted racial discrimination, so that white unions had already won important concessions before the Anglo-Boer War.[80] In the *Het Volk* and Union governments, Smuts faced the dual problem of limiting both union demands and the number of workers that these demands embraced. His endorsement of a racial franchise in the Transvaal thus suited industrial interests more than a nonracial qualified Cape franchise would have done. Although it enfranchised poor whites, these voters could be counted on not to insist on welfare benefits for the mass of nonwhite workers.

Hertzog also demanded that public schools teach Dutch and that the government hire white Dutch-speakers. Although Smuts favored English, he gave in to Hertzog on this issue because the country was developing a large enough internal economy to set its own language policy. In the nineteenth century, import-export businesses dominated commerce and required employees who could communicate with foreign customers. In the twentieth century, most South African business was domestic, and so a local language would suffice even for skilled jobs.

Malan's Nationalists wanted more protection than this, as did white labor unions. Smuts defended the employers' right to hire and fire as they saw fit, while white workers insisted that the higher paid jobs go to them. This demand did not affect the highest ranks of skill at first, for only European immigrants had mining experience. Boers and Coloureds were often indistinguishable except by color, and many Indians spoke English, so that mine companies against their will hired Boers to please the Transvaal government.[81]

Such white protectionism also extended to trade, the next step up from wage labor that workers aspired to reach. The Transvaal and Free State Boer governments had tried to prohibit nonwhite trading in the nineteenth century. Milner wanted trading licenses issued on a nonracial basis for high fees, with restricted quotas, in order to prevent poor individuals of any color from struggling along, unprofitably, trying to stay out of the labor market. The final compromise was strict but nonracial national trade laws, with local municipalities issuing the licenses. The country's white town councils then favored whites in granting licenses.[82]

The white franchise, Boer political influence, Smut's pragmatism and immigrant skills were not the only reasons for the success of urban racial discrimination in these early years of the Union. Whites were also in town to stay. When Boers left the land, they sold off their farms and could not return. Africans, in contrast, could return at any time to their fields and cattle, which relatives and friends managed in their absence, and they could not lose their land through the land market. African agriculture thus gave African workers unusual mobility, which the Rand mines exploited to the full. They signed men up on contract in their home districts, channeled them into regimented barracks on the mines, and sent them back to make room for the next batch of recruits. They thus maintained a steady flow of new laborers. Even if they returned to the same mine, these men met new fellow workers each contract, and so were unable to develop any organization that might grow into an independent union.[83]

Within South Africa and British colonies through to Central Africa, freely contract wage labor remained the principle of mine recruitment, enforced by 1911 Union regulations. That is, a man was free to sign or not to sign a contract. Joining a strike was a criminal breach of contract, however. The mine owners also formed a joint recruitment agency that offered uniform wages so that they would not compete against each other for workers, thereby keeping wages low. Moreover, the largest contingent of African workers came from Mozambique, whose Portuguese government would force men to sign contracts in return for which the South African government arranged to send a percentage of the miners' wages to Lisbon, in gold, at a special rate.[84]

Even through all these controls, black miners acquired mining skills and a knowledge of English and Dutch. Mine owners began to promote them, because they could pay nonunionized Africans less than unionized whites for the same job. The Smuts government passed a Mines and Work Act in 1911 that made the governor-general responsible for devising nonracial regulations requiring certificates of competency for skilled work and gave provincial governments responsibility for issuing them. As with trading licenses, Free State and Transvaal authorities favored whites.[85] White workers struck in 1913, winning the legal right to participate in formal collective bargaining and to strike. The government met a January 1914 strike with force, preventing any further concessions.[86] At the end of 1914, the Botha-Smuts government threw South Africa into World War I in alliance with Britain and proposed to invade German Southwest Africa. Some Boer veterans of the Anglo-Boer War mounted their horses and rose in anti-British rebellion: times had changed, however, and the government ran them down with motor cars in only a few weeks.[87]

It was in this climate of white hostility to the government that Hertzog launched his party. The strikes of 1913-14 drove poorer urban Boers into the white, largely English-speaking Labour Party, but they flocked to the National Party as soon as it was formed. Hertzog's men of capital dominated the party, but Malan's mass appeal provided the margin of victory. The Nationalists polled four-fifths as many votes as Smuts's party in the 1915 election.[88]

Rapid industrialization during World War I strengthened Hertzog's hand. The disruption of European production suddenly made local manufacturing competitive. Small factories sprang up to produce what South Africa hitherto had imported. European armies also demanded vast quantities of the low-quality meat that South Africa produced in abundance. More employers hired more workers, and then the war ended. White employers and white workers both demanded that the government protect their recent gains, and so voted for Hertzog.[89]

Smuts also gained from World War I. He joined the British war cabinet and won Southwest Africa under the Versailles mandate system that he helped devise. When Botha died in 1919, Smuts became prime minister. But the Nationalists became parliament's largest party in 1920, moving the old British party that Milner had once hoped would win the Transvaal to merge into Smuts's party, thereby keeping him in power.[90] The postwar slump came in 1921, moving mine owners to promote a large number of blacks to more skilled positions, eliminating costlier white labor. In January 1922, white workers rose in armed revolt across the Rand, and Smuts's troops fired on them. The National and Labour Parties formed an electoral coalition in 1923. In mid-1924 the Smuts government passed an Industrial Conciliation Act that empowered the government to make racial restrictions on job categories and wages in collaboration with industrial councils composed of employers and white unions. An election in mid-1924 gave 63 seats to the Nationalists, 53 seats to Smuts's party, and 18 to Labour. Hertzog became prime minister.[91]

The rise of a Nationalist party alarmed Britain. Narrow local interests, rather than comparative advantage, would now determine the direction of the South African economy. Smuts had taken the first step to incorporate neighboring territories when he won South-West Africa, and he offered money for Rhodesia when the BSAC charter ran out in 1919. The 1920 election and the Rand revolt then shook Britain's faith that Smuts could hold off the Nationalists. Rhodesia's white settlers voted for self-government over merger with the Union, and in 1923 Rhodesia became a self-governing colony with the Cape's nonracial laws. The status of Basutoland, Bechuanaland, and Swaziland remained unchanged, and it now became doubtful that they would ever be handed over to the Union.[92]

Although Hertzog immediately imposed high protective tariffs that included agricultural products,[93] we can see that he rose to power on nonagricultural issues. An important shift in government agricultural policy did occur in 1924, however, but we must look for its origins within the agricultural sector itself. The 1923 Report of the Drought Investigation Commission offered the first scientific evidence on the relative possibilities of intensive and extensive agriculture. The government already knew that intensification was making little progress. High-quality beef and dairy cattle had still not replaced the tough indigenous cattle that pulled plows and wagons and proved so resistant to drought. The discovery of gold began the diversion of Southern Africa's low-quality cattle from local circulation to the Rand market; World War I accelerated this demand, which collapsed when the armies disbanded. The postwar domestic market was thus flooded with cattle, few of which were of sufficient quality to compete as chilled beef on the world market.[94] As for grain, wheat had not replaced maize, so that the country still imported a quarter of its milling requirements by value: South African mills used £2.9 million of domestic maize, £2.1 million of domestic wheat, and £1.6 million of imported wheat, although the country also exported £3.1 million of maize.[95]

The government always knew that intensification was difficult. The Drought Commission now explained precisely how difficult. Careful measurement finally showed that only 1 percent of South Africa was irrigable.[96] The government's program of large-scale irrigation works had failed because so much of the country was too flat or dry to support irrigation. Farmers kept low-quality indigenous cattle because they could not grow the irrigated fodder, nor establish the permanent water sources that improved cattle required. They grew summer maize because they could not grow irrigated winter wheat.[97]

The findings of the Drought Commission were most ominous for the reserves. If intensive agriculture was so difficult, how could the densely populated reserves ever achieve commercial success? If maize and low-quality cattle were so well suited to the land, then there was no incentive for Africans to change their system of agriculture. Moreover, the 1922 Report of the Native Location Surveys showed that individual tenure, a prerequisite of intensive agriculture as the government envisioned it, had made almost no progress in the reserves. Even in Glen Grey District, the survey beacons had been overturned or moved, cultivators plowed where they wanted, and land changed hands outside the channels that the government prescribed. Enforcement of the Glen Grey Act required far more government staff than the district could pay for.[98] The tenure change had not stimulated intensive agriculture, and so much of the existing organization of agriculture remained intact.

The government was finally forced to accept that South Africa would have an extensive agricultural sector. In 1924, it threw up protective barriers to eliminate Rhodesian, Bechuanaland, and all other low-quality foreign cattle from its domestic market. The high-quality market, defined by the greater weight of good beef cattle, remained open.[99] Also in 1924, the Land Bank began granting farmers loans for their own small water works just to water their stock and perhaps to grow a little alfalfa, now that large-scale irrigation schemes had proved unrealistic.[100] Also in 1924, the government erected elevators along the railway to store maize and sorghum right after the harvest, thereby competing with traders who hitherto handled most crop sales. The railway elevators offered better prices to farmers and also operated tractor and truck services out beyond the railway to pick up grain closer to the farm.[101]

It is important to understand the economic logic of Hertzog's agricultural policies, and their similarity with Smuts's, because one of the new prime minister's agricultural proposals provoked considerable controversy. In 1926, Hertzog introduced four bills that embodied many of the remaining recommendations of the SANAC. One of these featured an important amendment of the 1913 Land Act, which had proposed separate black and white commercial areas as the SANAC urged. Whereas Smuts adhered to the original SANAC proposals, Hertzog's new land bill would allow white purchase in black commercial areas. The problem here was that blacks could not compete with white in the land market, except through group purchase, which only turned commercial land into reserve land. Commercial areas open only to black purchase reduced this competition, and thus reduced land prices to a level more individual blacks could afford. Hertzog favored an open, competitive land market in these areas instead. Certainly few if any Africans could ever aspire to owning and operating farms on the individual terms that the government demanded. Smuts wanted only to insure that those few blacks who might manage to obtain capital would be able to invest it effectively. Note, however, that strict segregation was deemed more beneficial for Africans: they had so little capital that they could only buy land shielded from white competition, as the SANAC, the 1913 act, and Smuts proposed.[102]

The other three "Hertzog Bills" of 1926 proposed to eliminate the Cape franchise, restricting direct African representation to reserve councils and adding a few at-large African seats to parliament. Although this was the original SANAC proposal, Smuts opposed it. His reasons were more pragmatic than principled, however, for he had already endorsed the Glen Grey reserve councils and created a Native Affairs Department in 1920 to extend these councils throughout the reserves. This Department received financial responsibility for the reserves in 1925, and its account was separated from the Union parliamentary budget in 1927.[103] Smuts's government also passed a Natives (Urban Areas) Act in 1923. This segregated urban areas, so that Africans could be more efficiently monitored for pass violations, and unified existing laws that empowered municipalities to evict unemployed Africans. Although these Africans could then look elsewhere for a job, the only place they could remain legally for long periods of unemployment was their home reserve, where local councils were planned to represent them. This formula was complicated by the fact that nearly half the rural African population hailed from commercial land and that second-generation urban residents had few rural ties at all.[104]

Smuts defended the nonracial Cape franchise for two indirect reasons. First, he did not want to constrain those few Africans who managed to acquire capital and education for fear that they might join forces with poorer Africans. Second, the rise of the Nationalists forced Smuts to count carefully the seats he commanded, and some of these in the Cape depended on nonwhite votes. All four Hertzog Bills thus stood unpassed.[105]

Over the years, however, Smuts and Hertzog found fewer and fewer issues dividing them. The tariff question was solved not domestically but internationally: at a 1926 imperial conference, Hertzog and Canada won greater financial freedom, and then the 1929 depression moved even Britain finally to turn protectionist. In 1932 another imperial conference in Canada arranged new tariff agreements, with each member of the commonwealth deciding its own policy.[106] With no imperial free trade left to defend, one of Smuts's major objections to Hertzog simply disappeared.

Hertzog's other policies also fell neatly into place. His 1925 Wage Act declared equal work for equal pay even in enterprises that did not have white unions to demand it, thereby inhibiting employers further from replacing high-paid white with low-paid blacks.[107] Hertzog's government built a steel mill in 1928, and in 1929 the Nationalists won an outright majority, although Labour leaders remained in the cabinet. Parliament now enfranchised all white women and then all white men, in 1930-31, giving poor whites the vote in the Cape and more than doubling the total white electorate. Smuts now faced the same dilemma as in the early days of the Union: Poorer whites were strongly protectionist, especially in the labor market; yet poorer whites could be counted on to exclude blacks from their own gains, thereby limiting the amount of national wealth diverted to welfare instead of to investment. Any franchise gains by blacks would now only move them toward equality with whites and eventually a universal, unqualified franchise.[108]

Smuts also found few reasons to oppose Hertzog's land bill. The 1930-32 Native Economic Commission reported that the battle against African agriculture was not going well. The 1913 tenancy restrictions were seldom observed, with most white landowners still negotiating illegal contracts with African tenants.[109] Despite the failure of individual tenure in the reserves, this Economic Commission still held that intensive methods would sustain more people than the present extensive system, but the reserves were overgrazed, overcrowded, and clearly too poor to pay for their own development.[110] The Economic

Commission reported that Africans throughout the country's rural and urban areas contributed only £3.3 million to public revenue in 1930-32, whereas government expenditure on Africans totaled £4.2 million.[111] The government began to dip African cattle en masse in 1913, and the reserves needed fences at least to control cattle movements to and from commercial areas.[112] The 1912 fencing law made neighbors share the cost of a fence between them, but with whom did a white farmer share expenses when his land adjoined a reserve? The Hertzog Bills amounted to a centralization of the functions of the Native Affairs Department to direct African revenue to reserve development. Individual reserve residents could not afford significant investments and had no authority over the commons. A collective state agency would now take control, and the first priority was to pay for fencing the reserves.[113]

Smuts's last reason to oppose Hertzog disappeared when the prime minister devaluated South Africa's currency in 1932 and so adjusted South African prices to the collapsed world market instead of continuing to try to pursue an independent financial policy. Only the Hertzog Bills now divided the two Boer generals. As we have noted, however, Smuts protected the Cape franchise to win seats against Hertzog. Without substantive issues dividing them, Smuts no longer had any reason to defend the franchise. After the 1932 devaluation, then, Smuts informed Hertzog that he would support his bills. Their two parties merged and won an overwhelming parliamentary majority in 1934. Hertzog remained prime minister, Smuts became deputy prime minister, and Malan broke away to form a Purified National Party.[114]

The Hertzog Bills passed in 1936. South Africa's political system was now unified according to the SANAC design. In the land market, groups of Africans were now allowed to buy land from whites again, but only in areas "released" for such purchase adjacent to existing reserves. Hertzog finally agreed to accept the original SANAC proposal to exempt these areas from white competition. Released land was to fall under the jurisdiction of the adjacent reserve administration for fencing, dipping, and other development. "Advanced and progressive" individuals or groups smaller than six, particularly "professional men and other highly educated natives" could gain exemption from reserve control.[115]

The Hertzog land bill also tightened tenancy on commercial land: labor contracts had to include 180 days of labor; absentee landlords paid higher taxes on African tenants; resident landlords paid higher taxes on Africans above the number needed to work their farms; and African men above the number themselves now paid an extra tax. Rural labor bureaus would now register every African to enforce these rules.[116]

These new bureaus did not begin operation in the period covered in this chapter, however. A Native Farm Labour Committee began preparations for the bureaus in 1937 and issued its first report in 1939. This Labour Committee stated explicitly that "the ultimate object should be the gradual development of a class of full-time agricultural labourers," who neither enjoyed grazing and cultivation rights nor worked periodically in town. Their concern was only commercial land with resident landlords, because they found no "information of value" in regard to the number of squatters in the Union. As the 1932 Economic Commission had found, the exact relations on the ground were very difficult to investigate.[117]

Nevertheless, the Labour Committee was able to discern that labor tenancy, that is, African grazing and cultivation rights, were still practically universal, except at the Cape. Most white farmers elsewhere also paid some cash and rations, so that the rudiments of wage labor were also nearly universal. White farmers were also able to limit the numbers of African stock on their land. On balance, cash and rations made the standard of living under tenancy somewhat comparable to that in the reserves: The Labour Committee found an average family of 5 owning about 3 cattle, 1 sheep, and 2 goats on white farms; and 5 cattle, 5 sheep, and 4 goats in the reserves.[118]

Until World War II, African agriculture dominated both commercial and reserve land. Although the 1913 and 1936 laws prevented the legal encroachment of the reserves onto commercial land, agriculture was still absorbing capital very slowly in both areas. The government had most success in promoting agriculture as a whole, as when it established grain, dairy, and meat marketing boards to hold up domestic prices in the depressed market of the early 1930s and to deal with the new British marketing boards of the same period.[119] On the farm, however, agriculture went on much as before. Even as fences, boreholes, dams, and dip tanks spread across commercial land, the need for tough, hardy oxen kept African agriculture in demand there as well. The oxen's ability to withstand drought and to pull plows and wagons kept them the most valuable investment for capital-poor farmers in the reserves or on commercial land.[120]

Alternative means of plowing would have eliminated the need for these oxen and the African agricultural system that produced them, thereby freeing valuable pasture for beef and dairy cows. The percentage of oxen in the national herd changed little before World War II. The first agricultural census in 1918 reported 80.7 oxen per 100 cows and heifers, and the last one in this period, in 1937, reported 83.7.[121] As for plowing, the modern tractor first received pneumatic tires and a diesel engine in the early 1930s and motor fuel was still expensive,[122] so that in 1937 there were only 6,000 tractors on South Africa's 100,000 commercial farms.[123] Even in the United States, the nursery of mechanized agriculture, the ratio of tractors to farms in 1940 was only 1 to 4.[124]

The last major act of the Hertzog-Smuts government was a 1937 amendment of the 1923 Natives (Urban Areas) Act. This new law enabled a list of municipalities to refuse entrance to African work-seekers because of labor surplus, that is, if the town judged that new entrants would only be unemployed. Although Johannesburg, the leading employer, was not yet on the list, this law completed the disenfranchisement of Africans from urban areas. Now if they lost their jobs in one town, they might find other towns closed to them as well. A reserve was now their only secure home. Again, there was no real enforcement before World War II, but as with the 1913 and 1936 land laws, the pattern was set for the future.[125]

By World War II, the essential elements of an agricultural industry were firmly in place: transport and marketing services, an effective agricultural department, a large local demand that encouraged domestic processing, and a body of laws that were firm if not yet enforceable. Wool was still the most valuable agricultural product, followed closely by maize. Cattle exports were insignificant, but local, protected production finally replaced wheat imports. Milk and dairy products almost equaled slaughtered cattle in value. Moreover, the total value of agricultural production rose from £38.9 million in 1911 to £72.9 million in 1940.[126]

African agriculture served in these years to provide produce, labor, and revenue for industrial development. We have seen that the government did not want to clear African agriculture off commercial land too suddenly, but rather endorsed a slow, legal transformation to industrial agricultural methods. Indeed, state agricultural policy had changed little from the nineteenth century. Laws of private tenure, freely contracted wage labor, vagrancy and passes remained much the same as under the British. Smuts turned out to be very loyal to British policy in general, while Hertzog's objections had little to do with agriculture. The assault on African agriculture showed remarkable continuity under the British, Smuts, and Hertzog. Agricultural development policy followed the demands of industrialization more than the narrow interests of any one domestic class.

## NOTES

1. See D. Denoon, *A Grand Illusion*, London, 1973; S. Marks and S. Trapido, "Lord Milner and the South African state," *HWJ*, 8, 1980.
2. South African Native Affairs Commission, *Report*, 1905, Vol. 1, p. 1. Henceforth SANAC.
3. Missionaries promoted the plow on their stations from the beginning of the nineteenth century. C. Bundy, *The Rise and Fall of the South African Peasantry*, Berkeley, 1979, p. 46, reports plows in the Ciskei at the time of the Great Trek. Colonel Griffith reported from Maseru, in Sotho territory, in 1874: "Hundreds of wagons criss cross the country in every direction, collecting the grain which it produces in order to import it to the Free State and the diamond mines. The growing of cereals has progressed apace and the plow everywhere has displaced the Kaffir hoe." R. Germond, *Chronicles of Basutoland*, Morija, Lesotho, 1967, p. 462. See also pp. 463-71.
4. The SANAC report has an excellent index, to which this chapter's footnotes will henceforth refer. For the state of African agriculture in the reserves, see vol. 5, Index, *Agriculture and Irrigation*: "Cultivation of Ground, Mode of"; "Natives as Producers"; "Produce, Nature and Value of."
5. SANAC, *Report*, vol. 5, Index, *Squatting*: "On Crown Lands, Conditions."
6. In South Africa proper, there were 5 18,000 rural whites.
7. SANAC, *Report*, vol. 5, Index, *Land Tenure*: "Purchase of Lands by Natives"; "Purchase of Lands in Community." In Natal, the joint title included stipulations that the land be broken up in the future into individual plots, as in the 1860 plan. SANAC, *Report*, vol. 3, p. 455.
8. SANAC, *Report*, vol. 5, Index, *Squatting*: "On Private Farms, Conditions, etc." See also Vol. 1, pp. 30-33.
9. SANAC, *Report*, vol. 5, Index, *Squatting*: "On Private Farms, Ploughing on Shares."
10. SANAC, *Report*, Index, *Labour and Industry*: "Farm Labour, in Lieu of Rent."
11. SANAC, *Report*, vol. 5, Index, *Labour and Industry*: "Farm Labour, Wages of." There were also a few small vegetable farms around the Rand carefully worked by recent immigrants, moving Owen Thomas to remark in 1904, "The best farm workers in the country are Italians." Thomas, *Agricultural and Pastoral Prospects*, p. 91. In the Cape, the 1911 census reported 88,000 African, 53,000 Coloured, and 82,000 white "farm workers," an ambiguous category that might or might not have included the entire households of tenants and sharecroppers. South Africa, Census Office, *1911 Census*, p. 1346.
12. For example, see SANAC, *Report*, vol. 2, p. 26; vol. 4, p. 650.
13. South Africa, *Agricultural Census*, 1925, reported 90,658 commercial farms actually occupied by their owners. Boer tenants paid the owner in cash or by shares, which they collected from the Africans whom they invited onto the land. See S. Trapido, "Landlord and tenant in a colonial economy," *JSAS*, 5, 1978.

14. See S. Trapido, "Reflections on land, office and wealth in the South African Republic, 1850-1900," in Marks and Atmore, *Economy and Society*.
15. See especially Goodfellow, *Modern Economic History*, pp. 53, 62, 120.
16. SANAC, *Report*, vol. 1, pp. 13-14.
17. SANAC, *Report*, vol. 1, p. 26.
18. Schapera, *Native Land*, p. 47.
19. SANAC, *Report*, vol. 1, p. 81.
20. SANAC, *Report*, vol. 5, Index, *Agriculture and Irrigation*: "Agricultural Training advocated."
21. Thomas, *Agricultural and Pastoral Prospects*, pp. 103-4.
22. Van der Poel, *Railway*, p. 55.
23. I. Phimister, "Meat and monopolies: beef cattle in Southern Rhodesia, 1890-1938," *JAH*, 19, 1978, pp. 404-8. See also A. Christopher, "The emergence of livestock regions in the Cape Colony," *SAG*, 5, 1976.
24. South Africa, Department of Agriculture, *Farming in South Africa*, 1924, pp. 201-229.
25. Spafford, *Agriculture*, pp. 82-118; Leppan, *Agricultural Development*, chs. 9, 11; C. Taylor, *Agriculture in Southern Africa*, United States Department of Agriculture, 1935, p. 78. But again, see note 3, Chapter 9 below.
26. South Africa, DoA, *Farming*, pp. 201-212; Barnes, "Cattle ranching," pp. 20-27.
27. Ralbot, "Land utilization," p. 324; Goodfellow, *Modern Economic History*, pp. 107-8; Thomas, *Agricultural and Pastoral Prospects*, p. 137. South Africa's first creamery was built in Bedforn, in the East Cape, in 1892, South Africa, *Official Yearbook*, 1910-25, p. 401.
28. Ransome, *Engineer*, pp. 297-304.
29. South Africa, DoA, *Farming*, p. 204.
30. Goodfellow, *Economic History*, p. 120; Thomas, *Agricultural and Pastoral Prospects*, p. 127.
31. South Africa, DoA, *Farming*, pp. 167-68.
32. South Africa, DoA, *Farming*, pp. 206-7.
33. South Africa, DoA, *Farming*, p. 210.
34. SANAC, *Report*, vol. 5, Index, *Agriculture and Irrigation*: "Cultivation of Ground, Mode of"; "Natives as Producers"; Goodfellow, *Modern Economic History*, pp. 119-24; Thomas, *Agricultural and Pastoral Prospects*, pp. 17, 161-70.
35. South African Railways and Harbours, *Farming Opportunities*, pp. 68-73.
36. Goodfellow, *Modern Economic History*, pp. 115-17.
37. See J. Gittinger, *Economic Analysis of Agricultural Projects*, Baltimore, pp. 3-8. Economists expect financial efficiency to decline only when an economy changes so quickly that producers must rely on trial and error to see what productive strategy to adopt. Mistakes are made until the right combination of resources is found. See T. Schultz, *Transforming Traditional Agriculture*, New Haven, 1964, for a general view of efficient but commercially unsuccessful producers.
38. But see P. Moock, "The efficiency of women as farm managers: Kenya," *AJAE*, 58, 1976; J. Heyer, *The Economics of Small-Scale Farming in Lowland Machakos*, Nairobi, 1967; B. Massell and R. Johnson, "Economics of smallholder farming in Rhodesia," *SFRIS*, 8, 1968.

39. South Africa, Native Affairs Department, *Report of the Native Location Surveys*, 1922, pp. 1-4. The 1879 vote was followed by a Commission in some ways similar to the SANAC: see Cape of Good Hope, Native Law and Customs Commission, *Report*, 1883.
40. SANAC, *Report*, vol. 1, p. 23. The first estimate in 1843 was 50,000; immigration from Zululand proper and better counting raised this figure to 100,000 in the 1860 plan. The SANAC found a population of 701,000 in these same reserves, that is, excluding Zululand.
41. See SANAC, *Report*, vol. 5, Annexure 12, from Acting Civil Commissioner, Glen Grey Division.
42. Goodfellow, *Modern Economic History*, pp. 148-58.
43. SANAC, *Report*, vol. 1, p. 26.
44. SANAC, *Report*, vol. 1, pp. 31-33.
45. SANAC, *Report*, vol. 1, pp. 32-33.
46. SANAC, *Report*, vol. 1, pp. 34-35.
47. Newton-King, "Labour market," p. 196.
48. S. van der Horst, *Native Labour in South Africa*, London, 1971, pp. 29-33, 161.
49. "Papers relating to the complaints of British subjects," *Parl. Papers*, 1899, p. 31.
50. SANAC, *Report*, vol. 1, p. 28.
51. SANAC, *Report*, vol. 1, p. 48.
52. D. Welsh, "The growth of towns," in Wilson and Thompson, *Oxford History*, vol. 2, p. 198; E. Brookes, *The History of Native Policy in South Africa*, Pretoria, 1927, ch. 9.
53. SANAC, *Report*, vol. 1, pp. 92-93. See also S. Trapido, "The origins of the Cape franchise qualifications of 1853," *JAH*, 5, 1963, and "Natal's non-racial franchise, 1856," *AS*, 22, 1963. The Transvaal Boer government had tried to keep English-speaking whites from voting by enforcing a residence requirement of several years. See "Papers relating to the complaints of British subjects," *Parl. Papers*, 1899, pp. 205-7.
54. Trapido discusses the importance of Cape African votes in "African divisional politics in the Cape Colony, 1894-1910," *JAH*, 9, 1968, and "The friends of the native," in Marks and Atmore, *Economy and Society*.
55. SANAC, *Report*, vol. 1, pp. 94-97.
56. T. Davenport, *South Africa: A Modern History*, Toronto, 1977, p. 148.
57. Appendix, "Correspondence respecting the terms of surrender of Boer forces in the field," *Parl. Papers*, 69, 1902. O. Pirow, *J.B.M. Hertzog*, Cape Town, n.d., p. 38, reports that Milner declared during the negotiations, "I want only one language in South Africa," to which Hertzog replied, "So do I."
58. Appendix, "Correspondence respecting the terms of surrender,"*Parl. Papers*, 69, 1902.
59. Denoon, *Grand Illusion*, chs. 2-3.
60. Thompson, "Compromise," pp. 337-62.
61. L. Gann, *A History of Southern Rhodesia*, London, 1965, pp. 215-216.
62. Thompson, "Compromise," p. 163. These territories remained in the customs union. See S. Ettinger, "The economics of the customs union between Botswana, Lesotho, Swaziland and South Africa," Ph.D., Michigan, 1974.

63. Denoon, *Grand Illusion*, pp. 63-72. The quitrent systems that the British tried to enforce in the Free State from 1848 to 1854 and in the Transvaal from 1877 to 1881 ended up based on area rather than value, so that the government did not raise rents as commerce developed. Also, a farmer could always buy a quitrent farm outright with one lump sum. Unlike the winter rainfall zone, the summer zone would fall into African hands if the government forced Boers off the land. South Africa, Select Committee on the Subject of the Apportionment of Quitrent (Further Amendment) Act, *Report*, 1927, paras. 3-5.

64. Goodfellow, *Modern Economic History*, p. 246.

65. Day, *Railways*, chs. 3-5.

66. Leppan, *Agricultural Development*, p. 15.

67. South Africa, Central Board of the Land and Agricultural Bank, *Annual Report*, 1941.

68. South Africa, *Census of Agricultural and Pastoral Production*, 1918.

69. Wilson, "Farming," pp. 126-36.

70. Goodfellow, *Modern Economic History*, ch. 3.1; Colonial Office, "Correspondence relating to the Native Land Act," *Parl. Papers*, 45, 1914-16.

71. See especially South Africa, Orange Free State Local Natives Land Committee, *Report*, 1918; South Africa, Select Committee on the Subject of the Union Native Council Bill, Coloured Persons Right Bill, and Natives Land (Amendment) Bill, *Report*, 1927, p. 11.

72. Select Committee, *Report*, 1927, pp. 4-5, 14. South Africa, Natives Land Commission, *Report*, 1916, vol. 1, p. 5, reported this distribution of African rural population:

| | |
|---|---|
| Reserves | 1.9 million |
| White-owned commercial land, occupied by whites | 1.3 |
| White-owned commercial land, unoccupied by whites | .3 |
| African-owned commercial land | .1 |
| Crown land | .1 |
| Mission land | .1 |
| Total | 3.9 million |

73. Select Committee, *Report*, 1927, pp. 2-3.

74. Goodfellow, *Modern Economic History*, p. 232; S. Plaatjie, *Native Life in South Africa*, London, 1916, chs. 3, 11.

75. B. Bozzoli, "The origins, development and ideology of local manufacture in South Africa," *JSAS*, 2, 1975; R. de Villiers, "Afrikaner Nationalism," in Wilson and Thompson, *Oxford History*, vol. 2, pp. 377-78.

76. S. Saul, *Studies in British Overseas Trade, 1870-1914*, Liverpool, 1960, ch. 6.

77. Davenport, *South Africa*, pp. 190-91, 208.

78. Saul, *Studies*, p. 174; F. van Biljoen, *State Intervention in South Africa*, London, 1939, pp. 91, 200.

79. De Villiers, "Afrikaner nationalism," pp. 368-86.

80. F. Wilson, *Labour in South African Gold Mines*, Cambridge, 1973, pp. 7-8.

81. W. Hutt, *The Economics of the Colour Bar*, London, 1964, p. 73.

82. B. Pillay, *British Indians in the Transvaal*, London, 1976, ch. 6.

83. Van der Horst, *Native Labour*, ch. 12.
84. This force came through a rural vagrancy law that did not recognize farming as gainful male employment. See J. Duffy, *A Question of Slavery*, Oxford, 1967; R. First et al., *The Mozambiquan Miner*, Eduardo Mondlane University, Maputo, 1977.
85. Wilson, *Labour*, pp. 7-8.
86. E. Kahn, "The right to strike in South Africa," *SAJE*, 11, 1943.
87. Davenport, *South Africa*, pp. 184-85.
88. Davenport, *South Africa*, pp. 186.
89. Van Biljon, *State Interference*, p. 92.
90. K. Hancock, *Smuts*, Cambridge, 1968, Vol. 1, pp. 30-35.
91. Davenport, *South Africa*, pp. 194-98.
92. R. Hyam, *The Failure of South African Expansion*, London, 1972, chs. 3-4; M. Chanock, *Unconsummated Union*, Manchester, 1977.
93. This was the 1925 Customs Tariff Act. Van Biljon, *State Interference*, p. 92.
94. DeKock, *Selected Subjects in the Economic History of South Africa*, Cape Town, 1924, pp. 217-18.
95. South Africa, *Official Yearbook*, 1926-7, pp. 571, 658. Meat exports in 1923 were only £16,000, down from a peak of £1,200,000 in 1919. *Official Yearbook*, 1910-25, p. 647.
96. South Africa, Drought Investigation Commission, *Final Report*, 1923, pp. 52.
97. Drought Commission, *Final Report*, pp. 20, 55-56.
98. *Report of the Native Location Surveys*, pp. 5-8. South Africa, Select Committee on the Carnavon Outer Commonage Settlement Bill, *Report*, 1913, shows how difficult it was to divide up a commons into smaller plots.
99. See S. Ettinger, "South Africa's weight restrictions on cattle imports from Bechuanaland, 1924-41," *BNR*, 4, 1972.
100. Central Board of the Land and Agricultural Bank, *Annual Report*, 1941.
101. South African Railways and Harbours, *South African Railways and Harbours*, 1924, pp. 106-8; T. Keegan, "Seasonality, markets and pricing: the South African maize trade in the early 20th century," *ULCSP*, 10, 1981.
102. R. Buell, *The Native Problem in Africa*, New York, 1928, vol. 1, p. 146.
103. Buell, *Native Problem*, pp. 114-17.
104. Buell, *Native Problem*, p. 56.
105. Davenport, *South Africa*, pp. 205-8.
106. Van Biljon, *State Interference*, pp. 201-2.
107. Hutt, *Economics*, p. 75.
108. Hancock, *Smuts*, ch. 6.
109. South Africa, Native Economic Commission, *Report*, 1932.
110. Native Economic Commission, *Report*, pp. 29-47.
111. Native Economic Commission, *Report*, p. 160. The contribution of African wages was not included here, because it fell under white employer taxes.
112. Buell, *Native Problem*, p. 100.
113. Select Committee, *Report*, 1927, p. 18; Native Economic Commission, *Report*, pp. 16, 47.
114. Davenport, *South Africa*, pp. 214-17.

115. South Africa, Native Affairs Commission, *Report*, 1937-38, Appendix B, pp. 10-11, in reference to section 18, subsection 2 of the Land Bill.
116. "Native Trust and Land Bill," Appendix A, Joint Committee on the Representation of Natives and Coloured Persons in Parliament and Provincial Councils and the Acquisition of Land by Natives, *Report and Proceedings*, South Africa, *Parliamentary Papers*, 1935.
117. South Africa, *Native Farm Labour Committee*, Report, 1939, pp. 11-15. But see E. Haines, "The economic status of the Cape Province farm native." *SAJE*, 3, 1935.
118. Native Farm Labour Committee, *Report*, pp. 29-43, 84. See also M. Morris, "The development of capitalism in South African agriculture," *ES*, 5, 1976.
119. J. Nagle, *Agricultural Trade Policies*, Westmead, 1976, pp. 5-10. The English-speaking business community feared that these price-fixing boards would keep more Boers in production than the economy actually needed. See E. Davis, "Some aspects of the marketing of farm products in South Africa," *SAJE*, 1, 1933; S. Frankel, "Some comments on price and marketing controls in South African agriculture," *SAJE*, 2, 1934; C. Richards, "Subsidies, quotas, tariffs and the excess cost of agriculture in South Africa," *SAJE*, 3, 1935; C. Richards, "The 'new despotism' in agriculture," *SAJE*, 5, 1937; P. Viljoen et al., "Planning and control in agriculture," *SAJE*, 6, 1938; J. Tinley, "Control of agriculture in South Africa" *SAJE*, 8, 1940.
120. South Africa, Office of Census and Statistics, *1936 Census*, p. xviii, reports the following distribution of African population:

| | |
|---|---|
| Commercial farms owned by non-Africans | 2,196,000 |
| Reserves | 2,420,000 |
| Commercial farms owned by Africans | 278,000 |
| Mission lands | 114,000 |
| Unsold Crown lands | 25,000 |

121. South Africa, Bureau of Census and Statistics, *Union Statistics for Fifty Years*, 1960, p. L-4.
122. F. Jones, *Farm Gas Engines and Tractors*, New York, 1952, ch. 3.
123. *Union Statistics*, p. I-22.
124. United States Department of Agriculture, *Farm Tractors*, Agriculture Information Bulletin, 231, 1960, p. 12.
125. Van der Horst, *Native Labour*, pp. 274-75. A 1930 amendment gave this authority to municipalities, but only 12 took advantage of it. The 1937 law gave control to the central government instead.
126. *Union Statistics*, p. I-23, reports gross value of agricultural production as follows (in £ million):

| | Maize | Wheat | Sorghum | Fodder Hay | Total Crops |
|---|---|---|---|---|---|
| 1911 | 4.0 | 1.6 | 1.0 | .6 | 12.7 |
| 1940 | 10.5 | 4.7 | 1.3 | 1.4 | 38.2 |

| | Wool | Cattle Slaughtered | Milk and Dairy Products | Total Livestock Products |
|---|---|---|---|---|
| 1911 | 3.2 | 2.4 | 3.1 | 16.3 |
| 1940 | 11.2 | 6.8 | 6.5 | 34.7 |

# 7

# Bechuanaland Agriculture, 1900–1940

This chapter explores in greater detail the conflict between African commercial agriculture and industrial agricultural development outlined in the previous chapter. Because colonial policy was exempt from the local political control that South Africa gained in 1910, we can perhaps see the logic of British economic planning more clearly here.[1] The territory's poverty kept developments on a very small scale in this period, despite its vast area, and this also makes Bechuanaland a good candidate for closer study. The first half of this chapter follows Bechuanaland's fortunes in Southern Africa's developing commercial markets, and the second half follows colonial agricultural development policy, which was important in this period more for what it set out to do than for what it accomplished. This policy was directed by officials on the spot. Although a tiny budget stifled their efforts, a thorough knowledge of the territory's agricultural problems informed their view of what agriculture needed.

## THE CATTLE MARKET

There was little doubt that cattle production was the best hope for commercial development in Bechuanaland in the early twentieth century. Tswana cattle were among the toughest and lowest-quality cattle in Southern Africa, however, and so had difficulty competing in the Rand market. There was so little local commerce either to tax or to promote with tax revenue that the Protectorate was a burden rather than a boon to the British treasury. Figure 7.1 shows how large

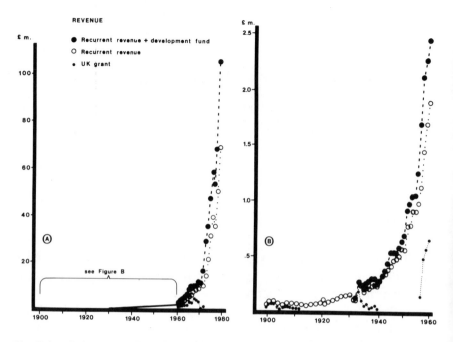

**Fig. 7.1.** Government Revenue: Bechuanaland and Botswana (See note to Fig. 5.2, p. 117.)

British grants and loans loomed in the revenue of the Protectorate before World War II. Revenue in this period was never more than £1 for each of Bechuanaland's citizens, who numbered some 300,000 by 1940.

With a slim budget, the government at first could do little else but tax and oversee the cattle trade. As in South Africa, the government restricted the number of trading licenses, fearing too many traders driving each other out of business. Indeed, the depression of the early 1930s moved the administration to reduce the number of licenses: there were 150 in 1921, but only 134 in 1934. The government also denied licenses to Africans until 1936.[2] Khama of the Ngwato financed a trading company managed by a white license holder, yet even this the government forbade in 1916.[3]

The government argued that the most likely candidates for African trading licenses were chiefs, who might pressure their people to trade only at their stores. If Khama was circumspect enough to trade fairly, Sebele II of the Kwena certainly was not. Sebele's 1926 request for a business license proved the administration's point, for no one doubted that he would coerce his people, least of all the Kwena themselves.[4] Whites were better candidates for trading licenses not only because they had fewer local followers than chiefs did: They were also able to operate freely in South Africa, where they obtained credit, picked up merchandise for their shops, and sold their Bechuanaland goods.[5]

Africans were granted a few licenses at reduced rates in 1936 and then freely in 1947, as trade began to improve.[6] Even if they had been allowed to trade earlier, only a few could have done so. In 1937 there was enough commerce in the Kweneng to support only 12 traders.[7] For all but 12 Kwena, then, trading was out of the question in the first place. Our 12 potential traders would certainly have been the wealthiest residents as well, like Khama and Sebele, and trading would only have helped them rise all the more quickly above their rural fellows. For the vast majority of Kwena, it did not matter whether the traders were white, black, or Indian, because they could never aspire to being traders themselves.

As Chapter 3 noted, most white traders also owned either commercial land or cattle posts in the reserves as holding grounds for the African cattle they purchased. Table 7.1 shows the distribution of cattle within the country as of 1921. All African cattle, all white-owned cattle within the reserves, and most cattle on commercial land was produced by African agriculture. Nevertheless, the government expected that traders would have the best chance of accumulating enough capital to establish proper ranches in the future. The land market was legally nonracial, but in practice the BSAC and Tati Companies sold title to their eastern land only to whites, and the Protectorate government did the same for Ghanzi farms.[8]

Before World War II industrial agricultural techniques made almost no progress in Bechuanaland. Commercial land remained unfenced, and traders remained almost completely dependent on African

**Table 7.1.** Bechuanaland Cattle Census, 1921

| Commercial Areas | European Owned | | African Owned | |
|---|---|---|---|---|
| | Reserves | | | |
| | Ngwato | 9,613 | Ngwato | 180,608 |
| | Kwena | 974 | Kwena | 23,727 |
| | Other | 9,018 | Other | 222,009 |
| Total    49,225 | Total | 19,389 | Total | 426,344 |

agriculture, thus serving the role that traders have done throughout history in most economic systems.[9] That is, they made profits by trading whatever their customers and suppliers demanded and offered for sale, and they tried to invest their profit wherever it could yield the highest return. Traders connected rural Botswana to the industrial world, and through them came the prices that rural citizens faced. These prices, not the trader, helped determine what and how they produced.

A look at the Southern African cattle market leaves little doubt as to why agriculture in Bechuanaland failed to become a modern industrial sector before World War II. If we considered only demand, we might expect South Africa's growing economy to offer a steadily rising price for meat. If we consider supply, however, we must take into account two other crucial developments. First, cattle filled Southern Africa's pastures before the Rand was discovered and continued to reproduce thereafter, at little cost to producers. This abundance of cattle reduced prices. Second, the industrial infrastructure beyond the pastures themselves, such as government veterinary controls, directed cattle as much as prices did.

Cattle producers thus faced fierce competition in the Southern African market and depended on their governments for success. The poverty of Bechuanaland's administration kept livestock services to a minimum and so kept its cattle industry in a poor competitive position. The first indication of these problems came when South Africa and Rhodesia imposed quarantine restrictions on Bechuanaland cattle imports during an outbreak of east coast fever in 1904-6. At that time the Protectorate had no agricultural staff, but relied on the Cape and Transvaal veterinary departments. South Africa loaned Bechuanaland one veterinary officer on a full-time basis to help implement the quarantine. Thus was born in 1905 the Bechuanaland Veterinary Department, predecessor of the Department of Agriculture.[10]

Thereafter cattle disease after cattle disease gave Rhodesia and South Africa reason to interrupt imports from Bechuanaland. The Veterinary Department struggled to prevent, control, and contain such outbreaks, but twenty years after its creation it boasted only one Veterinary Officer and three Stock Inspectors.[11] Disease continued periodically to close Bechuanaland's border to exports, giving an advantage to neighboring territories with wealthier governments and domestic demand.[12]

South Africa's 1924 controls on low-quality cattle, tightened again in 1926, struck Bechuanaland another serious blow. As of 1926, Bechuanaland oxen weighing less than 1,100 lbs. (500 kgs.) and cows weighing less than 840 lbs. (380 kgs.) were not allowed into South Africa, except to supply a Durban abattoir that won a contract to send low-quality meat to the Italian army.[13] Also in 1924, South Africa banned the import of cattle except by rail, so as to facilitate enforcement of its veterinary and weight controls. Rhodesia also fell under these controls, and like Bechuanaland, looked immediately to establish its own abattoir and cold storage works to move slaughtered cattle into South Africa and possibly the world market. Both colonies struck deals with Imperial Cold Storage Company (ICS), the largest meat processor in South Africa, to establish plants along their railways.[14]

The 1925 Protectorate agreement with ICS included price guarantees and a large land concession along the southern border for cattle holding grounds. The Lobatse abattoir was completed in 1927, but South Africa declared that it would accept only slaughtered meat that had come from animals above the prescribed weight limit. Because Bechuanaland had so few high-quality animals, Lobatse could not send its meat to South Africa, and the cost of refrigerated shipping was so high that only high-quality chilled meat could compete on the world market. Lobatse closed down without slaughtering a single animal and without even acquiring cold storage facilities.[15]

The early 1930s were particularly disastrous for the cattle trade, as Figure 7.2 shows. Official records date only from 1923, the year before the South African weight quota began. In that year 1,100 cattle walked across the northwest border to Angola; 3,269 walked across the northern border to the mines of the Congo and Northern Rhodesia; 1,089 walked across the eastern border to South Africa; and 16,635 walked onto rail cars up and down the rail line for transport to the Johannesburg abattoir.[16] Once the weight quota began in 1924, and cattle could no longer legally walk across the South African border, smuggling to the Transvaal increased.[17] Outbreaks of foot-and-mouth disease in the early 1930s then resulted in a total ban of Protectorate imports. Thereafter, the new South African meat marketing boards allocated Bechuanaland a fixed quota of heavy cattle, and prices improved in the postdepression recovery.[18] Rand cattle prices fell 40 percent from 1914 to 1924 but approached their pre-World War I level again by 1941, when the weight restriction on foreign cattle was removed.[19]

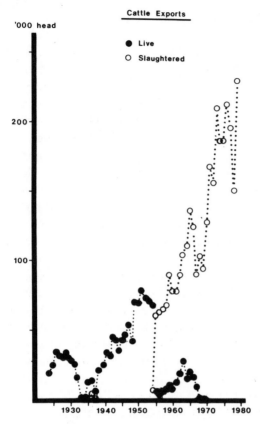

**Fig. 7.2.** Cattle Exports: Bechuanaland and Botswana (See note to Fig. 5.2, p. 117.)

The Lobatse abattoir began operating in 1934 but closed down after 1935. In 1939 an official "Report on the Cattle Industry of the Bechuanaland Protectorate" concluded that the abattoir could only compete on the South African market, and perhaps the world market, with a cold storage plant that would need an annual throughput of 25 to 30 thousand cattle to pay for itself.[20] The previous year's export total was only 21,750 head, however, whereas the official estimate for cattle smuggled into South Africa during 1935-38 was 75 to 100 thousand per year, almost all across the Transvaal border.[21] In order to divert these unofficial, smuggled exports to legal marketing channels along the rail line to Lobatse, the Bechuanaland government would have to take over the territory's cattle marketing system as the South African and Rhodesian governments had done in the 1930s.[22]

Before World War II the Protectorate lacked the processing facilities, veterinary services, and centralized marketing system that a modern cattle industry demanded. Although Bechuanaland was probably Africa's largest exporter of cattle per capita throughout the colonial era, neither African producers nor white landowners prospered enough from this trade to alter substantially their production techniques. Its vast herds of low-quality cattle had no outlet other than smuggling from 1924 to 1941, giving producers and traders alike a very low smuggler's price that inhibited investment in industrial production techniques.[23]

## THE GRAIN MARKET

In marked contrast to the cattle market, the South African grain market remained open to Bechuanaland throughout this period to 1940. The organization of this grain trade changed very little over these years. Traders still operated between the railway and Bechuanaland villages. South African maize controls of the early 1930s applied to African grain as well as white, whereas sorghum did not fall under marketing boards until after World War II. Because sorghum made a poor flour, its main industrial use was for beer brewing. Urban and rural African women also bought sorghum to make their own home brew for sale.[24]

Maize also required less labor than sorghum, because its closed cob kept birds out and thus obviated bird-scaring. It also had higher yields under a wider range of climatic conditions. In Bechuanaland's dry savanna, however, sorghum's resistance to drought kept it the most important crop for both consumption and sale. Figure 7.3 shows that grain imports consistently exceeded exports, most of which were also sorghum. As in the nineteenth century, producers continued to trade cattle for their neighbors' grain when their own harvests failed: Figure 7.4 shows that cattle exports more than paid for these grain imports. The only exceptions are the disastrous years of 1933 and 1934, when disease closed the border to legal cattle exports and drought eliminated harvests.[25]

## THE LABOR MARKET

Like most of rural Southern Africa, Bechuanaland sent not only cattle and grain but also labor to the region's growing industrial centers. At first, Bechuanaland's residents had the same access to South African jobs as South Africans did. A man required only a pass from

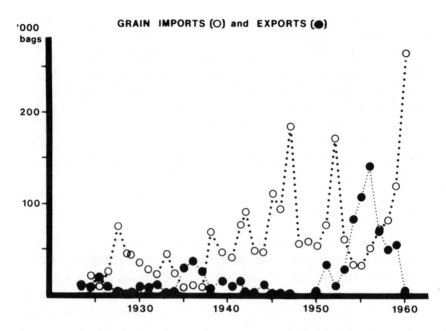

**Fig. 7.3.** Bechuanaland's Grain Imports and Exports (See note to Fig. 5.2, p. 117.)

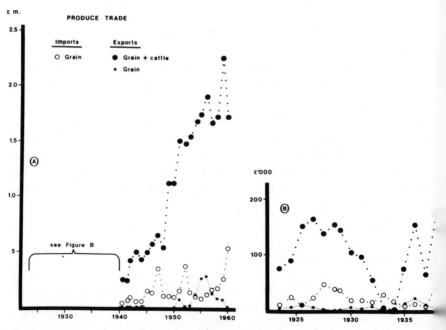

**Fig. 7.4.** Bechuanaland's Agricultural Trade (See note to Fig. 5.2, p. 117.)

his local district official to go to town, and women did not need passes at all. Men also walked across the border and bought passes in South African towns. Looking for work was expensive, however, because of the high cost of travel, urban rents, food, and taxes. Most men chose mine contracts instead, which guaranteed food, housing, and transport to and from the mine. Although mine wages were very low, a man was certain to arrive back home with at least some cash to invest in cattle or a plow. Moreover, there was not a single secondary school in Bechuanaland in 1940, while missionaries, the government, and black urban and rural communities supported African schools in South Africa. Bechuanaland men could not compete with black South Africans for nonmanual jobs, and so chose the guaranteed income of the mine contract.[26]

The first restriction on foreign workers to the Rand came in the first decade of the twentieth century, when the high death rate of miners from north of 22 degrees latitude moved the British colonial governments there to limit recruiting. In 1913 the South African government banned all recruiting north of 22 degrees, which included the northern half of Bechuanaland. This ban did not affect southern men, including the Kwena.[27]

The 1937 amendment of the 1923 Natives (Urban Areas) Act allowed a list of municipalities to deny access to Africans, but 1941 correspondence from the South African Secretary for Native Affairs summed up what this meant for Bechuanaland. First of all he thanked the Protectorate administration for following South African policy by refusing to issue a travel pass to the Rand unless a man could prove he had a job there. He then lamented that men simply entered South Africa without travel passes; they did not need them to ride the train, and upon arrival the Johannesburg pass office sold them a pass to look for work.[28] As the last chapter noted, Johannesburg was not on the list of restricted towns until 1947.[29] More than any other South African city, Johannesburg was the domain of English-speaking employers who had no desire to reduce the number of persons competing to work for them.

The number of Bechuanaland citizens working in South Africa was never much greater than 5,000 until the economic crisis of the early 1930s and the removal of the tropical recruiting ban in 1934. By 1934 the number had doubled to some 10,000, and by 1940 it had doubled again to 20,000. Competition for labor from manufacturing moved the mines to expand their search for recruits. Whereas they first paid local traders to sign men up for them, in 1936 they began establishing their own offices in the Protectorate. By 1940 some one-quarter of the adult working-age male population were in South Africa, and another quarter had been to South Africa at least once.[30]

## AGRICULTURAL DEVELOPMENT

The Protectorate administration was too poor to improve significantly the competitive position of its citizens in the cattle, grain, or labor markets in the first decades of the twentieth century. We have already noted its veterinary efforts and its deal with the ICS; in 1926 it appointed its first Dairy Officer, but the Protectorate could not compete with areas in South Africa and Rhodesia that were wetter, cooler, or nearer the urban market.[31] The most serious problem facing the cattle industry as a whole, however, concerned a more basic requirement: although grass covered Bechuanaland, cattle could not reach most of it because there was no water nearby to drink. The Kalahari separated some areas where there was water, such as Ngamiland and Ghanzi, from the railway and the South African market. Except when very good summer rain temporarily dotted the countryside with pools, cattle could not walk to market across these waterless pastures.

The government immediately began blasting wells in the hardveld rocks to provide water for its staff, but dynamite was useless in deep sand. And boreholes drilled by steam engine were expensive and risky. A 1910 estimate placed the cost per borehole at about £300, about the same as for an expensive well, but a tremendous amount of water was needed for drilling: 500 gallons per day.[32] A nearby water source was thus necessary or else ox carts had to return constantly to Gaborone to fetch water.[33] Cart and drill breakdowns threatened to drag out drilling and thus raise costs far beyond this 1910 estimate. More important, even if none of the boreholes yielded water, the cost of drilling still stood at £807. Wells were fairly certain to yield water because the surface rocks gave abundant clues about where to blast, whereas in the Kalahari a uniform layer of sand obscured such clues. There was no guarantee that a borehole would yield any water at all.

The first successful sandveld cattle boreholes were not deep in the Kalahari but along the railway line where the sandveld pushes almost to the Limpopo. In 1927 Chief Isang of the Kgatla imposed a special tribal tax to pay the South African government to drill for water in his Kgatleng District (see Maps 3.1 and 3.2). Carrying water along the railway was a relatively easy task. Two boreholes in his capital village of Mochudi and five in grazing areas proved successful.[34]

Meanwhile, in the same year the Protectorate administration bought its own drill, appointed its Public Work Department engineer to oversee its use, and began boring not to expand grazing but to facilitate the export of Ghanzi cattle.[35] The proposed path of boreholes led west from the rail at Gaborone to Molepolole to the last reliable water at Letlhakeng, and then across the Kweneng.[36] The first step was completed in 1929 with a successful borehole at Khudumelapye, twenty-five kilometers northwest of Letlhakeng. The rig and water took six months to travel from Gaborone, however, and the next two drillings failed, yielding only a dry hole at Lenake and brack water at Kuke. After spending £6,000, the project was abandoned.[37]

The year 1929 turned out to be promising in a different respect, when the British Parliament passed its first Colonial Development and Welfare Act.[38] The era of public spending had arrived in Britain and embraced its colonies as well. British grants and loans now augmented the Bechuanaland budget, which the cattle-trade crisis of the early 1930s further reduced. Along with the new funds came a special commissioner, Sir Alan Pim, to oversee its expenditure. With the 1933 "Pim Report," development planning replaced year-to-year budget balancing in Bechuanaland's government finances.[39]

Pim found a pitiful number of government staff in such a vast territory: 117 whites and 355 Africans. He also found revenue as presented in Table 7.2: we can see that income tax plummeted in 1931/2, pulling revenue down nearly to one-half pound per Bechuanaland resident. Only whites paid income tax, and most of these were traders dependent on African cattle sales to South Africa. Pim's most important recommendations were to give the Protectorate more staff and a larger budget for the staff to spend on development.[40]

Funding for Pim's development plan commenced in full in 1935; in 1938 the Protectorate administration evaluated this program, reporting that it had spent nearly half the budget shown in Table 7.3. In addition to this expenditure, the Veterinary Department grew from 11 white officers and 8 African assistants in 1933 to 29 white officers and 118 African assistants in 1938. The assistants were deployed as

**Table 7.2.** Bechuanaland Government Revenue, 1930-32 (£)

|         | Hut Tax | Income Tax | Customs | Other  | Total   |
|---------|---------|------------|---------|--------|---------|
| 1930-31 | 40,740  | 37,871     | 25,579  | 45,464 | 149,654 |
| 1931-32 | 31,921  | 2,686      | 26,313  | 45,815 | 106,735 |

Table 7.3. Bechuanaland Colonial Development Fund, 1935-38 (£)

| Water Development | Roads | Hospitals | Okavango Clearance | Small Stock and Dairy | Stud Farms in Reserves | Other | Total |
|---|---|---|---|---|---|---|---|
| 140,194 | 71,440 | 12,290 | 12,000 | 9,157 | 7,000 | 20,184 | 272,265 |

"cattle guards" in the reserve pastures to report immediately any disease outbreaks. The Protectorate had hired 3 African Agricultural Demonstrators (ADs) in 1930, and in 1938 it hired its first trained agronomist, who oversaw 12 African ADs and 8 AD assistants. The Dairy Department also had 2 white and 12 African staff in 1938.[41]

By 1938 state agricultural development policy had at last become a reality. Table 7.3 shows that water development was clearly its most important element. Even before this CDF program, the government had begun drilling boreholes instead of blasting wells in the hardveld, for once it owned a drill, boring was easier than blasting. As of 1933 these hardveld boreholes numbered only 16, and Khudumelapye remained the government's only sandveld success.[42] From 1935 to 1938 the government drilled 57 successful boreholes with 8 drills. Twenty-seven engine pumps, one windmill, and twenty-two hand pumps capped these holes. The CDF also built two major and nine minor dams in the hardveld.[43]

At first Pim suggested blasting wells and building dams instead of drilling boreholes, largely because he doubted that the government would be able to afford a proper program of aerial survey and full geological analysis as South Africa had done, where 20,000 boreholes had already been drilled.[44] Both the financial and technical problems proved smaller than Pim anticipated, however, and in 1939 the government declared that its well-blasting days were over.[45] From then on it drilled only holes instead, and most of these were in the reserve sandveld. By the end of 1940 there were some 120 government boreholes in Bechuanaland.[46]

Throughout the 1930s the borehole became conspicuous more for its promise than for its impact. The internal combustion engine finally replaced steam, reducing drastically the amount of water required for drilling, but the high cost of fuel, as well as the difficulties of proper site location and transport between sites, still made boreholes expensive. Although a motor vehicle crossed the Kalahari for the first time in 1928,[47] before World War II wagons dominated the traffic even on the few roads that the government maintained. Poor roads favored ox-drawn vehicles, and when a motor lorry stuck in the mud or sand, oxen pulled it out. Roads received the second largest allocation in the 1935-38 CDF budget shown in Table 7.8, and 300 kilometers were actually built in this period.[48] This could have little effect, however, in a country 900 kilometers long and 900 kilometers wide. In the Kweneng, the government maintained the 50-kilometer Gaborone-Molepolole road, which nonetheless remained impassable when the Metsemotlhaba River flooded its banks after a heavy rain.[49] As of 1937, the government itself owned only 52 internal combustion engines, including vehicles, borehole pumps, and drills.[50]

Well-financed South African transporters moved faster than the government in this period. In the early 1930s the South African railroad's road motor service ranged out from railheads in the western Transvaal to Bechuanaland's eastern hardveld villages.[51] When the ban on northern mine recruitment was lifted in 1934, the Witwatersrand Native Labour Association built a 500-kilometer road from Ngamiland to the railway in Tati District. Along this road it bused recruits to and from the mines. When the Rand's recruiting agency south of 22 degrees, the Native Recruitment Corporation, established a dozen offices in Bechuanaland from 1936, it ran two buses from the villages to the railway. The second of these offices was in Molepolole. Soon traders bought their own motor vehicles, so that the NRC relied on private contracting and stopped running its own buses.[52] By 1940 private motor vehicles plied the Gaborone-Molepolole road three times a week carrying goods and passengers, most of whom were miners.[53]

The high cost of transport before World War II helped keep traders in charge of the produce market. No individual African produced enough grain to fill a railway car. Instead, Africans sold grain to local traders, who transported grain in bulk to the railway, where other traders handled bulk shipments to and from South Africa. Traders thus reaped the transport profits of African grain. Lower transport costs might have allowed producers to deliver grain to traders along the railway themselves, or enabled the government to transport grain and hand the transport profits back to producers, as in South Africa.

Because the government could not help Africans garner a larger share of the profits from their produce, it urged them to increase their profits by increasing the size of their harvest through more intensive cultivation. When Protectorate officials announced the appointment of the first three ADs to the Native Advisory Committee in 1930,

Isang of the Kgatla asked, "If we do plow, where will we sell our kaffir corn* and crops? The market is very low. The railway rates are heavy." The ADs' official supervisor replied, "I know the market is low. You will make up for that by producing a larger quantity."[5][4]

We can recognize this strategy as that espoused by missionaries and South African governments through the nineteenth century and on into the twentieth: peasant farmers cultivate more intensively and invest their crop receipts in new technology, which expands their output, giving them more revenue to invest in more technology. Africans had to go to mission schools to learn new techniques, however, until Rhodesia began in 1926 to take the new techniques into the reserves. The pioneer of this new method was E. A. Alvord, an American missionary working in southeast Rhodesia along the Mozambique border. Alvord trained Africans to follow a prescribed "package" of techniques, and then to plow a field in a reserve to demonstrate these techniques to other Africans. The Rhodesian government hired Alvord in 1926 as its first "Agriculturalist for Instruction of the Natives," and in 1929 the South African Native Affairs Department adopted this system as well.[55] In 1930 Rhodesia passed a Land Apportionment Act that divided farmland according to the original SANAC formula as embodied in South Africa's 1913 Land Act; 37 percent of the country remained African land, but one-quarter of this was set aside as commercial land that Alvord's successful pupils might purchase without competition from white buyers.[56]

Of the 12 Bechuanaland ADs in 1938, one was posted in the Kweneng.[57] His demonstration package comprised the following: plowing during winter to leave the soil weedless, porous and ready to absorb the first summer rain; plowing on contours and ridging earth up on the field's borders to make a uniform, crumbly bed; when rain fell, sowing seed in a straight line with a mechanical ox-drawn planter rather than broadcasting seed all over the field before plowing; pulling tree stumps out of the field rather than guiding the plow around them; and storing stalks and refuse as silage for winter fodder.[58]

This package followed the Glen Grey system rather than the 1860 Natal plan, for it did not require enclosure of the commons. By increasing their reliance on cultivation, Africans would gradually depend less on cattle. This would make the pastures easier to enclose in the future. Virtually no one followed the AD's advice, however. Rather

---

*kaffir corn = sorghum.

than concentrating intensively on one field as the AD urged, cultivators continued to spread their resources over several fields, not all
of them their own, plowing extensively and quickly as much land
as possible.

More precisely, winter plowing wasted labor and cattle because
one could never be sure beforehand that enough rain would fall to
warrant plowing in the first place. Cultivators rather continued to
wait for one or two summer showers before beginning to plow. Moreover, dry winter soil was harder on the draft team than soft wet summer soil. As for contour plowing and ridging, soil erosion was not
much of a problem on the flat terrain. It was hard enough to drive
untrained cattle, taken out of the herd only to plow let alone along
an invisible contour. And ridging, like destumping, involved too large
a labor investment for a field that seldom received enough rain for a
good crop. Harrowing and planting with a mechanical planter only
wasted valuable labor and draft. Instead of going over one field three
times with a plow, then harrow, then planter, it made more sense to
plow under another field entirely, and so double the area plowed.[59]
Broadcasting followed by one pass of the plow was quick, and as yet
there was no dearth of arable land to till. As for winter fodder, summer rains did not produce enough vegetation to warrant storage, and
winter pasture was still available even in overgrazed areas.

This does not mean that the AD package was bad advice. If individual cultivators were eventually to intensify production, this path
was certainly the best to follow. Although cultivators found it more
profitable not to follow this advice, their reliance on many fields, and
on cattle instead of grain, made enclosure an increasingly unlikely
prospect, as more and more cultivators depended on more and more
low-quality cattle.

The government also bought six tractors and ran an experimental
tractor-plowing service in 1935. Some 3,000 acres were plowed in
Ngwato territory in return for one bag per acre payment at harvest.
Yields were very low, however, because the tractors plowed far more
area than field owners were able to weed, bird-scare and reap properly.
The government collected only 500 bags of grain, which did not even
begin to cover the high cost of fuel and equipment. The experiment
was declared a failure and the service abandoned.[60]

Despite the endurance of the commons, the government also promoted improved herding techniques: vaccinations, dipping, early castration, supplementary feeds like bonemeal, and sale of young oxen
and old cows. As of 1940, however, the only veterinary staff in the

reserves were the African cattle guards who reported disease out-breaks. Six guards roamed the Kweneng on foot, each covering 6,000 square kilometers. Although the Veterinary Department encouraged them to tell herders about these industrial herding aids, the guards could not have had a significant effect.[61] In any event, herders had good reason not to follow this veterinary advice. The government wanted them to rely on a smaller number of high-quality animals for sale on the cash market; the instability of this market and the constant threat of drought encouraged them to rely instead on large herds of tough, low-quality cattle that could also pull plows and wagons.

The government's most ambitious step to improve herd quality was the creation of a bull camp in each of the large reserves, including the Kweneng, upon imposition of the 1924 South African weight quotas. The camp was a fenced ranch stocked with exotic, high-quality bulls, to which cattle owners could bring their cows for breed-ing larger animals that might qualify for export.[62] The CDF budget in Table 7.3 includes additional funding for these camps. Hardly any herders went out of their way to interrupt their herding movements to drive a few cows to these bulls every year. Poor rains weakened these delicate animals, and the 1933 drought killed many of them outright.[63]

Nevertheless, we can see that the government took as many steps as it could afford to promote its agricultural industry. The dearth of basic infrastructure and the low level of commercial activity made large steps, such as dividing the commons or even granting negotiable arable titles, well beyond its means. The most successful government agricultural development policy was simply the provision of perma-nent water. The official water priorities were villages first and pasture second,[64] and an official inventory assembled by the District Com-missioner provides a good picture of progress as of 1938.[65] The gov-ernment had drilled boreholes at Molepolole (population 20,000), Gabane (3,000) and Kopong (450).[66] Molepolole had also received a large dam during the 1933 drought, and six wells.[67]

Although these were the only government water sources in the Kweneng as of 1938, the DC reported other village supplies as well. In the southern hardveld, Kumakwane (150) and Mogoditshane (300) depended on wells, while Thamaga (5,000) depended on the Metse-motlhaba River and Mankgodi (1,500) depended on its tributary, the Kolobeng. Lephepe (500) in the northern sandveld valley had five wells and its tiny satellite Boatlaname had two. The Letlhakeng Valley relied on its ancient sand pits at Letlhakeng village (4,000) and thirteen

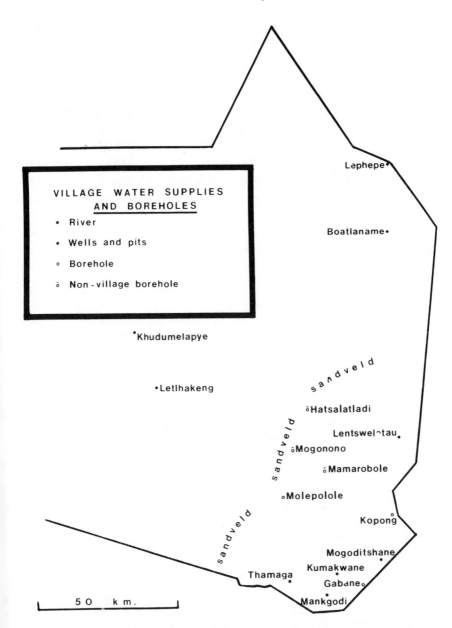

**VILLAGE WATER SUPPLIES
AND BOREHOLES**
* River
• Wells and pits
◦ Borehole
ᵒ̃ Non-village borehole

Lephepe•

Boatlaname•

•Khudumelapye

•Letlhakeng

s a n d v e l d

ᵒ̃Hatsalatladi

Lentswel⌃tau.

ᵒ̃Mogonono

ᵒ̃Mamarobole

◦Molepolole

Kopong◦

Mogoditshane

Kumakwane
•

Thamaga
*

Gabane◦

Mankgodi
*

s a n d v e l d

s a n d v e l d

50 km.

**Map 7.1.** Kweneng 1940: Village Water Supplies and Boreholes (From DC Mole-polole, BNA S 378/3/1; borehole sites from Wynne, "Preliminary report.")

wells along the valley. Four of these wells were at Khudumelapye, near the abandoned 1929 borehole. Because the DC's concern was village supplies, he missed some of the other permanent supplies in the Kweneng. Pits at Dutlwe still supported a permanent cattle population, and there were numerous wells scattered through the transitional hardveld, which the next chapter maps. The DC reported only the transitional hardveld wells at Lentsweletau village (100), and the unusual concentration of wells and pits at Suping. The transitional hardveld was not yet full with wells, plows, and wagons, however, and so this was where the government built the Kweneng's first nonvillage boreholes in 1940.[68] Map 7.1 shows the water sites mentioned above as of this year.

## NOTES

1. See J. Spence, "British policy towards the High Commission territories," *JMAS*, 2, 1964. More generally, see F. Pedler, "British planning and private enterprise in colonial Africa," in P. Duignan and L. Gann, *Colonialism in Africa: The Economics of Colonialism* (Vol. 4), Cambridge, 1975; C. Ehrlich, "Building and caretaking: economic policy in British tropical Africa, 1890-1960," *EHR*, 24, 1973.
2. Meeting of Resident Commissioner and Bechuanaland Indians, 1934, BNA DC Molepolole, Box 4, File M 262; Schapera, *Native Land*, pp. 90-92.
3. See N. Parsons, "Khama and Co. and the Jousse trouble, 1910-16," *JAH*, 16, 1975.
4. BNA DC Molepolole, Box 5, File M 313, 1926, discusses Sebele's request. RC Correspondence, 1925, BNA S 601/19 reports that Kwena headmen drew up a constitution of Kwena law that they wanted Sebele to sign.
5. If the government had expanded the number of licenses earlier, Indians probably would have snatched most of them up before Africans. Indians had more difficulty than whites, but less than Africans, in operating in the South African cattle market. There were 16 Indian traders in 1934. See Meeting of Resident Commissioner and Bechuanaland Indians, 1934; A. Best, "General trading in Botswana, 1890-1968," *EG*, 46, 1970.
6. Schapera, *Native Land*, pp. 90-92.
7. BNA DC Molepolole, Box 4, File M 299, 1937.
8. Schapera, *Native Land*, pp. 55-57. As of 1921, however, the government did allow the Malete and Tlokwa to expand their tiny reserves by buying commercial land. The cattle census is found in BNA S 4/9.
9. Some 7 percent of officially recorded cattle exports were "white-owned," a category that must have included African cattle purchases as immatures. RC Correspondence, 1934, BNA S 388/1/1.

10. BP, Veterinary Department, "Brief account of development, strength and method of organization," 1932, BNA S 294/11. Khama III of the Ngwato still had cattle grazing beyond the Rhodesian border, but these veterinary controls forced him finally to pull them into the Protectorate. GB CO, *ASD*, 802, 1902, 215.
11. BP, *Blue Book*, 1925/6.
12. The Veterinary Department's largest campaign in this period was the inoculation of 800,000 cattle during the 1933 foot and mouth outbreak. J. Falconer, "History of the Botswana veterinary service," *BNR*, 3, 1971; BNA S 338/1/4, 1939.
13. Veterinary Department, "Brief account." The export of cattle for the Durban trade began in 1926 and peaked at 17,000 head in 1929. The South African government dictated that 75 percent of exports from the Durban abattoir must be from South Africa, leaving Rhodesia, Bechuanaland, and Swaziland to compete for the rest. RC Correspondence, 1934, BNA S 338/1/1.
14. For Rhodesia, see Phimister, "Meat and monopolies."
15. The main Protectorate file on the embargo and abattoir is BNA S 18/4.
16. BP, Veterinary Department, "Brief account," 1932.
17. Although traders did most of the smuggling, Protectorate chiefs leased farms in the western Transvaal, with South African government approval, and the Protectorate administration claimed that they were smuggling cattle to these farms. RC Correspondence, 1928, BNA S 18/4.
18. RC Correspondence, 1939, BNA S 338/1/4.
19. Ettinger, "South Africa's weight restrictions," gives a 1910 base index of 100 for real Johannesburg cattle prices, and indexes of 117 for 1914, 69 for 1924, and 100 for 1942.
20. H. Walker and J. Hobday, "Report on the Cattle Industry of the Bechuanaland Protectorate," 1939, BNA S 388/2.
21. RC Correspondence, 1939, S 338/1/4. This smuggling killed the Bechuanaland trade to Durban, whose last shipments were in 1939.
22. Walker and Hobday, "Report."
23. Boer farmers in the western Transvaal sold their own cattle at the protected South African price and bought hardy, disease-resistant Protectorate cattle at the low smuggler's price to replace them. RC Correspondence, 1936, BNA S 446/7.
24. J. Tinley, *South African Food and Agriculture During World Wat II*, Stanford, 1954, pp. 5-17, 53.
25. If we subtract African taxes, we must add 1927 to the list of deficit years. E. Roe, "Development of livestock, agriculture and water supplies in eastern Botswana before independence," Cornell University, Table 2. Deducting trader profits would reduce the surplus even more, and counting the income from smuggled cattle would raise it.
26. Schapera, *Migrant Labour*, chs. 2-3.
27. Schapera, *Migrant Labour*, pp. 25-33.
28. South African Secretary for Native Affairs, Pretoria, to Government Secretary, Mafeking, 7 June 1941, BNA S 144/9.

29. RC Correspondence, 22 April 1948, BNA S 144/9.
30. Schapera, *Migrant Labour*, pp. 39-43, Appendix A. The Kweneng DC reported exactly this figure of 25 percent absentees in 1935. Kweneng District, *Annual Report*, 1935, BNA S 448/15.
31. From 1930, however, the new South African Dairy Industry Control Board offered fixed subsidized prices and included Bechuanaland in its orbit. Two white-owned creameries in the Tati area began ranging out 50 kilometers from the railway to buy separated milk from African suppliers. By 1932 there were more than 400 African-owned hand separators which provided separated milk to over 70 depots for pick-up by the creameries, but by 1938 the African separators numbered only 110. Some 1,000 cattle herders contributed milk. BP, *Annual Report*, 1935; BP, DoA, *Annual Report*, 1938. One of these separators was in the Kweneng at Mankgodi in 1930, but there was no quick transport to the rail. BNA DC Molepolole, Box 4, File M 292. See also J. Kneen, "The dairy industry in South Africa," *SAJE*, 3, 1965.
32. Townshend, "Development," GB, CO, *ASD*, 969, 1910, 98. In 1896 a government well cost from £200 to £500. GB, CO, *ASD*, 517, 1895-97, 222, 276. BP, *Blue Book*, 1921/2, reports a government well in Molepolole costing £250. These early government wells were much more expensive than private wells because they were contracted to South African professionals for set fees at specific sites. Transport costs featured largely in the fees. Private reserve wells were located by the prospective owner, who chose carefully a site certain to yield water at a reasonable depth, provided transport, and assisted the blaster.
33. Gaborone, which replaced Mafeking as the territorial capital in the early 1960s, was the first site in the Protectorate where the government tried drilling, unsuccessfully, in 1906-7. BP, *Annual Report*, 1906/7. The government's first successful borehole was at Mafeking headquarters, drilled in 1908-9 at a cost of £703. BP, *Annual Report*, 1908/9.
34. Isang spent £1,200 of tribal money plus a £500 government grant. BP, *Annual Report*, 1929; Schapera, *Native Land*, p. 242 and Map I, p. 128.
35. BP, *Annual Report*, 1927/8. Formerly, the Public Works Department comprised laborers plus a clerk to oversee their payment.
36. The government first tried blasting wells in Kweneng pans; some 300 spent at the beginning of the century yielded only two wells with good but seasonal water. BP, *Annual Report*, 1902-4. The government bridged the shorter gap from Ngamiland to the Ngwato hardveld with wells. BP, *Annual Report*, 1904/5, 1910-15.
37. BNA DC Molepolole, Box 6, File M 402A; BP Secretariat Correspondence, 10 July 1930, S 114/1. South African and Rhodesian government engineers did the drilling.
38. Pedler, "British planning," pp. 113-14.
39. Great Britain, *Financial and Economic Position of the Bechuanaland Protectorate*, 1933. Henceforth, "Pim Report."
40. "Pim Report," Appendixes 12, 15. This personnel count does not include a dozen administrative staff in Mafeking.
41. BP, "Progress report, 1933-38," BNA S 202/2; Veterinary Department, "Brief account"; BP, DoA, *Annual Report*, 1963/4. The government also began a poultry breeding plant at Lobatse and stationed a forestry officer at Kazangulu in 1935. BP, *Annual Report*, 1935.

42. "Pim Report," pp. 111-16.
43. BP, "Progress report, 1933-38."
44. "Pim Report," pp. 113, 156-58.
45. BNA DC Molepolole, Box 4, File M 274B, 1939.
46. Schapera, *Native Land*, p. 243.
47. B. Clifford, *Kalahari Desert Expedition*, Pretoria, 1928. The first motor vehicle, a Ford, reached Letlhakeng in 1926, driven by the Molepolole missionary. J. Burns, Correspondence, 25 April 1926, ZNA, BU 5/1/1/1.
48. BP, "Progress report, 1933-38." There were 3,250 kilometers of motorable road by 1940. BP, *Blue Book*, 1939/40.
49. Kweneng District, *Annual Report*, 1940.
50. BP, *Annual Report*, 1937.
51. BP, *Annual Report*, 1938, reported this service still operating from Mahalapye through Tuli to the Transvaal and from Lobatse to Zeerust. This service eliminated local wagons from the village-rail trade. NAC, May 1931. Because Rhodesia owned the Bechuanaland railway, South African Rail Road did not run the service from Protectorate railheads.
52. Schapera, *Migrant Labour*, pp. 77-81; J. Taylor, "Mine labour recruitment in the Bechuanaland Protectorate," *BNR*, 10, 1978.
53. Kweneng District, *Annual Report*, 1940.
54. NAC, April 1930.
55. Palmer, *Land*, p. 202; South Africa, Commission for the Socio-Economic Development of the Bantu Areas, *Summary of the Report*, 1955, p. 74. More generally, see G. Masefield, *A History of the Colonial Agricultural Service*, Oxford, 1972.
56. Palmer, *Land*, p. 185.
57. BP, DoA, *Annual Report*, 1938.
58. BP, DoA, *Annual Report*, 1938-39; NAC, 1937.
59. Cultivators did experiment with the harrow before rejecting it, as early as 1905. See BP, *Annual Report*, 1904/5.
60. BP, *Annual Report*, 1936; RC Correspondence, 1936, BNA S 446/1-2. Fuel cost 5 shillings per acre and each tractor unit cost £1,200.
61. A 1937 map of the six areas is in BNA S 487/2/1. See also Veterinary Department, "Brief account," 1932, and the discussion in the Serowe chief's *kgotla* in 1937, RC Correspondence, BNA S 487/2/1. Or reserve herders could journey to three Livestock Improvement Centers for medicines and advice.
62. BP, *Annual Report*, 1923/4.
63. BP, *Annual Report*, 1933.
64. BP, "Progress report, 1933-38."
65. Kweneng DC Correspondence, 1939-40, BNA A 378/3/1. The first Kweneng borehole was exploratory, drilled in a Metsemotlhaba tributary south of Thamaga, in 1923. It was never equipped for pumping.
66. Water sites are from Kweneng DC Correspondence, 1939-40, BNA S 387/3/1. Population figures are from BNA DC Molepolole, Box 5, File M345, 1939. 1939.
67. BP, "Progress report, 1933-38." Before World War II, hardveld dams were products of human labor, assisted by picks and shovels and ox-drawn wagons for carrying soil. Few dams were perennial.
68. See note 66.

# 8

# The Tractor, the Borehole, and the Truck, 1940–1980

This chapter completes the picture of Kweneng agriculture's failure to industrialize. The boom in the world economy in the decades following World War II raised the demand for agricultural products and improved technology, making it cheaper. Government revenue rose accordingly and funded development that brought industrial technology much closer to Bechuanaland's producers. The Protectorate gained independence in 1966, with a universal franchise and a fully representative parliament. The new Botswana government grew wealthy from high cattle prices and diamond discoveries in three remote sandveld sites in the 1970s, enabling it to deliver a wide range of services and infrastructure that has made the country a successful member of the South African industrial region.[1] Economic development policy changed very little. The problem of African agriculture remained unsolved, as this chapter shows, leaving the vast majority of Africans unable to take advantage of these technological advances.

## AGRICULTURAL PLANNING

Whereas missionaries in the nineteenth century claimed that African economies were like European economies centuries before and needed only a strong dose of commerce and education for them to evolve rapidly into a European-style peasantry, social anthropologists were called in during the twentieth century to explain why this evolution had not taken place. Pim's 1933 preliminary budget included a sum of £250 for an anthropologist, who turned out to be Isaac Schapera of the University of Cape Town.[2] His *Handbook of Tswana Law and Custom* appeared in 1938 and featured prominently in the first public discussion of African land tenure reform in the Protectorate, in 1940.

The outbreak of war aggravated official concern about Bechuanaland's large grain imports, which might otherwise be used to feed allied troops. The Resident Commissioner drew the attention of the March 1940 meeting of the African Advisory Council to a passage on page 207 of the *Handbook*, which explained what prevented a cultivator from producing more grain for the local market.

> . . .it is obvious that he has no security of tenure. This, more than anything else, has militated against improvement of the land such as fencing and attempts at irrigation.[3]

Chief Molema of the Rolong objected strongly to this statement. Schapera was present at this meeting, and replied thus:

> That statement is based on information given to me by the BaKgatla and particularly by Chief Isang. . . . If there is any inaccuracy in the statement, it must therefore be due to my informants.[4]

The problem here is that Isang and other chiefs were careful to insist that land was not held by negotiable private title, knowing that "security of tenure" also meant "insecurity of tenure," in that landowners with full control of their land could fall into debt and lose it. Chief Tshekedi of the Ngwato stated during the discussion:

> My opposition to any change in the present system is not due to the fact that I fear any change in the Chief's powers, but I fear that the Natives will lose their land.[5]

As we have already noted, Tswana tenure gave a cultivator full rights of occupation and benefit from investment but prohibited outright sale. Some of these legal subtleties were evidently lost in Schapera's exhaustive compilation. In any event, the RC summed up the discussion by stating that "Every speaker made it quite clear that in his opinion there is complete security of tenure by the individual users of the land," with the familiar exception of eminent domain for public use.[6]

Although the status of arable land sparked this discussion, the RC was also looking to the future of grazing land, inquiring "whether the present system of land tenure is not causing some modification in each tribal area of former customs."[7] When the war ended and food demands returned to normal, and when in the postwar boom cattle prices and exports rose rapidly, the government faced the decision of whether to modify African land laws to meet these new commercial opportunities. Figures 7.1, 7.2, 8.1 and 8.2 show the rise in prices, trade, and government revenue. Most immediate was the question of sandveld boreholes, which the government could now afford to deliver in greatly increased numbers. Efficient motor vehicles, powered by cheap fuel, could now convey more efficient drilling machines quickly and cheaply anywhere in the country. But what would prevent the new grazing areas from becoming as overgrazed as the hardveld?

The government had three choices. First, it could delineate and sell title to private, enclosed ranches around the new boreholes. The constraint here was that most of the sandveld, especially in its more accessible and better-watered eastern reaches, was part of the African reserves. Seizing more land for white settlement was politically impossible at this late date, especially while so much of the Crown Land beyond remained unsold; moreover, the government wanted to draw cattle from the overgrazed hardveld, and only a handful of Africans could afford to buy and invest further in a ranch.[8]

Second, the government could devise some sort of African group ranch, with a number of Africans pooling their cattle and money. The government could not waste funds on risky experiments, however.

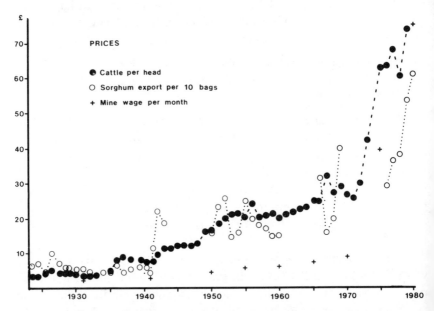

**Fig. 8.1.**  Prices: Bechuanaland and Botswana (See note to Fig. 5.2, p. 117.)

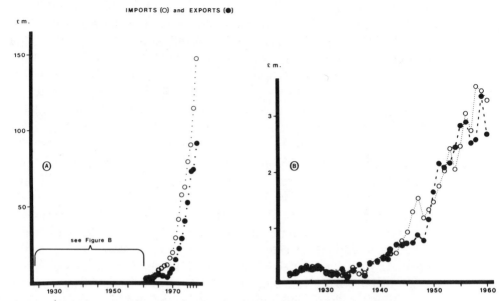

**Fig. 8.2.** Imports and Exports: Bechuanaland and Botswana (See note to Fig. 5.2, p. 117.)

No one knew how long the boom would last, and there were other necessary investments to make. The British Colonial Development Corporation bought the old Lobatse plant in 1949 and spent £750,000 on a new abattoir and cold storage works, which opened in 1954.[9]

The third possibility for pasture control at the new boreholes was to turn the responsibility over to local authorities. This turned out to be the cheapest and quickest option. Although Tswana law and custom did not foster industrial herding techniques, Schapera's second official study, *Native Land Tenure in the Bechuanaland Protectorate* (1943), reported that the overseers responsible for grazing areas had the power to limit cattle numbers there.[10] It is unclear whether the government actually accepted this proposition. Certainly the overgrazed hardveld testified loudly against it.[11] Surely this was another case of chiefs telling Schapera that the existing tenure system needed no revision. In any event, each reserve did have a strong tribal administration, with its own budget, capable of at least attempting to control stock at the new boreholes.[12]

There were two basic systems that the tribal authorities employed at their new boreholes: syndicates and quotas. The former were pioneered at the prewar Kgatla boreholes, for which a few herders accepted responsibility for paying pump fuel and repair costs and limiting cattle numbers.[13] Quotas were pioneered in the Kweneng in 1955-59, when the government began to contract South African drillers for an expanded reserve borehole program. The tribal authority paid for fuel and repairs but charged these costs to users per head of stock watered. Four hundred head were registered at each borehole. When these grew to five hundred, the largest owner had to take his herd elsewhere, thereby reducing the cattle population again.[14] Beyond the prevention of overgrazing, a distant borehole could at least in theory operate somewhat like a ranch, with a limited number of animals confined to the area around it and never mingling with adjacent herds watering elsewhere. This would aid breeding and disease control.

Another reason why the government did not build ranches in the reserves was that commercial landowners only just began to make substantial capital investments in this period. When the abattoir opened, white Bechuanaland residents still earned two and a half times more income from trade and transport, especially of African cattle, than directly from agricultural production.[15] Although they continued to buy African cattle, they quickly built up their own self-contained herds with hybrid bulls, medicines, fences, and boreholes. By 1958 they owned 146,000 cattle, three times as many as the 1921 cattle census reported on commercial land. They now purchased only 45 percent of their cattle from Africans, and one-sixth of the cattle exports were now born and bred on commercial land.[16]

The government thus had plenty of scope to develop commercial ranching on commercial land before turning to the more difficult problem of ranches in the reserves. In the early 1950s, the government added more Ghanzi farms, delineated ranches in the northern Crown Lands, and sold off plots in the southern Molopo tract that it had granted to ICS in the 1925 abattoir deal but repossessed along with the old Lobatse plant. It also converted all government and BSAC rental titles to outright freehold.[17]

A September 1959 memorandum from the Director of Geological Surveys offered the following report on the country's pasture. Since its first attempt at Khudumelapye, the government drilled or contracted 1,152 boreholes, of which 662 were successful. At the same time, freehold commercial landowners, reserve traders and a few wealthy African herders drilled 1,146 private boreholes, of which 823 were successful. He concluded:

In European farming blocks, the growth of the cattle population will probably tend to slow down over the next 5 to 10 years as farms become stocked to capacity. The greatest increase in the cattle population will thus be in the various African reserve areas and certain areas of Crown Lands, and it is here that the majority of new water points will be required. In nearly all areas development will have to take place in sandveld regions.[18]

If the reserve sandveld was the main hope for future expansion, however, the government had to find a new formula for reserve boreholes. There had been no significant progress with breeding or disease control, and overgrazing had not been prevented. Private, syndicate and quote borehole users did not castrate or sell cows or oxen earlier, continued to take in animals from other herds, and still used many of their cattle to plow in summer. All types of boreholes watered far more cattle than the official limit of 500. Reserve herding had simply expanded out into the sandveld to occupy the new boreholes.[19]

Part of the problem was simply the efficiency of boreholes themselves. A good borehole pumped 5,000 liters per hour: full-grown cattle need 30 liters per day per animal. Twelve hours of pumping fills a 60,000 liter reservoir alongside the borehole, enough for 2,000 cattle per day, or 4,000 cattle drinking every other day.[20] Borehole users watered as many cattle as they could, overgrazing the surrounding pasture while building up their herds to a size that would leave them with enough survivors to keep them in business after a serious drought. The pasture would be given a rest after the drought as herders struggled to rebuild their decimated herds.

New boreholes were added every year to draw off cattle from overgrazed areas, but once the entire country was filled, only industrial techniques, including fenced paddocks, could then raise the value of livestock exports. Once a borehole was occupied by reserve cattle, there was little hope of transforming the surrounding pasture into a ranch. Herders continued to accumulate low-quality cattle for plowing and insurance against drought. The government estimated in 1958 that 5 percent of reserve cattle were sold each year for export. The Kweneng had one of the lowest rates, 2.7 percent, and the highest was 7 percent in Ngamiland. Commercial freehold areas sold 12 to 15 percent.[21]

A final decision on African tenure was delayed by a severe drought that reduced the national herd from 1,352,000 in 1962 to 916,000 in 1966, a decline of 32 percent.[22] Figure 4.1 shows the extremely low level of rainfall in these years. As the pastures emptied of cattle, the government took the opportunity to revise its borehole policy, contracting individuals and partnerships directly to pay back drilling costs for new boreholes.[23] Its main focus, however, was to rebuild the national herd, fearing a decline in revenue if Lobatse did not receive enough cattle in the following years. The government also hoped that Africans would sell more cattle, to raise the total national commercial offtake to 10 percent. The goal of rebuilding the national herd to 2 million head was reached in 1970, but two years later offtake still stood at only 7.5 percent. Although the reserves contained 80 percent of the national herd in 1971, they contributed only 45 percent of the Lobatse total.[24]

The strategy of freehold ranches was evident, for by 1971 these were fully industrial enterprises: they now numbered 290, with 332 tractors, 212 trucks, 249 windmills, 1,171 water pumps, and 91 scoops for deepening their private dams. Even if Africans could not afford these investments, why did they sell so few cattle to the abattoir?[25]

Lobatse operated on a quota system so as to insure a regular flow of cattle: that is, it planned to slaughter a certain number of cattle on each day, and then contracted with suppliers to deliver this number at the proper time. The abattoir bought cattle only at its factory gate, so that suppliers had to cover their own transport costs and take the loss if any cattle died along the way. The railway would never and Lobatse would seldom accept cattle in lots of less than twelve, and very few Africans owned herds large enough to sell so many cattle at once. As for walking cattle to market, it was not economical for one herder to take several weeks off to march ten cattle the same distance that it took a train to travel in less than twenty-four hours.[26]

It thus made sense for African cattle owners to pool their sales and take a large quota and buy more space on the railway or assemble a large herd to walk to Lobatse.[27] From 1959, African cooperatives began to take advantage of these economies of scale, eliminating trader profits by dealing directly with Lobatse. Although there were 49 such African cooperatives by 1979, they did not solve the marketing problems of small cattle owners. The largest share of abattoir sales that the abattoir ever captured was 18 percent in 1977. In 1979 their share was 16 percent; 25 percent of the abattoir total comprised African cattle sold by traders or ranchers; Africans sold 31 percent directly to the abattoir; and ranches supplied the remaining 28 percent with their own cattle.[28]

Why did African cattle owners sell to traders rather than via co-ops, and how did so many manage to sell directly to Lobatse without co-ops? First of all, we must recognize that this figure of 31 percent is somewhat misleading. Most direct sales go through agents. Whereas a trader contracts a quota and then buys cattle to fill it, an agent contracts a quota and then transports the cattle to the abattoir without actually buying them. The abattoir pays the original owner, who pays the agent a fee. The agent therefore loses nothing if any cattle die en route to the abattoir. The agent's fee to ranchers is usually some two or three percent of the amount that the abattoir pays the owner, but many agents canvass the reserves for small lots of African cattle on short notice to fill their quotas, charging much more than the usual fee.[29]

Why would an African cattle owner pay a high agent fee or sell to a trader rather than through the local co-operative, which promised to return to the seller the agent fee and trader mark-up on their own cattle? The answer is found in the planning required to meet an abattoir quota. A co-op takes out a quota and then parcels it out to its members, who thus contract well in advance to deliver to coop headquarters a certain number of cattle at a certain time. Only the largest cattle owners can plan in advance; the rest sell on short notice to traders or through agents.[30]

Why are small owners unable to plan their cattle sales? The reason is that they try not to sell any cattle at all. They are trying to hold onto them, to build up their herds, and carefully plan their budgets accordingly. Then emergency cash needs, the bane of the world's poor, force them to sell on very short notice. And because most rural producers still need each other, the emergency might come from a wide range of relatives and friends. Thus a cattle owner might sell a cow on short notive to pay the school fees of a niece whose parents' fields failed and who have exhausted other sources of cash.

We can catch a glimpse of this shoestring budget in Table 8.1, which is an updated version of Table 5.2. Precious few cattle are available for sale even in year 10: A small owner keeps even old oxen so as to be able to plow more hectares and old cows in the hope of a good rainy season enabling it to bear another precious calf. We have accurate national surveys only in the 1970s, so that we do not know for sure how cattle were distributed among the rural population before then. The Rural Income Distribution Survey's 1975 figure of 45 percent of rural households cattleless, although we must remember

**Table 8.1.** A Growing Herd's Income, 1980

The herd here is as in Table 5.2, with the following prices:
  (a) The 1980 Botswana Agricultural Marketing Board sorghum price was P10 for a 70 kg. bag. (1P = approximately 1 $ U.S.)
  (b) Cattle value was estimated more precisely than in Table 5.2: using the 1980 Lobatse grade 3 price of P91; assuming a five-year peak weight of 440 kg. for oxen and 330 kg. for cows (the latter is just above the 320 kg. required for calving); depreciating value after year 6 by P10 per year; estimating mortality rates and oxen depreciation and increased mortality owing to inspanning; deducting P10 marketing charge for transport to Lobatse. This produces the following schedule of cattle value:

| Net Cattle Value | Year | | | | | | | |
|---|---|---|---|---|---|---|---|---|
| | 5 | 6 | 7 | 8 | 9 | 10 | 11 | 12 |
| Cows | | | | | | | | |
| Gross value | 150 | 150 | 140 | 130 | 120 | 110 | 100 | 90 |
| Mortality (%) | 5 | 10 | 10 | 15 | 15 | 20 | 25 | 30 |
| Net value | 133 | 125 | 116 | 101 | 92 | 78 | 65 | 53 |
| Oxen | | | | | | | | |
| Gross value | 200 | 200 | 190 | 180 | 170 | 160 | 150 | 140 |
| Mortality (%) | 0 | 0 | 0 | 5 | 5 | 5 | 10 | 10 |
| Net value (a) | 190 | 190 | 180 | 161 | 151 | 142 | 125 | 116 |
| Inspan | | | | | | | | |
| Depreciation (%) | 5 | 5 | 5 | 5 | 5 | 10 | 10 | 10 |
| Mortality (%) | 0 | 0 | 0 | 5 | 5 | 5 | 10 | 10 |
| Net value (b) | 180 | 180 | 161 | 144 | 135 | 119 | 98 | 91 |

We then take year 9 as an average, yielding P92 per cow and P135 per ox. Inspanning cows, a common practice, would reduce herd growth and cow value well below those represented here.

| Year | Total Herd | Draft Animals | Grain (bags) | Grain Value (P) | Value of Mature Cattle (P) |
|---|---|---|---|---|---|
| 1 | 2 | – | – | – | – |
| 2 | 4 | 1.0 | 2.5 | 25 | 184 |
| 3 | 6 | 1.5 | 3.8 | 38 | 184 |
| 4 | 6 | 2.0 | 5.0 | 50 | 184 |
| 5 | 9 | 3.0 | 7.5 | 75 | 411 |
| 6 | 11 | 4.5 | 11.3 | 113 | 638 |
| 7 | 14 | 5.0 | 12.5 | 125 | 638 |
| 8 | 17 | 7.5 | 18.8 | 188 | 957 |
| 9 | 23 | 9.0 | 22.5 | 225 | 1319 |
| 10 | 24 | 11.0 | 27.5 | 275 | 1362 |

that most of the cattleless aspire to owning cattle and probably will do so at some time in their lives.[31] Different households constantly struggle up to join the ranks of the cattle holders and then fall down again among the cattleless. The 1980 agricultural survey reported 90 percent of rural producers owning fewer cattle than year 10 in Table 8.1.[32] In 1974 only 10 percent of abattoir sales came from owners selling five cattle or fewer. These sellers totaled less than 15 percent of all rural households.[33] Very few cattle owners are able to plan cattle sales.

Managing a cooperative under these circumstances has proved very difficult indeed. Lobatse fines unfilled quotas, and administrative costs under such uncertainty are often higher than agent fees. All in all, neither the abattoir nor co-ops have solved the problems of poor African producers, nor could we expect them to do so.

## MASTER FARMING

Table 8.2 shows that crop income is of decisive importance for households trying to hold onto their cattle. It gives them food and cash to enable them to postpone selling cattle. The government also sought to assist the commercial grain market. The export of grain to South Africa in good years and the import of grain in bad years raised the question of domestic storage instead. That is, traders reaped profits importing and exporting that might be saved if the grain never left the country. In 1966 an official report disputed this notion, however, estimating that the costs of domestic storage would be greater than trader profits. Bechuanaland actually benefited from the tremendous economies of scale afforded by the South African economy. So much grain circulated in South Africa that Bechuanaland grain was efficiently absorbed and Bechuanaland shortfalls were quickly met without extra costs along the way.[34]

The government also considered domestic milling, which, unlike storage, turned grain into a more valuable product. A local mill would give the national economy the extra income earned from processing. Commercial sorghum milling was still not perfected, so that the government concentrated on maize instead. From 1954 the Department of Agriculture (DoA) began assembling bulk supplies to mill in Mafeking, and then in 1960 it shifted this supply to the Protectorate's first mill at Lobatse. The private firm that built the mill received government price and supply guarantees which the drought of the early 1960s immediately erased. Suddenly Bechuanaland produced no maize surplus for processing, so that the mill bought South African grain to grind.[35]

The most important government assistance to grain production was expansion of its extension services. The Rhodesian program now entailed ADs enrolling cultivators as pupils that practiced the prescribed techniques, in steps, on their own fields. In 1947, the Kgatla chief helped the DoA to begin such a scheme in his district. In the 1950s, this program was extended to other areas, and in 1959 there were 58 ADs in the country, 10 of whom were in the Kweneng, and 694 total pupils, 64 of whom were Kwena.[36]

The technical package grew somewhat more sophisticated as well. To enroll as a Pupil Farmer, a cultivator needed to own a plow and two oxen, to have more oxen readily available, to reside permanently at the fields or employ a manager who did so, and to destump at least half an acre. A Pupil Farmer who then used a harrow and cow dung on the field graduated to an Improved Farmer. Then came the leap to Progressive Farmer, which required all of the above plus full crop rotation without interplanting, the ownership or a share in a mechanical row planter and cultivator, and planting in rows rather than broadcasting. After this, the addition of mechanical weeding with the cultivator, a scotch cart or wagon or trailer, a tool shed, winter or early spring plowing, good stock care, and full ownership of a set of implements qualified a Progressive Farmer of two years to become a Master Farmer.[37]

In 1965, however, the DoA lamented that ADs reached only 2.5 percent of the country's 100,000 cultivators, at a rate of 22 per AD. In 1967 the DoA further reported that of those pupils enrolled in the program, only 9 percent of their acres were winter plowed, only 5 percent were manured, and only 5 percent were destumped. The most popular of the program's techniques was mechanical row planting, which 59 percent of the pupil acreage received.[38] The government phased out the Master Farming hierarchy in the mid-1970s, encouraging ADs to spread their advice around rather than concentrate it on their enrolled farmers.[39]

Why did so few cultivators become Master Farmers? Let us approach this question another way: How did the program manage to attract anyone at all? We have seen why cultivators plowed as much land as possible and loaned widely their labor, tools, and cattle for the cultivation of fields other than their own. Master Farming, in contrast, required a cultivator to concentrate all available resources on one fixed field. But where could a Master Farmer turn when that one field failed? Certainly Master Farmers had to possess more wealth than most in order to insure themselves against drought, and a recent study in the

Kgatleng reports that Master Farmers there were mostly older men who had invested in their farming operations with cash from years of urban wage labor.[40] But why would those with extra cash or other resources invest them in crops? Did it not make more sense to invest them in cattle? There were three reasons to become a Master Farmer. First, Table 8.1 shows how important crop production could be on the way to accumulating cattle. If herders in year 10 raised their crop output, they would need to sell fewer cattle to meet their food and cash needs. Once they had enough cattle to pay for well or borehole rights, they could sell cattle without threatening the further growth of their herds. A second reason for investing in crops rather than in cattle was that cattle accumulation was becoming harder in the hardveld, making crop production a more attractive alternative.

Yet even if it did make sense to invest in crops, why do so through Master Farming? The ADs techniques certainly raised yields per hectare, but they also raised costs per hectare. Row planting required more oxen-time than broadcasting; manuring and fencing required more labor time; harrows and mechanical equipment cost money as well as time. It was also difficult for most cultivators to bring their cattle to their fields at exactly the right time to plow, plant, and harrow: pasture around crop fields was the worst overgrazed, so that cattle owners were in a constant dilemma about whether to keep their cattle away from the field eating better grass or to bring them in to plow and grow thin. If the cultivator decided to do the latter and then the rains stopped, the cattle weak from plowing and poor grazing would have no nearby fresh grass to speed their recovery, and neither would the plowed field yield any income.

Master Farmers looked beyond their immediate profit, however, and this was the third reason for cultivators to join the program. They became participants in a new state agricultural development project: prices, transport, and state assistance were improving every year, and they looked to the day when these things might turn them into full-fledged commercial farmers. For two or three years Pupil Farmers borrowed the AD's equipment, and then they qualified for loans to buy their own. An American revolving fund established in 1960 financed these loans.[41] Everyone aspired to buying a wagon or someday even a tractor through this program. Indeed, the ADs found that after participants qualified for their loans, they tended to revert to their old ways.

Moreover, the expectation of commercial success was not an entirely unrealistic one. In the Rolong reserve, a number of Master

Farmers actually achieved it. Although there are some eight to nine times as many Kwena cultivators as Rolong, as of 1964 there were 370 Rolong Pupil Farmers to Kweneng's 317.[42] In 1966, the year of independence, the Rolong numbered 2.3 percent of the country's cultivators, but accounted for 33 percent of the extension loans, by value.[43] Whereas 2 percent of Kweneng cultivators planted in rows in 1980, and the national figure was 6 percent, 50 percent of Rolong cultivators planted in rows.[44] The Rolong accounted for most of Botswana's commercial grain sales throughout the 1970s.[45]

The reasons for the Rolong success are several: their climate is the most temperate in the country; the terrain is transitional hardveld that remained sparsely settled until wells and boreholes opened it up; cultivators could travel to nearby Mafeking to buy equipment; they could transport their own grain to Mafeking or to the nearby Lobatse mill without the mediation of traders. Moreover, the area achieved crucial economies of scale in transport and tractor-plowing; that is, cultivators unable to buy a truck or tractor hired the services of neighbors, thereby helping the area to acquire more of these vehicles than if individuals relied on only their own fields. The most successful Rolong cultivators earned most of their income from using their tractors and trucks to plow and transport for hire to others.[46]

This was the trend elsewhere in the country as well, although on a much smaller scale, because tractors and trucks moved so much faster than ox teams. When a government tractor plowed a demonstration plot in the Kweneng in 1936, Chief Kgari Sechele voiced this popular assessment of the machine: "We like it because it does not require many hands."[47] Whereas three ox-plowers could cover a quarter hectare in one morning, one tractor driver could cover as much as a hectare an hour and continue through the night as well. As for transport, a tractor can move produce and workers to and from their fields faster than an ox wagon and requires no stops for water or grass.

After six years of experiments, however, the government decided against tractor-plowing, in 1966. The costs of purchase, fuel, and repairs could not be offset by higher yields by pulling increasingly sophisticated machinery quickly and efficiently across the field. It made sense to plant quickly as much area as possible, but subsequent operations with the tractor did not raise yields enough to make them worthwhile. In other words, the tractor would make Tswana farming more extensive, rather than more intensive as the DoA desired. Tractor owners plowed their own large fields and then hired out their services to others, plowing quickly over a field that someone had broadcast with seed. In this way, the tractor simply increased the area that could be planted during the brief summer rains. Weeding and harvesting were still done by hand. Ox plowing was more intensive, in that the team moved more slowly and carefully, adjusting the depth of the plow to slight irregularities in the field. This was why the DoA preferred it to tractor plowing.[48]

The 1970/71 Agricultural Survey reported that 14.5 percent of cultivators used tractors for plowing, although nearly half of these used oxen as well; 13.4 percent hired the tractor, so that only 1.1 percent used their own.[49] The 1980 Agricultural Statistics is the first survey to report on district tractor use in categories somewhat different from earlier surveys. Tractors plowed more than 20 percent of cultivated fields in the country: The highest figure was 55 percent in the agricultural district surrounding the Ngwato capital, Serowe; the Kweneng's figure was only 5 percent. On the one hand, this revealed the poverty of the Kweneng, in that few of its producers could afford to buy and operate tractors. On the other hand, the persistence of ox plowing also meant that most Kweneng producers could still muster enough cattle to make a team. In the tiny Malete hardveld reserve, squeezed between the Lobatse and Gaborone commercial blocks, overgrazing was so severe that its producers were going out of the cattle business. In 1980, 45 percent of its cultivated fields were plowed by tractors.[50]

We can see now how the tractor fit into the general pattern of Tswana agriculture. It enabled its owner to earn income from a wide range of fields, so that if its owner's field failed there would still be income from hire-plowing and transport fees. It moved more people and plowed more land faster so as to increase the chance that some might catch the rain. By replacing ox plowing, the tractor separated cultivation from herding, as had been the case in the time of the hoe and as British missionaries and governments had always urged.

Trucks also moved more, faster, but they could neither plow nor travel off the beaten track. Where there were roads, however, trucks were cheaper to run. The government gave high priority to road building, which is much easier in the flat, dry hardveld than in most of sub-Saharan Africa. Kalahari sand posed a special problem, however, for trucks needed especially powerful engines to push through the sand, and there were no nearby gravel pits for making a harder surface. To this day, almost all sandveld roads are simply single tracks maintained only by the wear of the vehicle tires traversing them. The longest sandveld road built by the government dates from 1957, running from

Ghanzi to Lobatse, allowing trucks to carry cattle these 600 kilometers in only two days.[51] Alongside this road runs a government trek route, which consists of boreholes and cattle holding pens to water and quarantine cattle on the long walk to the abattoir. The government built three such trek routes to the railway line after World War II, but as overgrazing advanced, cattle grew thin along the way.[52] Improved trucks, roads, and cattle prices made it increasingly economical to truck cattle rather than walk them over poor pasture to the railway. In the Kweneng, the graveling of the Letlhakeng-Molepolole road in the mid-1970s, and the tarring of the Molepolole-Gaborone road thereafter, assisted this development.

Most trucks still carried not cattle, however, but South African imports. These comprised both consumer and productive goods such as cement and motor fuel. The number of vehicles operating in the country rose from 4,000 at independence in 1966 to 20,000 in 1978, reflecting partly the boom in demand for imports. Again the government led the way, as 22 percent of the total at independence and 14 percent of the 1978 total were government vehicles. Private trucking remained the business of South African operators, however, who carried 70 percent of the country's road haulage traffic.[53]

The transport boom on and off the beaten track completed the Kweneng's integration into the Southern African industrial economy. Yet this progress was double-edged. On the one hand, it made essential consumer and productive goods cheaper and thus more abundant. On the other hand, it gave a direct advantage to those able to buy and run expensive motor vehicles. A 1971 survey of Molepolole's 3,200 households reported 387 wagons, 129 ox and donkey carts, 1,001 bicycles, 12 motor cars, 24 tractors, and 35 trucks. Although wagons now come in an improved model with metal frame and rubber tires, they are slowly losing ground.[54] Their speed cannot match a truck or even a tractor. The new vehicles require no cattle, and thus need no water or grass to sustain them but only cash for fuel and repairs. As such they require nothing produced in the rural economy. Despite their speed in moving people, grain, and other goods across the countryside, they partly discourage rural production as well. Cheap South African maize meal now reaches regularly every village in the Kweneng. This has made it economical for more Kweneng residents to use cash from wages or cattle sales to buy food rather than to produce their own. The National Development Plan reported in 1979 that "Typically about one half of Botswana's basic grain needs have to be met from imports." *Agricultural Statistics* for 1980, a good agricultural year, reported that fewer than one-fifth of the country's 66,000 cultivators planted more than the six hectares needed to feed an average household of six members.[55]

## THE CULTIVATOR AS HEROINE

The recent improvement in Botswana's economic fortunes has brought improvements in information as well, so that at the very end of our inquiry we can at last fix firm figures to the forces and trends that in earlier periods we could only highlight. Although Schapera compiled a few invaluable but small surveys before World War II, only in the 1970s do we have accurate data for the rural economy on the national and district levels. Even within this recent period there are few serial statistics. Although the Ministry of Agriculture's *Agricultural Statistics* has appeared every year since independence, the method and coverage of its 1980 version is so superior that we must treat it as the first comprehensive national agricultural survey.

The 1974/5 Rural Income Distribution Survey (RIDS) gives some detail on the poorer half of Botswana's rural population, who figure so slightly in earlier records. Table 8.2 shows the four income group profiles that RIDS presented in addition to its summary national figures. From the first two groups, the poorest 10 percent of rural

**Table 8.2.** Rural Income Distribution Survey, 1974/5

| | | Percentile Among All Rural Households | | | | | | | |
|---|---|---|---|---|---|---|---|---|---|
| | | (I) 0-10 | | (II) 15-50 | | (III) 60-95 | | (IV) 97-99.7 | |
| Income Source | | R | (%) | (R) | (%) | (R) | (%) | (R) | (%) |
| Crops | (A) | 10 | 6 | 38 | 9 | 78 | 4 | 16 | 0 |
| Livestock | (B) | 9 | 5 | 29 | 7 | 531 | 32 | 5,841 | 64 |
| Gathering | (C) | 28 | 18 | 34 | 8 | 31 | 2 | 20 | 0 |
| Employment | (D) | 24 | 15 | 156 | 36 | 612 | 36 | 796 | 9 |
| Transfers | (E) | 34 | 21 | 60 | 14 | 70 | 4 | -15 | 0 |
| Other | (F) | 56 | 35 | 113 | 26 | 347 | 21 | 2,485 | 27 |
| Total Income | (G) | 161 | 100 | 430 | 100 | 1,669 | 100 | 9,143 | 100 |
| Cash | (H) | 47 | | 218 | | 960 | | 7,178 | |
| In Kind | (I) | 114 | | 212 | | 709 | | 2,695 | |

*Source*: RB, CSO, "Rural Income Distribution Survey, 1974/5," 1976.

households (column I) and those in the 15 to 50 percentile (II), it appears that the rural poor are not so poor after all. With the value of the Pula somewhat more than a US dollar at the time, P161 and P430 seem high by world standards of poverty (row G). RIDS's accounting was very thorough, however, so that firewood (C), a new grass roof (F), a new calf born or even the weight gained by an older animal (B), and all other such cashless accruals were priced and included as income. The survey computed a poverty datum line of P304 for group I and P572 for group II, well above their average incomes. Nevertheless, they both receive a surprising amount of cash, which shows how much they are members, albeit poor ones, of the industrial world.

As for sources of income, almost all values increase as total income increases. That is, the wealthier have more income of all types than the poor do. The two exceptions are crops (A) and gathering (C) for the wealthiest of rural households (IV) who buy their food and firewood or cook with bottled gas. By world standards the cash income of this group, although still derived chiefly from cattle, is high enough to put them squarely in the ranks of the middle class.

Crops (A) and livestock (B) refer to production on one's own field. Our poorer half clearly earn most of their income in other ways, especially wage employment (D). RIDS did not ask households about working on the fields of others for payment other than cash, and so this source of income ended up mostly in the "Other" category (F). The largest source of income for the lowest 10 percent was "Transfers" (E), under which the survey intended to comprise wages sent home by an urban worker, government food relief, or other gifts. "Transfers" as well as "Others" probably picked up some of the casual labor and other lending and borrowing that we have hitherto described as reciprocity.

Now that we have some idea of what and how much income our poorer rural half receives, can we identify who they are? A 1970/71 agricultural survey yielded the data in Table 8.3, which shows differences between male- and female-headed households. Women headed 30 percent of rural households: 72 percent of these female-headed households were cattleless and 34 percent were unable to plow in the previous year. The rural poor are overwhelmingly women.

Why are so many poor women on their own in rural Botswana? The answer is simply that men have needed women less and less in the postwar era. On the one hand, men have had increasing access to wages, which they earn independently of wives: In 1978 there were 69,200 wage employees in the country, 26,300 of whom worked for

**Table 8.3.** Male and Female Cultivators, 1970/71

|  | Rural Households | | |
|---|---|---|---|
|  | Total | Male Head | Female Head |
| Total Households | 100% | 70% | 30% |
| Households holding no cattle | 45% | 33% | 72% |
| Cattle per household | 18.0 | 23.5 | 5.6 |
| Households not plowing last year | 24% | 19% | 34% |

*Source*: Food and Africulture Organization, "Study of constraints on agricultural development in the Republic of Botswana," MoA, 1973.

the government. South African mine contracts peaked at 40,390 in 1976, falling afterwards to 23,195 in 1978, to make a total of 22 percent of the adult workforce in formal employment inside and outside the country out of a total population of 805,000. This is a high percentage for an African country, but half the total work outside the country or for the government.[56]

Wage employment within Botswana itself has been open to women as well, and a 1974 survey of poor residential areas on the outskirts of the three main urban areas of Selibe-Phikwe, Gaborone, and Francistown reported an adult male-female ratio of 52:48. This does not mean that women held 48 percent of jobs. Rather, 61 percent of men and only 16 percent of women held wage jobs.[57] The city promised at least a chance at a job, even short-term occasional ones, and also greater access to men with cash incomes. Cooking, cleaning, and performing other domestic chores for wage-earning men paid better for some than doing the same work for a poor rural household.

Another reason that women are on their own in rural Botswana is that men invest their wages in what will bring them the greatest return. In earlier decades they invested back home in rural production: cattle, fields, and wives and children to tend them. Nowadays, overgrazing has seriously reduced the income that a woman and her children can promise to contribute to the household. Making a living off the land becomes harder, and a man who buys 5 cattle for his hardveld cattle post can no longer expect them to grow quickly to 20, plowing a dozen hectares and yielding fat oxen for sale. Cattle success requires access to an open sandveld borehole, which requires paying a calf or cash for someone else to graze and water the herd, or paying borehole maintenance expenses. Neither of these herding arrangements involves women. Men can no longer start out small in cattle accumulation with a small hardveld herd that earns much of its income from crops. Women suffer, because it is their fields and children in which working men once invested.[58]

If poor women have difficulty attracting income-earning men, how do they stay in production at all? Their strategies are many, but most include some form of reciprocity. They borrow here, help someone there, feed a neighbor's child, and generally immerse themselves in as wide a network as possible. When they have built up enough favors and cash, they might try to plow a large field with borrowed or hired oxen, and then use the sorghum to make beer to sell.[59] This is a reason for staying in the hardveld: The large villages give a poor woman most opportunity for finding willing borrowers and lenders.

Reciprocity has always worked on mutual self-interest, however, and rural women have difficulty borrowing when they have so little to offer in return. This is one reason why wagon, tractor, plow-team, and borehole owners increasingly demand cash for their services. What could a poor woman lend them in return? Many women thus invest in the education of their children, especially their daughters, who will support them if they later find a wage job. This mutual dependence of mothers and daughters is a dangerously narrow base of reciprocity, however, for if either suffers misfortune there is only one other person to bear the extra weight. Those suffering economic misfortune are no longer helped back onto their feet, for they have so little to offer their helpers in return.[60]

This decline of reciprocity is difficult to chart. Cash fees for water, transport, and plowing are one sign, as is a widely acknowledged reluctance to give *mafisa*.[61] The plow had already reduced *mafisa*, as owners became fearful that the borrowers would work their cattle to death instead of using their own. The permanence of borehole water and the efficiency of modern machines also reduced the need for wealthier cattle owners to spread their cattle around.

The dispersal of population is another indication of declining reciprocity. The 1971 census reported 53 percent of the Kweneng's 72,000 residents living outside the district's 22 villages of more than 500 persons. There are three reasons for this move away from the villages.[62] First, there are more permanent water sites in the hardveld and sandveld to sustain producers throughout the year. Second, overgrazing has forced herders to keep their cattle dispersed among these scattered water points, rather than concentrating them around the larger villages in winter. Third, negotiations for lending, borrowing, *mafisa*, marriages, and other reciprocal arrangements once occupied the winter months of July and August. As reciprocity declines, there is less reason to return to the village in winter.

Even Molepolole has changed. Map 8.1 shows the village in 1976, by which time two new wards, Borakalalo and Boribamo, had grown to rival the five nineteenth century wards alongside them. Borakalalo, which means "where people meet from different places," grew up as a way station for Kalahari men signing mine contracts at the traders and then the recruiting office in the ward. Its population is largely Kgalagari and follows no established *kgotla* formation. Boribamo, also known as New Town, is Molepolole's largest ward and sprang from population growth spilling out from the older wards. Its earliest residents formed *makgotla* subordinate to those in the older wards, but more recent settlement has been haphazard. Since this map was drawn, a third new settlement has grown up west of Borakalalo, and Boribamo has nearly doubled in area.

Despite this decline in *kgotla* organization, the rise of cash demands, the emergence of the female-headed household, and the escape of the wealthiest to distant boreholes, most rural producers still need each other to produce, especially beyond the hardveld. We can still travel out to the sandveld and up the Letlhakeng Valley to Khudu-

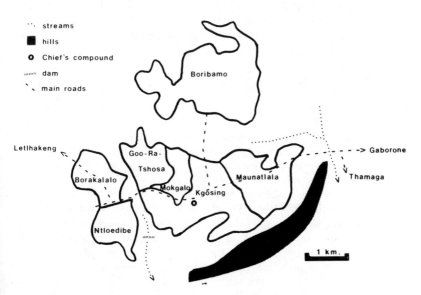

**Map 8.1.** Molepolole's Wards, 1976

melapye, site of the 1929 borehole, to catch a glimpse of the old system remarkably intact. In December 1980 a citizen of the village conducted a survey of 85 cultivators plowing their fields outside the village.[63] In the sandveld land is poorer but less crowded, making cattle herds and fields larger than the national averages. Area plowed in this survey averaged 8.7 hectares, while the national average for the previous year was 4.1; median herd size was 16, while the national median was 13. Of the 85 cultivators surveyed, 20 owned no cattle, yet 30 used none of their own cattle to plow. That is, 10 owned cattle but did not use them to plow. These 10 owned an average of more than 10 cattle each. Only 18 of the 85 used only their own cattle. Clearly, then, borrowing and lending plow-cattle were the rule.

As for labor, only 76 cultivators reported who helped them plow. Exactly half of these 76 had no nuclear family member assisting them. Another 22 had a nuclear family helper but also borrowed someone else's labor as well. This left only 16 plowing teams composed of only nuclear family members. If we take both cattle and labor together, we find that only 6 of 76 cultivators used only nuclear family labor and nuclear family cattle. Everyone else borrowed. No one hired a plow team or tractor, and not a single transaction involved any cash.[64]

## NOTES

1. For details on national politics, see J. Parson, "The political economy of Botswana," D. Phil., Sussex, 1979; C. Colclough and S. McCarthy, *The Political Economy of Botswana*, Oxford, 1980. Kweneng politics are discussed in R. Vengroff, *Botswana: Rural Development in the Shadow of Apartheid*, Cranbury, 1977.
2. "Pim Report," p. 156.
3. AAC, March, 1940.
4. AAC, March, 1940.
5. AAC, March, 1940.
6. AAC, March 1940. The government secretary confirmed this view in 1945 correspondence to Lord Hailey, who met with Protectorate officials in that year as part of his review of British African policy. The secretary added: "The Bechuana, as is natural, are intensely jealous of their control of the land but they have on several occasions been warned that their control can only be allowed to continue if government is satisfied that the best use is being made of the land and they do not by their action or neglect contribute to its deterioration; that the land does not, in fact, belong to them but to future generations, and that they are entitled to the use of it during their lifetime and must strive to leave it in no worse condition than they found it." This is a curious ideological twist: The government here invokes the same "communalism" that it usually decried. BNA S 401/6.

7. AAC, March 1940.

8. Before independence, the debate about further ranch development was actually confined to Crown Land. See A. Gaitskell, *Report of a Mission to the Bechuanaland Protectorate*, London, 1954, which advocated such development on a large scale, and Great Britain, *Economic and Financial Report on the High Commission Territories*, London, 1954, which overruled Gaitskell, giving priority instead to water supplies in the reserves and in existing commercial areas.

9. There are several files on the abattoir. Most informative is the 1949 RC memorandum, "Preliminary Proposals for the Establishment of an Abattoir and Cold Storage Plant in the Bechuanaland Protectorate by the Colonial Development Corporation," BNA S 518/1. See also the CDC's own magazine, *Colonial Development*, Winter 1954.

10. Schapera, *Native Land*, pp. 224-38.

11. As did Interviews 2, 18, 32.

12. This delegation of authority was evident already in NAC, March 1938.

13. Schapera, *Native Land*, pp. 247-49, 153.

14. The file for the Kweneng water program is DIV COM S 4/6. The final rules were drafted by the Bakwena Development Committee on 12 July 1956, and issued in 1958.

15. D. Erasmus, "The national income of the Bechuanaland Protectorate, 1955," in L. Samuels, *African Studies in Income and Wealth*, London, 1963, pp. 282-83. Erasmus also calculated that 50 percent of net national income came from agriculture, 14.7 percent came from trade and transport, 12.1 percent came from government, and 8.2 percent came from migrant labor.

16. G. Ryan, "Report on the Livestock Industry," BP, 1958.

17. The government added 49 Ghanzi and 13 Molopo farms. BP, "Development Plan, 1960-64." The CDC also built its own holding-ground ranches in Molopo and the northern Crown Lands. Ryan, "Report."

18. Director, Geological Surveys, 26 September 1959, "Memorandum on the Potentialities for Underground Water Development in Relation to the Development of the Livestock Industry," BNA S 381/6. By 1959, there were 95 government and 39 private boreholes in the Kweneng. S. Wynne, "A preliminary report on borehole drilling for Kweneng District," District Office, Molepolole, July 1979.

19. Kweneng District, *Annual Report*, 1958, BNA S 574/15, reported that the 500-head limit was broken from the very first. For the Kgatla, see P. Peters, "Preliminary findings and observations on borehole syndicates in Kgatleng District," MLGL, 1980.

20. RB, APRU, "Beef production," p. 128.

21. Ryan, "Report."

22. RB, *Statistical Abstract*, 1968. See also J. Ingersoll, *Historical Examples of Ecological Disaster*, Hudson Institute, 1965, and A. Campbell, "The 1960s drought in Botswana," in Hinchey, *Symposium*.

23. As of 1966, the cost of R2,800 per borehole was to be paid by R200 (£100) down and five years' repayment at 6 percent interest. F. Homan, "Some Aspects of Land Tenure Reform in the Tribal Territories of Bechuanaland," BP, 1966.

24. RB, "National Development Plan, 1973-8," Vol. 1, pp. 33, 171-75. The Kweneng contained 10 percent of the national herd but contributed only 1 percent of the Lobatse total.
25. RB, CSO, "Freehold Farm Survey, 1970/1," 1971.
26. G. Bond, "A Report on Livestock Marketing," MoA, 1975, p. 38.
27. D. Ansell, *Cattle Marketing in Botswana*, Reading, 1971, pp. 30-32, 35-42. See also G. Cole, "Livestock marketing in the Kalahari," in Botswana Society, *Sustained Production*.
28. RB, "National Development Plan, 1979-85," pp. 145-47. See also RB, MoA, "A handbook of livestock statistics," 1978.
29. Ansell, *Cattle Marketing*, pp. 32-34; Bond, "Report," pp. 27-31. Some Africans did manage to sell direct to South African abattoirs once the South African Meat Control Board began a quota system in 1932; in that year Bechuanaland Africans sold directly 317 out of 10,840 Protectorate cattle exported. RC Correspondence, 1935, BNA S 266/6.
30. Ansell, *Cattle Marketing*, ch. 4; Bond, "Report," p. 52; L. Syson, "A profile of cattle sales in the Shoshong area," UNDP, Gaborone, 1971.
31. RB, CSO, "Rural Income Distribution Survey, 1974/5," p. 111.
32. RB, MoA, *Agricultural Statistics*, 1980, Tables 2, 13.
33. Bond, "Report," pp. 29-30.
34. H. Biggs, "Report on the marketing of agricultural produce in Bechuanaland," Ministry of Overseas Development, London, 1966, BNA. See H. Morley, "Grain storage in Bechuanaland," DoA, 1965, for farm storage problems.
35. Biggs, "Report."
36. Great Britain, *Basutoland, Bechuanaland Protectorate and Swaziland: Report of an Economic Survey Mission*, London, 1960, pp. 162, 187.
37. BP, DoA, *Annual Report*, 1964/5. See B. Lever, *Agricultural Extension in Botswana*, Reading, 1970, for a fuller technical discussion of Botswana's extension program.
38. BP, DoA, *Annual Report*, 1964/5; RB, DoA, *Annual Report*, 1966/7.
39. RD, "National Development Plan, 1976-81," pp. 163-64.
40. D. Massey, "Labour migration and rural development in Botswana," Ph.D., Boston, 1981, ch. 7. For similar profiles in Rhodesia, see A. Weinrich, *African Farmers in Rhodesia*, London, 1975.
41. BP, DoA, *Annual Report*, 1964/5; A. Harrison, *Agricultural Credit in Botswana*, Reading, 1967.
42. BP, DoA, *Annual Report*, 1964/5.
43. Harrison, *Agricultural Credit*, p. 7. The Kwena numbered 15.8 percent of cultivators but only 9 percent of loans.
44. RB, MoA, *Agricultural Statistics*, 1980, Tables 93-94.
45. See Comaroff, "Class and culture."
46. Comaroff, "Class and culture," pp. 98-103; F. Wande, "Agro-economic survey of the Barolong farms," BP, 1949.
47. NAC, May, 1936.
48. RB, MoA, "Sedibeng Experimental Unit Farms: Six-year report," 1971. Compare M. Kolawole, "Economic aspects of private tractor operations in the savanna zone of Western Nigeria," *Sa*, 1974. The British had always hoped for mechanization; see especially J. Raeburn et al., *Report of a Survey of Problems of Mechanization of Native Agriculture in Tropical African Colonies*, Colonial Office, 1950.

49. RB, Agricultural Survey, 1970/1.

50. *Agricultural Statistics*, 1980, Tables 91-92.

51. M. and M. Russell, *Afrikaners of the Kalahari*, Cambridge, 1976, ch. 3. Wealthier South African Boers bought out many of the old Ghanzi Boers during this period.

52. Correspondence relating to the Economic Survey Mission, 1961, BNA S 575/15. Bond, "Report," p. 45. The two other trek routes were Ngamiland to Francistown and Werda (southwest of Molopo) to Lobatse.

53. "National Development Plan, 1979-85," pp. 228, 241.

54. See D. Eding, "Report on village studies," MoA, 1972, for this detailed survey of Molepolole; and D. Eding, "Moshupa catchment survey," MoA, 1970, and D. Eding and M. Sekgoma, "Kweneng resource survey," Gaborone, 1972, for valuable data on hardveld agriculture.

55. RB, "National Development Plan, 1979-85," p. 137; *Agricultural Statistics*, 1980, Table 50. Six hectares planted yielded some four and a half hectares harvested, at two and a half bags per hectare, and two bags per person per year. The costs and benefits of regional integration are discussed in Ettinger, "Economics of the customs union"; L. Green and T. Fair, *Development in Africa*, Johannesburg, 1962; P. Selwyn, *Industries on the Southern African Periphery*, Sussex, 1975; P. Robson, "Economic integration in Southern Africa," *JMAS*, 5, 1967.

56. "National Development Plan, 1979-85," pp. 12-29. See also Lipton, "Employment," and W. Elkan, "Labour migration from Botswana, Lesotho and Swaziland," *AP*, 1, 1978.

57. RB, CSO, "A social and economic survey of three peri-urban areas in Botswana," 1974, discussed in C. Bryant et al., "Rural to urban migration," *AStR*, 21, 1978. Urban-rural income gaps are discussed in D. Jackson, "Income differentials and unbalanced planning," *JMAS*, 8, 1970; P. Landell-Mills. "Rural incomes and urban wage rates," *BNR*, 2, 1969; S. Johns, "Botswana's strategy for development," *JCPS*, 11, 1973.

58. See C. Kerven, "Rural and urban female-headed households' dependence on agriculture," NMS, 1979; B. Brown, "The impact of male labour migration on women in Botswana," African Studies Association conference paper, Bloomington, 1981; W. Izzard, "Rural-urban migration of women in Botswana," NMS, 1979; C. Bond, "Women's involvement in agriculture in Botswana," MoA, 1974; L. Syson, "Unmarried mothers in Botswana," *BNR*, 5, 1973; D. Cooper, "How urban workers in Botswana manage their cattle and lands," NMS, 1980; F. Bettles, "Women's access to agricultural extension in Botswana, MoA, 1980.

59. See D. Curtis, "Cash brewing in a rural economy," *BNR*, 5, 1973.

60. Izzard, "Rural-urban migration," pp. 25-30.

61. See T. Hertel, "On the system of mafisa," MoA, 1979, for a Kweneng hardveld survey.

62. See also R. Field, "Patterns of settlement at the lands," MoA, 1980.

63. This was Gordon Mokgwathi. Cultivators within the area were chosen on the basis of a simple random cluster sample, that is, everyone in one location was interviewed. W. Duggan, "The economics of ploughing in Botswana," MoA, 1981, discusses the results of this survey in greater detail. Other studies that emphasize rural economic interdependence are D. Curtis, "The social organization of ploughing," *BNR*, 4, 1972; Ø. Gulbrandsen, "Agro-

pastoral production and communal land use in Botswana," MoA, 1980; N. Mahoney, "Contract and neighborly exchange among the Birwa of Botswana," *JAL*, 21, 1977; H. Vierich, "Majako," NMS, 1979.

64. The 1971 national survey in Food and Agricultural Organization, "Study of constraints," p. 45, reported the origin of plow animals that year as follows:

| Own or Mafisa | Borrow | Hire | Total Households |
|---|---|---|---|
| 50% | 26% | 24% | 100% |

*Agricultural Statistics*, 1980, Table 90, reported this:

| Own | Mafisa | Borrow | Hire | Total Households |
|---|---|---|---|---|
| 48% | 5% | 15% | 25% | 100% |

# 9

# Crisis on the Commons, 1940–1980

The post-World War II boom in the world economy brought new prosperity to a number of the world's poor agricultural regions as industry demanded more produce and agricultural technology improved. In the 1960s the Green Revolution brought a leap in yields and output through the adaptation of advanced technology to small peasant farms. The most important element of this technology was high-yielding hybrid grain seeds that required carefully controlled applications of water. Even in rainy areas, some irrigation was usually necessary to deliver the right amount of water at precisely the right time. With more arid land than any other continent, and 52 percent of its surface area devoid of any permanent stream running to the sea,[1] Africa had little hope of a Green Revolution.[2]

Along with this postwar boom came the promotion of individual land ownership that might take most advantage of the new opportunities for investment. Even drier, unirrigable areas became candidates for "land-to-the-tiller" campaigns, which sought to eliminate both landlord-tenant and communal obligations.[3] In Southern Africa, we can recognize this land reform as merely part of the ongoing assault on African tenure. The postwar economic climate gave the region's governments new resources to fight this war, as this chapter explains.[4]

## THE NEW RURAL ORDER

As noted in Chapter 2, overcrowding and overgrazing first appeared in the Ciskei before the 1856-57 cattle-killing. The 1913 Land

211

Act acknowledged that the current area owned by Africans was insufficient to sustain its occupants. Relief was to come from Africans buying more land, the government allocating more Crown Land as reserves, and intensive agricultural techniques reducing the amount of land needed. Indeed, land pressure was seen to be a partly beneficial influence because it would speed intensification and eventually lead to the spontaneous rise of a commercial land market in the reserves.

As previous chapters explained, the plow made cultivation more extensive and dependent on cattle herding. Population growth added more Africans struggling to hold on to enough cattle for plowing and to sell for cash. Although good arable land was scarce, another poor-quality field could always be carved out from the commons, reducing further the available pasture. As population grew, people were forced to spread out to fill up land between permanent streams, making it difficult to move plow teams quickly from water to fields. This was true even in relatively well-watered areas like the Transkei. Moreover, as Professor W. M. MacMillan observed in 1924:

> It is well-known from bulletins of the Department of Public Health that typhus has for years been endemic in a great many parts of the Union. Typhus is due to dirt, and the native is not naturally filthy in his habits. But washing becomes a luxury when every drop of water for domestic use has to be fetched four miles or more, and that is the fact about parts even of the Transkei.[5]

The South African Department of Native Affairs (DNA) switched from agricultural education to Rhodesian-style demonstration plots in 1929, but it was clear that intensive agriculture would not develop without more direct government intervention. The 1930-32 Native Economic Commission proposed that the government advance communal loans for fencing and paddocking reserve commons rather than continue to wait for spontaneous privatization of land.[6] The DNA began a few reserve irrigation schemes in 1932 and then began experimental paddocking on land that it acquired adjacent to reserves after 1936. From 1938 to 1947, the DNA subsidized the purchase of plows, harrows, and mechanical planters in the reserves, and in 1946 it began to sell high-quality seed at cost price, as well as subsidized fertilizer and manure.[7]

In 1949, the DNA finally decided on a complete model for agricultural development in the reserves. It now selected an area, fenced it in, and divided it into rotational paddocks with permanent water supplies. Cattle grazed in one paddock in summer and were then led to another in winter, thus allowing the first paddock to rest. The DNA calculated the number of animals that the land could sustain without overgrazing and then reduced the stock accordingly, forcing owners to kill or sell those over the limit. Arable blocks within the paddocks were marked out and beaconed off, with each cultivator receiving a plot. No more arable fields were allocated thereafter. Villages were also planned, with concentrated residential sites reducing the amount of arable and grazing land devoted to compound space. Residents could only increase their agricultural incomes by increasing the quality rather than the quantity of their stock, or by increasing the yields rather than the area of their fields. Future population growth would have to be accommodated in wage employment elsewhere or as unemployed in the planned villages.[8]

In 1954, the Commission for the Socio-Economic Development of the Bantu Areas Within the Union of South Africa proposed extending this model throughout African-held land. Map 9.1 shows the final delimitation, which left Africans some 13 percent of the country. Known by its head, J. R. Tomlinson, this commission issued a report that amounted to a comprehensive development plan embracing all economic sectors. The main problem that the Tomlinson Commission addressed was the deterioration of land, which threatened to reduce the reserves' contribution to the national economy. As of 1951, some 45 percent of the country's Africans were on African land. These 3.6 million persons amounted to 600,000 families averaging 6 members. Each family occupied a total of 21 hectares of land, 3 of which were arable, and owned 6 cattle, 6 sheep, and 5 goats. This was a fall in livestock per family of nearly 50 percent from 1930. Average agricultural income was £29 per family, whereas the commission calculated that £60 was the minimum necessary for subsistence. More than 40 percent of reserve males between the ages of 15 and 64 were away earning wages to supplement this paltry rural income.[9]

Although the average, predominately female reserve family had far too few livestock to earn a decent living, the reserves as a whole held 50 percent more animals than the land could safely sustain. Whereas virtually all ranch cattle died in abattoirs, more than two-thirds of the cattle that died in the reserves from 1946 to 1952 were not slaughtered: 39 percent died from thirst and hunger, and 23 percent died from disease.[10] If the reserves were fenced, paddocked, and destocked down to safe limits, the average reserve family would own 50 percent fewer cattle. The Tomlinson Commission, then, planned not for the average farming family, but for the "self-sufficient" farming family. That is, it calculated that the minimum subsistence income

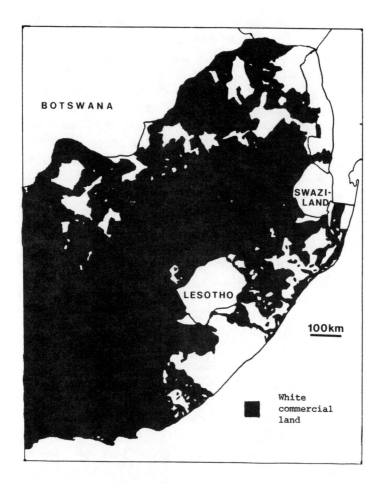

BOTSWANA

SWAZI-
LAND

LESOTHO

100km

White
commercial
land

**Map 9.1.** South Africa's Final Enclosure (From South Africa, Commission for Socio-Economic Development of the Bantu Areas, *Summary of the Report*, Map 5.)

of £60 required 44 hectares of land, or more than twice the amount available to the average reserve family. In order to accommodate families at £60 each, half the reserve population would have to be removed from the land.[11]

Where would these people go? The Rand and other urban centers could employ some of them, but most would live in new rural townships that the commission planned for the reserves. Here the government would promote commerce and industry to complement agricultural development.[12] The commission planned for diversified beef, dairy, and irrigated farming industries, many of whose essential services the government had already introduced in the reserves.[13] All together, the Tomlinson Commission report offered a comprehensive plan for bringing the reserves, although not the majority of their population, finally and completely into the national industrial economy.

But who would pay the bill? The commission calculated that annual direct government expenditure on Africans amounted to £28.6 million, and indirect expenditure amounted to £16.2 million. Africans paid only £9.7 million in taxes. As the Native Economic Commission found in 1930-32, the problem here was that African wage labor, as well as the vast natural resources of gold, farmland, and other minerals, contributed to the taxes of white employers, not African employees, and so did not result in revenue for African development. This was explicit government policy, unchanged from the days of British rule. The Tomlinson Commission now proposed a ten-year expenditure of £104.5 million, which would double the DNA budget. The commission expected that only 53 percent of this sum could be repaid. That is, £49.2 million would be permanently transferred to African areas from central government revenues.[14]

Perhaps in different political circumstances the Tomlinson Commission plan would have been accepted. Hertzog died in 1942, and the white electorate flocked to Malan's newly militant National Party, which defeated Smuts in the 1948 national election. Again, the most important issues were urban. Whereas the British, Smuts, and Hertzog had allowed African men to stay in town indefinitely as long as they remained employed (women did not need a job or even a pass to stay in town), the rush of Africans to take up new jobs in the booming economy heightened the white electorate's fear of black competition. The urban black population finally surpassed the urban white population during World War II, and by 1951 it totaled 25 percent of the country's total African population. Malan's National Party promised to freeze the number of permanently settled urban Africans, leaving the rest to be migrant contract workers, as in the mines, forcing them to return to reserve homelands between contracts. This would further inhibit Africans from gaining skills, organizing unions, or otherwise capturing economic opportunities that whites wanted for themselves. Women too now had to carry passes and so faced eviction from town if they could not prove that they were employed.[15]

We cannot know whether a British, Smuts, or Hertzog government would have accepted the Tomlinson Commission report. Malan's National Party did not. Such a large transfer of funds to African development was now out of the question. Beyond the high cost, however, there was little objectionable to Malan in the Tomlinson plan. Agricultural development in the reserves continued much as the plan prescribed, but very slowly, within the narrow budget supplied largely by African taxes.[16] The government also built rural townships for the landless unemployed and tried to attract private industry to build factories near them. Without the infrastructural investment proposed by the Tomlinson Commission, and probably even with it, firms found no reason to leave the fully industrial centers of the Rand, Durban, Cape Town, and Port Elizabeth.[17]

A more rapid tenure change came to commercial land in South Africa in this postwar era. Figure 9.1 shows the boom in the total economy after the war, with manufacturing leading the way but with agriculture growing extremely rapidly as well.[18] Whereas most white landowners previously engaged African tenants, who plowed their own fields and herded their own cattle, wage labor now became the rule. White farmers finally fulfilled the government's wishes and ended their landlord-tenant relations with Africans. As we noted in Chapter

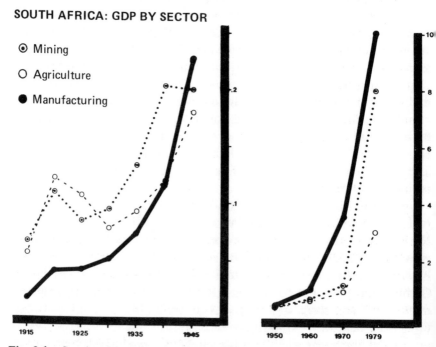

**Fig. 9.1.** South Africa: Gross Domestic Product by Sector (From South Africa, *Official Yearbook*, 1980/1, pp. 26, 32, 327.)

6, the laws for this change were enacted in 1899, 1913, and 1936, but one important element was missing until after World War II. This was the tractor. There was only 1 tractor for every 17 commercial farms in 1937; the ratio of 1 to 1 was reached in 1957.[19] The United States achieved this ratio only in 1955.[20] By 1980, there were more than 4 tractors for every 1 commercial farm in South Africa.[21]

Tough, hardy oxen were no longer needed for plowing, and so white farmers could keep high-quality beef and dairy cows instead. The ratio of oxen to cows and heifers in the national herd fell from .84 in 1937 to .71 in 1946 to .37 in 1957.[22] Herding was finally separated from cultivation. Africans were no longer needed to handle oxen and plow carefully at just the right time. A farmer could rely on his tractor instead. White landowners expanded their fields, took all their pasture for their own herds, and became fully industrial farmers at last. African fields and herds disappeared from commercial land. The sudden demand for wage labor exceeded the supply from the former tenants; the government solved this problem temporarily in the early 1950s by channeling men caught unemployed in the city into prison labor gangs for white farms.[23]

Despite its only partial acceptance, and the stark contrast of white farming's commercial success, the Tomlinson Commission report offered a model for agricultural development that other British colonies also adopted in part. Ring fences and paddocks would completely enclose the commons. This was a step beyond the Glen Grey allocation of arable plots and rights to communal pasture. A paddocked reserve could function much like a ranch, at least in theory, with controlled breeding and disease prevention, even though the herd comprised animals owned by many different individuals. The costs of establishing such a scheme, and providing permanent water for each paddock, remained great drawbacks.

We noted in Chapter 6 that Rhodesia allocated nearly 10 percent of its farmland for individual African purchase in 1930; in 1944 a Native Production and Trade Commission advocated extending individual title finally throughout the reserves.[24] The 1951 Native Husbandry Act, first implemented in 1954, amounted to the Tomlinson Commission plan without the ring fences and paddocks. An area was marked off and stock within it were reduced to a safe limit. Arable plots were beaconed off, and thereafter no more fields could be carved out of the commons. Each farming family received a field and a stock limit calculated to make them agriculturally self-sufficient. Rural townships would absorb the landless unemployed.[25]

Although the Husbandry Act included provisions for reducing the number of landless by reducing field size and individual stock quotas below self-sufficiency, these were expected only to be necessary in exceptional cases. The exception turned out to be the rule, however. Although Rhodesian industry prospered after the war, it did not absorb enough Africans to relieve land pressure in the reserves; population grew rapidly in the 1950s; and the 1960 census revealed that the reserve population was actually much larger than the government had thought. In any event, political events finally overtook the Husbandry Act. A £2 million loan from the World Bank in 1961 helped speed its implementation, and the government proposed in the same year gradually to open all commercial land to black purchase. But a settler party won the 1962 election and declared independence from Britain in 1966. As with the 1948 Nationalist victory in South Africa, expenditure on African agriculture was now confined to African tax revenue, and the commercial land market remained closed to blacks.[26] Ring fencing and paddocking was tried in Victoria Province in the late 1960s, with some success,[27] but the Husbandry Act was officially abandoned in 1969, and then guerrilla war ravaged the countryside in the 1970s.[28]

By the 1970s, then, the problem of African agriculture in Southern Africa remained unsolved. The Tomlinson Commission found on the farms that the Department of Native Affairs bought after 1936 that the cost of fencing, paddocking, arable allocation, plus the cost of purchase, amounted to £1,430 per self-sufficient family in pastoral areas, £1,082 per family in mixed farming areas with stock income exceeding crop income, £376 in mixed farming areas with stock equaling crops, and £165 in irrigated areas. In other words: "The settlement costs per farming family are thus in inverse ratio to the intensiveness of the type of farming practised."[29]

African agriculture in Southern Africa, based so firmly on cattle, was simply very expensive to develop. This was the dilemma facing Botswana's planners in the early 1970s. The commercial ranches were fully stocked with cattle and capital improvements, while the African commons was overgrazed and still depended on low-quality oxen and old cows. It was time to turn to African land for further agricultural intensification, but the costs would be high. Two questions remained: Which model would the government follow, and where would the money come from?

## ENCLOSING THE KWENENG

British administrators throughout East, Central, and Southern Africa met in Arusha, Tanganyika in February 1956 to discuss implementing the Glen Grey Act in their territories, as Rhodesia and Kenya had already begun to do.[30] As a result of this meeting, the Bechuanaland administration set up a committee in 1958 formally to study the question. Although the Protectorate gained a reprieve from overcrowding through the expansion of water supplies into new sandveld pastures, the government knew that it would have to face the question of land reform eventually. This 1958 committee concluded that arable land pressure had not grown serious enough to generate a commercial market in arable land. As for pasture:

It is considered that policy should be designed to encourage the individual rancher and the syndicates who develop their own water supplies to encourage the extension of the grant of individual rights to water to groups of individuals in the allocation of/the new underground water supplies now becoming available. Such groups of individuals will become in effect syndicates themselves and experience in the Bakwena reserve suggests that it may be possible to allocate the new boreholes on conditions limiting the number of cattle to be watered from them. In this way greater definition can be given to tenure in grazing areas which is considered essential to improved animal management.[31]

The government, then, confined its immediate hopes for tenure reform to the new uncultivated sandveld pastures. The overgrazed, overcrowded hardveld was to be left to evolve a commercial land market through arable land pressure. Despite the immediate failure of the Kweneng formula, the government continued to look to the evolution of group ranches and for individual borehole owners to become ranchers.[32]

As we noted in the previous chapter, drought postponed the question of grazing control until the early 1970s, when the national herd surpassed two million head. The final model for tenure reform was now influenced by a change in government funding. Britain began offering grants and loans to independent countries in 1959, as "Commonwealth" rather than "Colonial" Development Funds, and other international aid agencies made contributions to Botswana in the 1960s.[33] In 1971, the United Nations reclassified twenty-five poor countries for special assistance as "least developed among the developing countries." There were three primary criteria for this list of

"Fourth World" countries: per capita gross domestic product of $100 or less; share of manufacturing in total gross domestic product of 10 percent or less; and a literacy rate of 20 percent or less. Sixteen of these twenty-five nations were African, and one was Botswana.[34]

Botswana's new aid money was then augmented by diamond discoveries and high beef prices in the 1970s.[35] Figures 7.1, 7.2, 8.1, and 8.2 show the dramatic rise in prices, trade, and government revenue in this decade. As the administration expanded to deliver a full range of industrial services to its mining, agricultural, and urban sectors, there emerged a new class of well-paid civil servants who could also claim citizenship in the reserves. Private ranches in the reserves, owned by reserve citizens, at last became a possibility. In 1973 an official "Report on Rural Development" advocated precisely this formula, with government revenue derived from this development diverted to pay for social services in the unaffected, unenclosed remainder of the country.[36] The government formally endorsed this plan in 1975 as the Tribal Grazing Land Policy (TGLP).[37]

Although this TGLP encouraged group ranches, it was apparent that only a few wealthy, salaried individuals would be able to sustain the huge investment required for a ranch. Indeed, the actual investment model developed by the Ministry of Agriculture began with a single herd at a private cattle post at a private borehole, self-contained and segregated from neighboring herds and from *mafisa*-type relations. This herd of 550 head had a ratio of oxen to cows and heifers of .61. Over 10 years, the herd composition was to change to younger, healthier animals sold earlier, with a ratio of oxen to cows and heifers of .44.[38]

The goal of TGLP was explicitly to convert sandveld boreholes to ranches. Beyond the tenure change, a series of Livestock Development Projects was designed to provide the technical requirements of a ranching industry that the existing freehold areas already enjoyed. In the words of a World Bank expert who helped design the program:

> The freehold farmers had security of tenure, markets and executive and technical skills. The Tribal Grazing Land Policy will try to help the tribal farmers acquire the same advantages [through] the creation of ranches and grazing schemes with defined boundaries and identifiable ownership. . . . The second Livestock Development Project will help provide the other essentials for the farmers to become self-sufficient agricultural businessmen.[39]

Map 9.2 shows the initial zoning for commercial ranch expansion; this should be compared to Maps 3.2 and 9.1. As of 1980, 5 percent of Botswana stood as pre-TGLP freehold land, whose ranches now numbered 349; 12 percent was zoned TGLP commercial land for 700 to 900 new ranches; and 30 percent was zoned for occupation by the nonranching African population. The remaining land was game reserve (27%), forest (1%), and unzoned (25%).[40]

Implementation of TGLP has been very slow, however, for a number of reasons. As long as a rancher has access to the commons as well

TRIBAL GRAZING LAND POLICY · 1980

■ Proposed commercial
   ranch land

KWENENG

**Map 9.2.** Botswana's Proposed Enclosure (From RB, "National Development Plan, 1979-85," Map 6.1.)

as a ranch, he can pack cattle around an unfenced ranch borehole and shift them back to the commons when the ranch becomes overgrazed. The low rent that the government charges, 5 cents per hectare for a 6,400 hectare ranch, encourages this misuse, which has already struck some new ranches.[41] The Ministry of Agriculture also estimates that a complete ranch costs more than $50,000 to establish, a figure beyond the means of even most well-paid civil servants. Moreover, few individuals own the 550 cattle required for a ranch; half the existing freehold ranches do not own this many, and only 7 percent of rural Africans own more than even a hundred cattle.[42] Those few Africans who do own more than 500 cattle already own their own boreholes, whose cattle numbers they control completely. They have avoided the great expense of fencing and piping water into paddocks.

TGLP's logic extends to the future, however, even if its present seems uncertain. Once the hardveld and older sandveld pastures are completely overgrazed, a wealthy cattle owner can look only to increasing the yield of the pasture around his private borehole. Fences, paddocks, and the full range of industrial techniques will then remain the only available alternative. TGLP thus captures the last frontier of reserve sandveld before African agriculture can occupy it fully.

In the Kweneng, there were 68 private and 144 government boreholes by 1970. By 1980 these figures were 117 and 202.[43] Map 9.3 shows that by 1976 boreholes had allowed the occupation of nearly all the open sandveld beyond the hardveld and sandveld valleys. The open sandveld had never had permanent water before. The remaining waterless areas were not unexplored, but rather failed to yield water after careful searching.[44] This map also shows the proposed enclosure in the Kweneng, amounting to some 50 ranches of 6,400 hectares each, covering 22 percent of the district.[45]

A preliminary compound count for the 1981 census indicates approximately how many Kweneng citizens have ended up in each of the district's geographical zones.[46] About 40 percent of the population remained in the southern hardveld, and some 25 percent in the transitional hardveld. Sandveld households are concentrated in the two old valleys of Letlhakeng and Lephepe, leaving 20 percent in the open sandveld beyond. Most of these 20 percent are clustered at the small but public and thus crowded water points like Motokwe, Dutlwe, and Ngware. Even in the open sandveld we can expect that only private boreholes, each watering one large herd, can escape overgrazing. These might number 200 at most, or some 1 percent of Kweneng households.

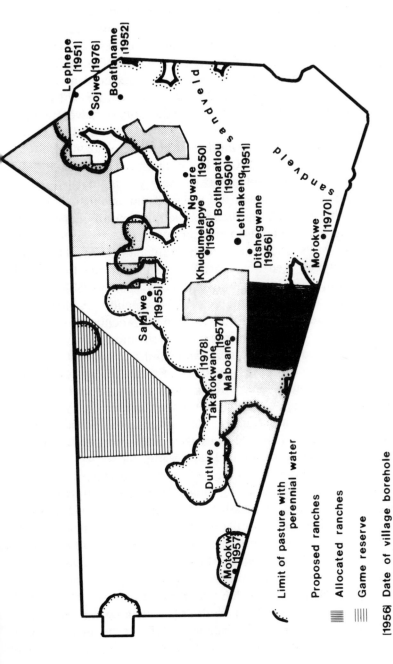

**Map 9.3.** Kweneng Sandveld, 1980 (From W. Duggan and L. Ellsworth, "Communal area development in the Kweneng," MLGL, 1981.)

Lephepe
|1951|

Sojwe|1976|

Boatlaname
|1952|

sandveld

sandveld

Ngware |1950|

Botlhapatlou
|1950|●

Khudumelapye
|1956|●

Letlhakeng|1951|
●

Ditshegwane
|1956|

Motokwe
● |1970|

Salajwe
|1955|

Takatokwane |1978|
Maboane |1957|
●

Dutlwe

Motokwe
|1957|

50 km.

⌒  Limit of pasture with
     perennial water

     Proposed ranches

▦  Allocated ranches

▥  Game reserve

|1956| Date of village borehole

223

The government continues to hope that smaller herd owners will pool their cattle and invest in ranches. Experimental group ranches have already failed, however, and it is not difficult to see why.[47] The operating costs and loan repayments of a modern commercial ranch require a steady, planned stream of cattle sales. A recent study of Kgatleng syndicates shows that cattle owners have difficulty planning expenses and sales even when borehole maintenance costs are divided among a dozen or so fairly large cattle owners. An owner of 100 head tries to hold on to his cattle, so that even if a drought halves his herd he will have some cattle left to sell. This is why tribal and syndicate borehole users have not tried to limit their herds.[48]

From its inception in 1905 the Veterinary Department has preached an answer to this dilemma: Increase yields, that is, reduce the time it takes cattle to reach full weight from five or six years to two or three. This would more than double the yield of beef per hectare grazed. The requirements for this are earlier castration and fast-growing hybrid bulls, medicines, food supplements, and constant, abundant water. Yet even large cattle owners continue to rely on local slow-growing but drought-resistant bulls selected from young males after two long uncastrated years. They spend very little cash on medicine or feed. The transition to modern ranching encouraged by the government simply requires more cash and more risk from drought than even most large herders can afford.

What will become of the vast majority of rural Africans unable to afford a ranch? Although some poorer producers lease their land to tractor owners for a share of the crop, population pressure has not led to a real arable land market. The commons has not enclosed itself. Overcrowding has not encouraged intensive cultivation, although the government continues to do so. In 1980 it launched an Arable Lands Development Programme, which subsidizes the purchase of various aids to cultivation. The "package," however, is essentially the same as the ADs have peddled for nearly half a century. This remains excellent technical advice, which still only a few cultivators can afford.[49]

So what does the future promise for Botswana's commons? The government has kept to its promise of using revenue gained elsewhere to pay for social services in overgrazed areas.[50] This is one of the many ways Botswana's citizens have been more fortunate than Africans in South Africa or Rhodesia. Neither has the government forced anyone to kill their stock.[51] Nevertheless, TGLP is the only substantial agricultural program in the country, and it is confined to open sandveld pastures. Nothing more is planned for the hardveld and sandveld areas that still combine cultivation and herding, where almost all the rural population reside.[52] In this way areas crowded with fields and small herds remain similar to most Southern African reserves: The commons endures, and the industrial world leaves it behind.

## NOTES

1. Hance, *Geography*, pp. 49-54.
2. United States Department of Agriculture, Economic Research Service, *Food Problems and Prospects in Sub-Saharan Africa*, 1981, pp. 105-7. For one of the few Green Revolution successes in Africa, see J. Gerhart, *The Diffusion of Hybrid Maize in Western Kenya*, Mexico City, 1975.
3. See K. Parsons, et al., *Land Tenure*, Madison, 1956; J. Timmons, "Improving agricultural tenancy," *FAOAS*, 35, 1957; K. Parsons, "The owner-cultivator in a progressive agriculture," *FAOAS*, 39, 1958; E. Jacoby, "The interrelationship between agrarian reform and agricultural development," *FAOAS*, 26, 1953; B. Binns, "Cadastral surveys and records of rights in land," *FAOAS*, 18, 1953; L. Mair, "Agrarian policy in African colonies," in Afrike Instituut, Leiden, *Land Tenure Symposium*, Leiden, 1950; D. Warriner, *Land Reform in Principle and Practice*, Oxford, 1969. But contrast G. Clauson, "Communal land tenure," *FAOAS*, 17, 1953.
4. For reviews of postwar African agricultural development, see J. de Wilde, *Agricultural Development in Tropical Africa*, Baltimore, 1967; U. Lele, *The Design of Rural Development*, Baltimore, 1975; R. Bates and M. Lofchie, *Agricultural Development in Africa*, New York, 1980.
5. W. MacMillan, *The Land, the Native and Unemployment*, Johannesburg, 1924, cited in Buell, *Native Problem*, p. 78. C. Simkins, "Agricultural production in the African reserves," *JSAS*, 7, 1971, shows that already by the first agricultural census in 1918 the reserves did not produce enough food to feed themselves. See also A. Hall, *The Improvement of Native Agriculture in Relation to Population and Public Health*, London, 1939.
6. Native Economic Commission, *Report*, p. 16.
7. South Africa, Commission for Socio-Economic Development of the Bantu Areas, *Summary of the Report*, 1954, pp. 71, 84.
8. Commission for Socio-Economic Development, *Summary*, pp. 74-75, 82, 117.
9. Commission for Socio-Economic Development, *Report*, pp. 28, 49, 53, 77-78.
10. Commission for Socio-Economic Development, *Report*, p. 81. The remaining 11 percent died from "miscellaneous causes, such as wild animals, lightning, etc."
11. Commission for Socio-Economic Development, *Report*, pp. 77, 114. "The aim of the Department is to help the Bantu to develop an efficient and self-supporting 'peasant farmers' class in their own areas, as part of a well balanced and diversified economy. This aim cannot be realised unless the Bantu radically change their present attitude towards their land and livestock." (p. 77). The figure of £60 (pp. 77, 113) changes somewhat mysteriously to £70 (p. 114). The first figure considered was £120 (p. 113), which would have left fewer than 20 percent of reserve Africans on the land.

12. Commission for Socio-Economic Development, *Report*, chs. 33-38.

13. Commission for Socio-Economic Development, *Report*, pp. 80-86. These included 17 bull camps and 84 tractor plowing schemes.

14. Commission for Socio-Economic Development, *Report*, pp. 38, 206. The budget was as follows:

| | £ million |
|---|---|
| Agricultural development | 33.9 |
| Forestry and mining | 4.0 |
| Secondary and tertiary | 30.0 |
| Urban development | 12.0 |
| Basic facilities | 13.0 |
| Health, education, and welfare | 11.6 |
| Total | 104.5 |

15. Welsh, "Growth," pp. 190-92. For the Smuts position, see South Africa, Department of Native Affairs, *Report of the Native Laws Commission*, 1948.

16. Whereas Glen Grey instituted one plot per cultivator in order to encourage increased investment on one fixed unit of land rather than in more extensive areas, the Tomlinson Commission suggested modifying this rule to let wealthier Africans buy more lots on a limited basis. Commission for Socio-Economic Development, *Report*, p. 152. The government held to the Glen Grey principle instead. The eviction to rural townships in the 1960s is described by Father Cosmas Desmond in *The Discarded People*, Hammondsworth, 1971.

17. See T. Bell, *Industrial Decentralization in South Africa*, Cape Town, 1975.

18. For the rise of manufacturing, which attracted substantial foreign investment after the war, see W. Busschau, "The expansion of manufacturing industry in the Union," *SAJE*, 13, 1945; G. Palmer, "Some aspects of the development of secondary industry in South Africa since the depression of 1929-32," *SAJE*, 22, 1954; N. Pearsall, "Some aspects of the development of secondary industry in the Union of South Africa," *SAJE*, 5, 1937; J. Suckling, "Foreign investment and domestic savings in the Republic of South Africa," *SAJE*, 43, 1975. For official agricultural marketing policy in this era, see T. Waasdijk, "Agricultural prices and price policy," *SAJE*, 22, 1954; R. Brits, "The marketing of South African maize," *SAJE*, 37, 1969; H. Behrmann, "Agricultural price policy in South Africa," *RJE*, 6, 1972.

19. *Union Statistics*, p. I-22.

20. United States Department of Agriculture, *Farm Tractors*, p. 12.

21. South Africa, *Official Yearbook*, 1980, pp. 559-60, reports 75,563 commercial farms and 320,000 tractors in use. Because of South Africa's more fragile soils, these tractors are much smaller and lighter than the average American variety.

22. *Union Statistics*, p. I-4.

23. See M. Lipton, "White farming: a case study of social change in South Africa," *JCCP*, 1, 1974. The removal of "surplus" African families to the reserves commenced in full force in the 1960s. See A. Baldwin, "Mass removals and separate development," *JSAS*, 1, 1975. In 1971, an official commission judged that white farming was sufficiently advanced to eliminate the various supports that kept the poorest third of white farms in production. See South Africa, Commission of Enquiry into Agriculture, *Report*, 1971.

24. Southern Rhodesia, Native Production and Trade Commission, *Report*, 1944.

25. Southern Rhodesia, *What the Native Land Husbandry Act Means to the Rural African and to Southern Rhodesia*, 1955, p. 4.

26. W. Duggan, "The Native Land Husbandry Act and the rural African middle class of Southern Rhodesia," *AfA*, 82, 1981.

27. J. Danckwerts, "A socio-economic study of veld management in the tribal areas of Victoria Province," University of Rhodesia, Department of Agriculture, 1970?

28. The African government that came to power in 1980 seemed to have returned to the agricultural policies of 1961. In addition finally to throwing commercial land open to black purchase, the government's first rural development proposal for the reserves, beginning with Victoria Province, entailed dividing the land into self-sufficient units and relocating the resulting landless unemployed in rural townships. The plan was ultimately withdrawn. Republic of Zimbabwe, "Integrated Rural Development Plan for Victoria Province," 1980.

29. Commission for Socio-Economic Development, *Report*, p. 116. The cost of land purchase should not have skewed this formula, for land prices should have reflected the land's value. That is, the cost of land for each family should have been about the same because in drier areas a family needed more hectares but each hectare cost less.

30. The proceedings were published in *Journal of African Administration*, Special Supplement, October, 1956. See also Special Supplement on "Land Tenure," October, 1952, and C. Meek, *Land Law and Custom in the Colonies*, London, 1946. For Kenya, see R. Swynnerton, *A Plan to Intensify the Development of African Agriculture in Kenya*, Nairobi, 1954; M. Sorrenson, *Land Reform in the Kikuyu Country*, Nairobi, 1967; J. Heyer et al., *Agricultural Development in Kenya*; N. Humphrey, *The Kikuyu Lands*, Kenya Colony and Protectorate, 1945, and *The Liguru and the Land*, Kenya Department of Agriculture, 1947. For Lesotho and Swaziland, see P. Scott, "Land policy and native population of Swaziland," *GJ*, 117, 1951; Sheddick, *Land Tenure*; J. Sterkenburg, "Agricultural commercialization in Africa south of the Sahara: the cases of Lesotho and Swaziland," *DC*, 11, 1980.

31. Homan, "Some aspects of land tenure reform."

32. Great Britain, Ministry of Overseas Development, *The Development of the Bechuanaland Economy*, 1965, p. 26, suggests group ranches, as does Homan, "Some aspects of land tenure reform," and RB, "National Development Plan, 1970-5," p. 29.

33. K. Jones, "Britain's contribution to Botswana's public debt," *BNR*, 9, 1977.

34. United Nations Conference on Trade and Development, *Special Measures in Favour of the Least Developed Among the Developing Countries*, 1971.

35. By the mid-1970s, Botswana was the largest per capita recipient of foreign aid in sub-Saharan Africa: $67 per person per year in 1974-76. G. Hunter, *Aid in Africa*, London, 1979, p. 28. For details on Botswana, see D. Jones, *Aid and Development in Southern Africa*, London, 1977, chs. 6-9; Colclough and McCarthy, *Political Economy*; S. McCarthy, "The administration of capital aid," *DD*, 1, 1978.

36. R. Chambers and D. Feldman, "Report on rural development," MFDP, 1973, p. 4.

37. RB, "National Policy on Tribal Grazing Land," Government Paper no. 2, 1975. For political discussions, see J. Parson, "Cattle, class and the state in rural Botswana," *JSAS*, 7, 1981; L. Picard, "Bureaucrats, cattle and public policy," *CPS*, 13, 1980; L. Cliffe and R. Moorsom, "Rural class formation and ecological collapse in Botswana," *RAPE*, 15/16, 1980; R. Hitchcock, "Tradition, social justice and land reform in Central Botswana," *JAL*, 24, 1980.

38. APRU, "Beef Production," p. 160. This ideal model of a solitary cattle post is very different from the complex reality described in R. Hitchcock, "Kalahari cattle posts," MLGL, 1978. Hitchcock reports that the rural economy extends even to these private boreholes, whose conversion to ranches would displace several thousand persons, mostly Sarwa, throughout the country. See also L. Wily, "Official policy towards San hunter-gatherers in modern Botswana," NIR, 1979.

39. R. von Kaufmann, "The Second Livestock Development Project," in B. Weimer, "A Policy for Rural Development," NIR, Discussion Paper no. 6, 1977, p. 30. See also R. von Kaufmann, "The Tribal Grazing Land Policy's relevance in a drought-prone environment," and N. Buck, "Beef cattle production research in Botswana and its relevance to drought conditions," in Hinchey, *Symposium*; T. Jarman and K. Butler, "Livestock management and production in the Kalahari," H. Martens, "The effect of tribal grazing patterns on the habitat of the Kalahari," and R. Martin, "Livestock production in relation to the maintenance of habitats in the Kalahari," in Botswana Society, *Sustained Production*.

40. S. Sanford, "Keeping an eye on TGLP," NIR Working Paper no. 31, 1980, p. 4; RB, "National Development Plan, 1976-81," p. 148. Hitchcock, "Tradition," p. 14, notes that there is one transitional hardveld area zoned for new ranches: This is Lepasha, in Ngwato territory.

41. Hitchcock, "Tradition," p. 17; M. Odell, "Botswana's First Livestock Development Project," Gaborone, 1980; RB, MoA, "Monitoring and progress report of the Second Livestock Development Project," 1979.

42. *Agricultural Statistics*, 1980, Table 13.

43. Wynne, "Preliminary report."

44. J. Farr and P. Spray, "Groundwater search for the extension of livestock grazing, DGS, 1980, gives an example of the difficulties of drilling in the northern Kweneng.

45. As of 1980, 8,100 of the Kweneng's 36,800 square kilometers were zoned for TGLP ranches, 8,200 were zoned as game reserve, and 19,500 were zoned "communal." Sanford, "Keeping an eye," p. 5. The first Kweneng ranch plan is RB, MoA, "Planning for development, Western Kweneng District," 1979.

46. W. Duggan and L. Ellsworth, "Communal area development in the Kweneng," MLGL, 1981. A more detailed breakdown is as follows:

| Hardveld Households | | | Sandveld Households | | | | |
|---|---|---|---|---|---|---|---|
| Southern | Transitional | Total | Letlhakeng | Lephepe | Open Sandveld | Total | Total Kweneng |
| 7,214 (39%) | 4,781 (26%) | 11,995 (64%) | 2,019 (11%) | 954 (5%) | 3,671 (20%) | 6,644 (36%) | 18,639 (100%) |

47. See also C. Fumagalli, "An evaluation of development projects among East African pastoralists," *AStR*, 21, 1978.
48. Peters, "Preliminary findings." Extensive networks of hardveld water use, with each herd owner depending on a number of water sites rather than one, as in a ranch, are described in L. Fortmann and E. Roe, "The water points survey," MoA, 1981.
49. "National Development Plan, 1979-85," pp. 150-55. A national marketing board began to collect, mill, and sell produce in 1974, but it still handles almost as much South African as Botswana grain. "Development Plan, 1979-85," p. 139. See also M. Eakes, "Crop pricing and protection in Botswana," MoA, 1978.
50. See for example R. Chambers, "Botswana's Accelerated Rural Development Programme, 1973-6," RB, 1976; L. Picard, "Rural development in Botswana," *JDA*, 13, 1979; J. Holm, "Rural development in Botswana," *RA*, 1972; A. Osborne, "Rural development in Botswana," *JSAS*, 2, 1976.
51. The 1972 Agricultural Resources Conservation Act, however, gives the government the power to do so. See RB, "National policy for rural development," 1973.
52. That is, extension advice and services remain the model here. Group drift fencing has also been encouraged, but to keep cattle out of dense arable areas after plowing rather than to enclose and rotate. "Development Plan, 1979-85," ch. 6, describes recent agricultural policy.

# 10

# Conclusion

This book has discussed the economic history of Southern African agriculture from a firmly neoclassical perspective. Although agricultural history based on the labor theory of value provides valuable insights into labor relations, to an agricultural economist this is only one-third of the story. Farming combines labor with land and capital. This study has shown how geography (land) and technology (capital) shaped indigenous agriculture and official agricultural policy.

This study further argues that the indigenous agricultural system's resistance to full commercialization sprang from concrete technical problems. African farmers themselves readily adjusted production to take advantage of new commercial opportunities. They proved too poor in land and capital, however, to make massive changes in the organization of their commons-based system and so achieve full commercialization before population pressure overcame them. Modern technology demanded a very different agricultural system. Southern Africa is not the only example in the world of an indigenous agricultural system well suited to its local economic environment but unable to make the leap to a modern agricultural industry.

Just because an agricultural system is rational, rational agricultural planners do not necessarily favor it. Its ability to absorb and profit from modern technology is more important. This study reveals that the British were committed to commercial development above all, and so they chose enclosed farming over the African commons. The British government promoted African agricultural development

230

when it seemed to pay to do so. As rational investors, the British channeled funds to wherever they thought would yield the highest return. In this their judgment was consistently good. The social costs, of course, were monstrous.

This study, then, offers an alternative to the wishful thinking that presently characterizes much of African agricultural economic history. In general, scholars rush to the defense of African farmers and search for someone to blame for the dismal poverty of African agriculture. The culprits are variously venal colonial rulers, venal white settlers, venal multinational corporations, venal African independent governments, or even venal chiefs. One or more of these criminals stole the economic surplus that should have funded African agricultural development.

Without blaming or exonerating any of the above, this study defends African farmers in a more realistic way. The key methodological mistake that all the views above share is their assumption that agricultural development is a natural process, that it fails to occur only when someone stifles it. Hence the list of stiflers above. This study begins with the more fundamental question of what are the requirements of agricultural development in the first place. It analyzes how an indigenous agricultural system fits and how it conflicts with the technology of modern commercial agriculture appropriate to a specific geographical area. Even if the fit is a good one, and in Southern Africa it was not, high transport costs, low local and world prices for the product, or other strictly economic factors can inhibit agricultural development. Only after such technical and economic factors have been assessed should African agricultural economic historians turn to examine whether the culprits listed above stifled African agriculture or, more often, promoted it in specific, self-interested ways.

There are lessons here not only for historians but also for economists interested in African agricultural development. The most important lesson is simply that African agriculture has a history, that it has changed considerably, especially in the last hundred years. Partial commercialization, population pressure, and state agricultural policy had already helped shape the agricultural systems that international development agencies encountered when they began to assist newly independent African governments in the 1960s. African agriculture looked traditional, but it was not. Economists viewed African farmers as self-sufficient, subsistence producers who, as commercial markets spread, would become commercial, surplus producers. More often than not, however, commercial markets had already spread, some for hundreds of years, especially in West Africa. Farmers already took account of these commercial prices to plan production; some produced less than subsistence, some produced more. Colonial governments had already promoted commercial agricultural development. The countryside that development economists faced in the 1960s, and still today, was not a noncommercial world ripe for the introduction of market forces but a complex economic system that had already adapted to the modern commercial world. That adaptation was largely unsuccessful not because market forces were slow in coming or encountered resistance from African farmers. Rather, the modern market economy did not bring with it an agricultural technology appropriate to both the environment and the limited resources of poor African farmers.

It should come as no surprise, then, that recent economic research in African agriculture consistently shows that seemingly noncommercial farming practices usually reflect prevailing market forces. This has led to a greater appreciation of the logic of African agricultural systems. New research programs seek to understand African agriculture, and then to develop a series of appropriate technological improvements to help increase its productivity. This study certainly supports such a change. Now more than ever, however, economic researchers must appreciate history, because the present agricultural systems, for all their logic, face a modern world not of their making. They fit an earlier economic environment much better than they fit the present one. Appreciating their logic requires understanding that previous economic environment, that is, history.

This study also warns that the original basis of African agriculture was not a self-sufficient peasant farm family but a household involved intimately with others in the production and distribution of crops and livestock. Their interactions with other households are not noneconomic relations. Rather, they are the heart of the agricultural system, directly economic and crucial to any future success in African agricultural development.

# BIBLIOGRAPHY

This bibliography is presented in these sections:

   I. Archives
  II. Official and Semi-Official Reports, Bechuanaland and Botswana
 III. Published and Secondary Sources
     A. Southern Africa
     B. Botswana
     C. Africa and General

At the beginning of each section is a list of abbreviations used in the notes to the text.

## SECTION I: ARCHIVES

*BNA —Botswana National Archives, Gaborone*

| | |
|---|---|
| AAC | African Advisory Council |
| AC | Acting Commissioner |
| DC | District Commissioner |
| HC | High Commission |
| NAC | Native Advisory Council |
| RC | Resident Commissioner |
| RM | Resident Magistrate |
| S | Government Secretary |
| V | Veterinary Department |
| VO | Veterinary Officer |

*LMSA —London Missionary Society Archives, London University*

| | |
|---|---|
| ASC | Africa, South, Correspondence |
| ASR | Africa, South, Reports |

*ZNA —Zimbabwe National Archives, Harare*

| | |
|---|---|
| BU | J. Burns, Correspondence |
| GB, CO, *ASD* | Great Britain, Colonial Office, *Africa South, Despatches* |

## SECTION II: OFFICIAL AND SEMI-OFFICIAL REPORTS, BECHUANALAND AND BOTSWANA

*Abbreviations Used*

| | |
|---|---|
| APRU | Animal Production Research Unit |
| BP | Bechuanaland Protectorate |

CSO    Central Statistics Office
DoA    Department of Agriculture
DGS    Department of Geological Survey
MoA    Ministry of Agriculture
MFDP   Ministry of Finance and Development Planning
MLGL   Ministry of Local Government and Lands
NIR    National Institute of Research
NMS    National Migration Survey
RB     Republic of Botswana
UNDP   United Nations Development Programme, Botswana

Bailey, C., "Keeping cattle and the cost of water in eastern Botswana," MoA, 1980.

Beetles, F., "Women's access to agricultural extension services in Botswana," MoA, 1980.

Biggs, H., "Report on the marketing of agricultural produce in Bechuanaland," Great Britain Overseas Development Ministry, 1966.

Bond, C., "Women's involvement in agriculture in Botswana," MoA, 1974.

Bond, G., "A report on livestock marketing," MoA, 1975.

Botswana Society, *Sustained Production From Semi-Arid Areas*, Gaborone, 1970.

BP, *Annual Report*, 1902-65.

———, *Blue Book*, 1910-47.

———, "Conduct and Development of the Livestock Industry," 1964.

———, "Development Plan, 1960-4."

———, "Development Plan, 1963-8."

———, "Transitional Plan for Social and Economic Development," 1966.

BP, DoA, *Annual Report*, 1937-66.

Buck, N., "Beef cattle research in Botswana and its relevance to drought conditions," in Hinchey, *Symposium*, 1979.

Campbell, A., "The 1960s drought in Botswana," in Hinchey, *Symposium*, 1979.

Chambers, R., "Botswana's Accelerated Rural Development Programme, 1973-6," 1977.

Chambers, R., and D. Feldman, "Report on rural development," MFDP, 1973.

Cole, G., "Livestock marketing in the Kalahari," in Botswana Society, *Sustained Production*, 1971.

Comaroff, J., The structure of agricultural transformation in the Barolong," MoA, 1977.

Cooper, D., "How urban workers in Botswana manage their cattle and lands," NMS, 1980.

Curl, S., and J. Schuster, "Ecological and physiological constraints," in Botswana Society, *Sustained Production*, 1971.

Devitt, P., "Drought and poverty," in Hinchey, *Symposium*, 1979.

Duggan, W., "The economics of ploughing in Botswana," MoA, 1981.

———, "Informal markets, technology and employment on arable land in Botswana," MoA, 1979.

Duggan, W., and L. Ellsworth, "Communal area development in the Kweneng," MLGL, 1981.

Eakes, M., "Crop pricing and protection in Botswana," MoA, 1978.

Eding, D., "Moshupa catchment survey," MoA, 1970.

Eding, D., and M. Sekgoma, "Kweneng resource survey," Gaborone, 1972.

Eding, D., et al., "Report in village studies," MoA, 1972.

Farr, J., and P. Spray, "Groundwater search for the extension of livestock grazing," DGS, 1980.

Field, D., "A handbook of basic ecology for range management in Botswana," MoA, 1978.

Field, R., "Patterns of settlement at the lands," MoA, 1980.

Food and Agriculture Organization, "Study of constraints on agricultural development in the Republic of Botswana," MoA, 1973.

Fortmann, L., and E. Roe, "The water points survey," MoA, 1981.

Fosbrooke, H., "Man in the Kalahari tribal area," in Botswana Society, *Sustained Production*, 1971.

Gulbrandsen, Ø., "Agro-pastoral production and communal land use in Botswana," MoA, 1980.

Hamilton, A., "Review of post-harvest technologies in Botswana," MoA, 1975.

Hertel, T., "The system of mafisa," MoA, 1977.

Hinchey, M., *Symposium on Drought in Botswana*, Botswana Society, 1979.

Hitchcock, R., "Kalahari cattle posts," MLGL, 1978.

Homan, F., "Some aspects of land tenure reform in the tribal territories of Bechuanaland," BP, 1966.

Hyde, L., "Groundwater supplies in the Kalahari area," in Botswana Society, *Sustained Production*, 1971.

Izzard, W., "Rural-urban migration of women in Botswana," NMS, 1979.

Jarman, T., and K. Butler, "Livestock management and production in the Kalahari," in Botswana Society, *Sustained Production*, 1971.

Kerven, C., "Rural and urban female-headed households' dependence on agriculture," NMS, 1979.

Lightfoot, C., "Broadcast planting in perspective," MoA, 1981.

Lipton, M., Employment and labour use in Botswana," MFDP, 1978.

Lucan, R., "The distribution and efficiency of crop production in tribal areas of Botswana," Rural Income Distribution Survey seminar, Gaborone, 1979.

Martens, H., "The effect of tribal grazing patterns on the habitat of the Kalahari," in Botswana Society, *Sustained Production*, 1971.

Martin, R., "Livestock production in relation to the maintenance of habitats in the Kalahari," in Botswana Society, *Sustained Production*, 1971.

Morley, G., "Grain storage in Bechuanaland," DoA, 1965.

Odell, M., "Botswana's First Livestock Development Project," Gaborone, 1980.

Parish, E., "Crop survey of the Bechuanaland Protectorate," DoA, 1948.

Peters, P., "Preliminary findings and observations on borehole syndicates in Kgatleng District," MLGL, 1980.

Pike, J., "Rainfall and evaporation in Botswana," UNDP, 1971.

RB, "National development plan, 1968-73."
_____, "National development plan, 1970-75."
_____, "National development plan, 1973-78."
_____, "National development plan, 1976-81."
_____, "National development plan, 1979-85."
_____, "National policy on tribal grazing land," Government paper no. 2, 1975.
_____, "National policy for rural development," 1973.
RB, CSO, "Freehold farm survey," 1971.
_____, "Report on the population census, 1971," 1972.
_____, "Rural income distribution survey, 1974/5," 1976.
_____, "A social and economic survey in three peri-urban areas in Botswana," 1974.
_____, *Statistical Abstract*, 1966-79.
_____, "Transport statistics, 1976-8," 1978.
RB, MoA, *Agricultural Statistics*, 1979-80.
_____, *Agricultural Survey*, 1967-78.
_____, "Evaluation of farming systems and agricultural implements project: Report No. 3," 1978.
_____, "A handbook of livestock statistics," 1978.
_____, "Integrated farming pilot project: Annual Report," 1977.
_____, "Monitoring and progress report of the Second Livestock Development Project," 1979.
_____, "Planning for development, Western Kweneng District," 1979.
_____, "Sedibeng experimental unit farms: Six-Year Report," 1971.
RB, MoA, APRU, "Beef production and range management in Botswana," 1980.
Ryan, G., "Report on the livestock industry," BP, 1958.
Sanford, S., "Keeping an eye on TGLP," NIR, 1980.
Sheppard, C., "Coping with drought in Botswana," MoA, 1979.
Smith, C., "An analysis of the factors affecting district primary school enrolment," MFDP, 1977.
Solway, J., "Report on Dutlwe village," MoA, 1979.
Syson, L., "A profile of cattle sales in the Shoshong area," UNDP, 1971.
_____, "Some agricultural data from the Shoshong area," UNDP, 1972.
_____, "Some aspects of 'traditional' and 'modern' village life in Botswana," UNDP, 1972.
Vierich, H., "Majako," NMS, 1979.
Von Kaufman, R., "The Second Livestock Development Project," in B. Weimar, "A Policy for Rural Development," NIR, 1977.
_____, "The Tribal Grazing Land Policy's relevance in a drought-prone environment," in Hinchey, *Symposium*, 1979.
Walker, H., and J. Hobday, "Report on the cattle industry of the Bechuanaland Protectorate," BP, 1939.
Wande, F., "Agro-economic survey of the Barolong Farms," BP, 1949.
Weare, P., "Vegetation of the Kalahari," in Botswana Society, *Sustained Production*, 1971.

Wilson, B., "A mini-guide to the water resources," in Hinchey, *Symposium*, 1979.

Wily, L., "Official policy towards San hunter-gatherers in modern Botswana," NIR, 1979.

Wynne, S., "A preliminary report on borehole drilling for Kweneng District," District Office, Molepolole, 1979.

## SECTION III: PUBLISHED AND SECONDARY SOURCES

*Journals Cited—Abbreviations*

| A | Africa |
|---|---|
| AfA | African Affairs |
| AmA | American Anthropologist |
| AEH | African Economic History |
| AER | American Economic Review |
| AJAE | American Journal of Agricultural Economics |
| AP | African Perspectives |
| AS | African Studies |
| ASoR | African Social Research |
| AStR | African Studies Review |
| BJPS | British Journal of Political Science |
| BNR | Botswana Notes and Records |
| BS | Bantu Studies |
| CJAS | Canadian Journal of African Studies |
| CPS | Comparative Political Studies |
| DC | Development and Change |
| DD | Development Dialogue |
| Ec | Economica |
| Ek | Ekistics |
| EAJRD | East African Journal of Rural Development |
| EDCC | Economic Development and Cultural Change |
| EG | Economic Geography |
| EHR | Economic History Review |
| ES | Economy and Society |
| FAOAS | Food and Agriculture Organization Agricultural Studies |
| GJ | Geographical Journal |
| H | Hadith |
| HWJ | History Workshop Journal |
| JAH | Journal of African History |
| JAI | Journal of the Anthropological Institute |
| JAL | Journal of African Law |
| JCCP | Journal of Commonwealth and Comparative Politics |
| JCPS | Journal of Commonwealth Political Studies |
| JDA | Journal of Developing Areas |
| JDS | Journal of Development Studies |

JEH       Journal of Economic History
JMAS      Journal of Modern African Studies
JPE       Journal of Political Economy
JSAS      Journal of South African Studies
JTG       Journal of Tropical Georgraphy
M         Man
MSESS     Manchester School Economic and Social Studies
O         Optima
P         Pula
RA        Rural Africana
RAPE      Review of African Political Economy
RH        Rhodesian History
RJE       Rhodesian Journal of Economics
Sa        Savanna
Sc        Science
SAG       South African Geographer
SAJE      South African Journal of Economics
SFRIS     Stanford Food Research Institute Studies
TGSSA     Transactions of the Geological Society of South Africa
ULCSP     University of London Collected Seminar Papers

## A: SOUTHERN AFRICA

Armstrong, J., "The slaves, 1652-1795," in Elphick and Gilliomee, *Shaping*, 1979.

Arrighi, G., "Labour supplies in historical perspective: the proletarianization of the African peasantry in Rhodesia," *JDS*, 6, 1970.

Axelson, E., *Portugal and the Scramble for Africa*, Johannesburg, 1967.

Baldwin, A., "Mass removals and separate development," *JSAS*, 2, 1975.

Barber, W., *The Economy of British Central Africa*, London, 1961.

Barnes, D., "Cattle ranching in the semi-arid savanna of East and Southern Africa," in B. Walker, *Management of Semi-Arid Ecosystems*, Amsterdam, 1979.

Barnes, L., *The New Boer War*, London, 1932.

Barnes, T., *The Gold Regions of Southeast Africa*, London, 1877.

Beach, D., "The Shona economy," in Palmer and Parsons, *Roots*, 1977.

Behrmann, H., "Agricultural price policy in South Africa," *RJE*, 6, 1972.

Beinart, W., "Production, labour migrancy and chieftaincy: aspects of the political economy of Pondoland," Ph.D., London, 1979.

Bell, T., *Industrial Decentralization in South Africa*, Cape Town, 1973.

Bergman, L., "Technological change in South African manufacturing industries, 1955-64," *SAJE*, 36, 1968.

Blainey, G., "The lost causes of the Jameson Raid," *EHR*, 18, 1965.

Bley, H., "Social discord in South West Africa," in P. Gifford and W. Louis, *Britain and Germany in Africa*, New Haven, 1967.

Bozzoli, B., "The origins, development and ideology of local manufacturing in South Africa," *JSAS*, 2, 1975.

Brits, R., "The marketing of South African maize," *SAJE*, 37, 1969.

Brookes, E., *The History of Native Policy in South Africa*, Pretoria, 1927.

Brown, R., "Aspects of the scramble for Matabeleland," in E. Stokes and R. Brown, *The Zambesian Past*, Manchester, 1966.

Brownlee, C., *Reminiscences of Kaffir Life and History*, Lovedale, 1896.

Buell, R., *The Native Problem in Africa*, Vol. 2, New York, 1928.

Bundy, C., *The Rise and Fall of the South African Peasantry*, Berkeley, 1979.

——, "Emergence and decline of a South African peasantry," *AfA*, 71, 1972.

Busschau, W., "The expansion of manufacturing industry in the Union," *SAJE*, 13, 1945.

Butler, G., *The 1820 Settlers*, Cape Town, 1974.

Cape of Good Hope, Native Law and Customs Commission, *Report*, 1883.

Casalis, E., *My Life in Basutoland*, Cape Town, 1971.

Chanock, M., *Unconsummated Union*, Manchester, 1977.

Chase, J., *The Cape of Good Hope and the Eastern Province of Algoa Bay*, London, 1843.

Christopher, A., "The emergence of livestock regions in the Cape Colony," *SAG*, 5, 1976.

Christopher, A., *Southern Africa*, Folkestone, 1976.

Dachs, A., "Missionary imperialism—the case of Bechuanaland," *JAH*, 13, 1972.

Danckwerts, T., "A socio-economic study of veld management in the tribal areas of Victoria Province," University of Rhodesia, Department of Agriculture, 1970?

Davenport, T., *South Africa: A Modern History*, Toronto, 1977.

——, "The consolidation of a new society," in Wilson and Thompson, *Oxford History*, vol. 1, 1969.

Davenport, T., and K. Hunt, *The Right to the Land*, Cape Town, 1974.

Davis, E., "Some aspects of the marketing of farm products in South Africa," *SAJE*, 1, 1933.

Day, J., *Railways of Southern Africa*, London, 1963.

DeKiewiet, C., *A History of South Africa: Social and Economic*, Oxford, 1941.

——, *The Imperial Factor in South Africa*, New York, 1966.

DeKock, M., *The Economic Development of South Africa*, London, 1936.

——, *Selected Subjects in the Economic History of South Africa*, Cape Town, 1924.

Denoon, D., *A Grand Illusion*, London, 1973.

Desmond, C., *The Discarded People*, Hammondsworth, 1971.

DeVilliers, R., "Afrikaner nationalism," in Wilson and Thompson, *Oxford History*, vol. 2, 1971.

Duffy, J., *A Question of Slavery*, Oxford, 1967.

Duggan, W., "The Native Land Husbandry Act and the rural African middle class of Southern Rhodesia," *AfA*, 82, 1981.

Duly, L., *British Land Policy at the Cape, 1795-1844*, Durham, 1968.

Edwards, I., *The 1820 Settlers in South Africa*, London, 1934.

Elphick, R., "The Khoisan to c. 1770," in Elphick and Gilliomee, *Shaping*, 1979.

Elphick, R., and H. Gilliomee, *The Shaping of South African Society*, Cape Town, 1979.

First, R., et. al., *The Mozambiquan Miner*, Eduardo Mondlane University, Maputo, 1977.

Frankel, S., *Cooperation and Competition in the Marketing of Maize in South Africa*, London, 1926.

_____, "A national economic policy," in E. Brookes et al., *Coming of Age*, Cape Town, 1930.

_____, "Some comments on price and marketing controls in South African agriculture," *SAJE*, 2, 1934.

Galbraith, J., *Crown and Charter*, Berkeley, 1974.

_____, *Reluctant Empire*, Berkeley, 1963.

Gann, L., *A History of Southern Rhodesia*, London, 1965.

Garlake, P., *Great Zimbabwe*, Aylesbury, 1973.

Germond, R., *Chronicles of Basutoland*, Morija, Lesotho, 1967.

Gilliomee, H., "The burgher rebellions on the eastern frontier, 1795-1815," in Elphick and Gilliomee, *Shaping*, 1979.

_____, "The eastern frontier, 1770-1812," in Elphick and Gilliomee, *Shaping*, 1979.

Goodfellow, D., *A Modern Economic History of South Africa*, London, 1931.

Gordon, C., *The Growth of Boer Opposition to Kruger*, Cape Town, 1970.

Great Britain, *Parliamentary Papers*:

 — "Report from the Select Committees on the Disposal of Lands in the British Colonies," 11, 1836.

 — "Papers relative to the establishment of the settlement of Natal," 42, 1847-48.

 — "Despatches from the Governor of Natal," 36, 1862.

 — "Papers relating to the complaints of British subjects in the South African Republic," cmd. 9345, 1899.

 — "Report of the South African Land Settlement Commission," 24, 1901.

 — "Correspondence respecting the terms of surrender of Boer forces in the field," 69, 1902.

 — Lord Blyth, "Report on agriculture and viticulture in South Africa," 59, 1909.

 — "Correspondence relating to the Natives Land Act, 1913," 45, 1914-16.

Green, L., and T. Fair, *Development in Africa*, Johannesburg, 1962.

Greenberg, S., *Race and State in Capitalist Development*, New Haven, 1980.

Guelke, L., "The white settlers, 1652-1780," in Elphick and Gilliomee, *Shaping*, 1979.

Haines, E., "The economic status of the Cape Province farm native," *SAJE*, 3, 1935.

Hancock, K., *Smuts*, Vol. 2, Cambridge, 1968.

Henning, C., *Graaf-Reinet*, Cape Town, 1975.

Holleman, J., *Shona Customary Law*, London, 1952.

Horwitz, R., *The Political Economy of South Africa*, London, 1967.

_____, "The restriction of competition between road motor transport and the railways in the Union of South Africa," *SAJE*, 5, 1937.

Houghton, D., *The South African Economy*, London, 1964.

_____, "Economic development, 1865-1965," in Wilson and Thompson, *Oxford History*, vol. 2, 1971.

Hutt, W., *The Economics of the Colour Bar*, London, 1964.

Hyam, R., *The Failure of South African Expansion*, London, 1972.

Kahn, E., "The right to strike in South Africa: an historical analysis," *SAJE*, 11, 1943.

Katzen, M., "White settlers and the origin of a new society, 1652-1778," in Wilson and Thompson, *Oxford History*, vol. 1, 1969.

Keegan, T., "Seasonality, markets and pricing: the South African maize trade in the early 20th century," *ULCSP*, 10, 1981.

Kirk, T., "The Cape economy and the expropriation of the Kat River Settlement," in Marks and Atmore, *Economy and Society*, 1980.

Kneen, J., "The dairy industry in South Africa," *SAJE*, 3, 1935.

Knowles, L., *The Economic Development of the British Overseas Empire: South Africa* (Vol. 3), London, 1936.

Kolb, P., *The Present State of the Cape of Good Hope*, Vol. 2, New York, 1968.

Laight, J., "Railway expansion during the post-war period," *SAJE*, 25, 1957.

_____, "Road transport of goods in South Africa," *SAJE*, 27, 1959.

Legassick, M., "The northern frontier to 1820," in Elphick and Gilliomee, *Shaping*, 1979.

Leppan, H., *The Agricultural Development of Arid and Semi-Arid Regions*, Pretoria, 1928.

_____, *Agricultural Policy in South Africa*, Johannesburg, 1931.

Lipton, M., "Men of two worlds," *O*, 29, 1980.

_____, "White farming: a case study of social change in South Africa," *JCCP*, 1, 1974.

Logan, K., "Land utilization in the arid regions of South West Africa," in Stamp, *History*, 1961.

Marks, S., and A. Atmore, *Economy and Society in Pre-Industrial South Africa*, London, 1980.

_____, "Firearms in Southern Africa," *JAH*, 12, 1971.

Mills, M., and M. Wilson, *Keiskammahoek Rural Survey: Land Tenure* (Vol. 4), Pietermaritzburg, 1952.

Morris, M., "The development of capitalism in South African agriculture," *ES*, 5, 1976.

Neumark, S., *Economic Influences on the South African Frontier*, Stanford, 1957.

_____, "The war and its effect on agricultural prices and surpluses in South Africa," *SAJE*, 8, 1940.

Newton-King, S., "The labour market of the Cape Colony, 1807-28," in Marks and Atmore, *Economy and Society*, 1980.

Noer, T., *Boer, Briton and Yankee*, Kent, 1979.

Palmer, G., "Some aspects of the development of secondary industry in South Africa since the depression of 1929-32," *SAJE*, 22, 1954.

Palmer, R., *Land and Racial Domination in Rhodesia*, Berkeley, 1977.

Palmer, R., and N. Parsons, *The Roots of Rural Poverty in Central and Southern Africa*, Berkeley, 1977.

Pearsall, N., "Some aspects of the development of secondary industry in the Union of South Africa," *SAJE*, 5, 1937.

Philip, J., *Missionary Researches in South Africa*, Vol. 2, London, 1828.

Phimister, I., "Meat and monopolies: beef cattle in Southern Rhodesia, 1890-1938," *JAH*, 19, 1978.

Pillay, B., *British Indians in the Transvaal*, London, 1976.

Pirow, O., *J.B.M. Hertzog*, Cape Town, n.d.

Plaatje, S., *Native Life in South Africa*, London, 1916.

Pollock, N., and S. Agnew, *An Historical Geography of South Africa*, New York, 1963.

Pursell, D., "Bantu real wages and employment opportunities in South Africa," *SAJE*, 36, 1968.

Ranger, T., *Revolt in Southern Rhodesia*, London, 1967.

Ransome, S., *The Engineer in South Africa*, London, 1903.

Republic of Zimbabwe, "Integrated Rural Development Plan for Victoria Province," 1980.

Richards, C., "The 'new despotism' in agriculture," *SAJE*, 5, 1937.

———, "Subsidies, quotas, tariffs and the excess cost of agriculture in South Africa," *SAJE*, 3, 1935.

Robson, P., "Economic integration in Southern Africa," *JMAS*, 5, 1967.

Ross, R., *Adam Kok's Griqua*, Cambridge, 1976.

Rutherford, J., *Sir George Grey*, London, 1961.

Sansom, B., "Traditional economic systems," in W. Hammond-Tooke, *The Bantu-Speaking Peoples of Southern Africa*, London, 1974.

Schlemmer, L., and E. Webster, *Change, Reform and Economic Growth in South Africa*, Johannesburg, 1978.

Schumann, C., *Structural Changes and South African Business Cycles*, London, 1938.

Scott, P., "Land policy and native population of Swaziland," *GJ*, 117, 1951.

Selwyn, P., *Industries on the Southern African Periphery*, Sussex, 1975.

Sheddick, V., *Land Tenure in Basutoland*, London, 1954.

Simkins, C., "Agricultural production in the African reserves," *JSAS*, 7, 1981.

South Africa, *Official Yearbook*, 1910-80.

South Africa, Bureau of Census and Statistics, *Union Statistics for Fifty Years*, 1960.

South Africa, Census Office, *1911 Census*.

South Africa, Central Board of the Land and Agricultural Bank, *Report*, 1941.

South Africa, Commission of Enquiry into Agriculture, *Report*, 1971.

South Africa, Commission for the Socio-Economic Development of the Bantu Areas, *Summary of the Report*, 1955.

South Africa, Commission to Enquire into Co-operation and Agricultural Credit, *Report*, 1934.

South Africa, Department of Agriculture, *Agro-Economic Survey of the Union*, 1948.

——, *Farming in South Africa*, 1924.

South Africa, Department of Native Affairs, *Report of the Native Laws Commission*, 1948.

——, *Report of the Native Location Surveys*, 1922.

South Africa, Drought Investigation Commission, *Final Report*, 1923.

South Africa, Native Affairs Commission, *Report*, 1937-38.

South Africa, Native Economic Commission, *Report*, 1932.

South Africa, Native Farm Labour Committee, *Report*, 1939.

South Africa, Natives Land Commission, *Report*, 1916.

South Africa, Office of Census and Statistics, *Agricultural Census*, 1918, 1925.

——, *1936 Census*.

South Africa, Orange Free State Local Natives Land Committee, *Report*, 1918.

South Africa, *Parliamentary Papers*, 1935.

South Africa, Select Committee on the Carnavon Outer Commonage Settlement Bill, *Report*, 1913.

South Africa, Select Committee on Native Custom and Marriage Laws, *Report*, 1913.

South Africa, Select Committee on the Subject of the Appointment of Quitrent (Further Amendment) Act, *Report*, 1927.

South Africa, Select Committee on the Subject of the Union Native Council Bill, Coloured Persons Rights Bill, and Natives Land (Amendment) Bill, *Report*, 1927.

*South African Journal of Economics*, 33, 1965, Special Issue on "Economic Growth and Investment in South Africa."

——, 35, 1967, Special Issue on "Inflation."

——, 47, 1979, Special Issue on "Economic Policy in South Africa."

South African Native Affairs Commission, *Report*, 1903-5.

South African Native Races Committee, *The Natives of South Africa*, London, 1901.

South African Railways, *The South African Railways*, 1947.

South African Railways and Harbours, *Farming Opportunities in South Africa*, 1926.

——, *South African Railways and Harbours*, 1924.

Southern Rhodesia, *What the Native Land Husbandry Act Means to the Rural African and to Southern Rhodesia*, 1955.

Southern Rhodesia, Native Production and Trade Commission, *Report*, 1944.

Stamp, L., *A History of Land Use in Arid Regions*, Paris, 1961.

Sterkenberg, J., "Agricultural commercialization in Africa south of the Sahara: the cases of Lesotho and Swaziland," DC, 11, 1980.

Strockenstrom, A., Autobiography, Cape Town, 1887.

Suckling, J., "Foreign investment and domestic savings in the Republic of South Africa, 1958-72," SAJE, 1975.

Talbot, W., "Land utilization in the arid regions of South Africa," in Stamp, History, 1961.

Taylor, C., Agriculture in Southern Africa, United States Department of Agriculture, 1935.

Theal, G., History of South Africa, London, 1926.

Thomas, O., Agricultural and Pastoral Prospects of South Africa, London, 1904.

Thompson, L., "Co-operation and conflict: the high veld," in Wilson and Thompson, Oxford History, vol. 1, 1969.

_____, "Co-operation and conflict: the Zulu kingdom and Natal," in Wilson and Thompson, Oxford History, vol. 1, 1969.

_____, "Great Britain and the Afrikaner republics, 1870-1899," in Wilson and Thompson, Oxford History, vol. 2, 1971.

_____, "The subjection of the African chiefdoms," in Wilson and Thompson, Oxford History, vol. 2, 1971.

Thompson, W., Moisture and Farming in South Africa, Pretoria, 1936.

Tinley, J., South African Food and Agriculture in World War II, Stanford, 1954.

_____, "Control of agriculture in South Africa," SAJE, 8, 1940.

Trapido, S., "African divisional politics in the Cape Colony, 1884-1910," JAH, 9, 1968.

_____, "The friends of the natives," in Marks and Atmore, Economy and Society, 1980.

_____, "Landlord and tenant in a colonial economy," JSAS, 5, 1978.

_____, "Natal's non-racial franchise, 1856," AS, 22, 1963.

_____, "The origins of the Cape franchise qualifications of 1853," JAH, 5, 1964.

_____, "Reflections on land, office and wealth in the South African Republic, 1850-1900," in Marks and Atmore, Economy and Society, 1980.

_____, "South Africa in a comparative study of industrialization," JDS, 7, 1971.

Van Biljon, F., "Competition and centralized planning," SAJE, 5, 1937.

Van Biljon, R., State Interference in South Africa, London, 1939.

Van der Horst, S., Native Labour in South Africa, London, 1971.

Van der Poel, J., Railway and Customs Policy in South Africa, London, 1933.

Van-Helten, J., "German capital, the Netherlands Railway Company and the political economy of the Transvaal," JAH, 19, 1978.

Van Onselen, C., "Reactions to rinderpest in Southern Africa," JAH, 13, 1972.

Viljoen, P., et al., "Planning and control in agriculture," SAJE, 6, 1938.

Voigt, J., Fifty Years of the History of the Republic of South Africa, London, 1899.

Waasdijk, T., "Agricultural prices and price policy," SAJE, 22, 1954.

Walker, E., The Great Trek, London, 1934.

Warwick, P., *The South African War*, London, 1980.

Weinrich, A., *African Farmers in Rhodesia*, London, 1975.

Welsh, D., "The growth of towns," in Wilson and Thompson, *Oxford History*, vol. 2, 1971.

Wellington, J., *Southern Africa*, Cambridge, 1955.

Wilson, F., *Labour in South African Gold Mines*, Cambridge, 1972.

———, "Farming, 1866-1966," in Wilson and Thompson, *Oxford History*, vol. 2, 1971.

Wilson, M., "Co-operation and conflict: the eastern Cape frontier," in Wilson and Thompson, *Oxford History*, vol. 1, 1969.

———, "The growth of peasant communities," in Wilson and Thompson, *Oxford History*, vol. 2, 1971.

———, "The hunters and herders," in Wilson and Thompson, *Oxford History*, vol. 1, 1969.

———, "The Nguni people," in Wilson and Thompson, *Oxford History*, vol. 1, 1969.

———, "The Sotho, Venda and Tsonga," in Wilson and Thompson, *Oxford History*, vol. 1, 1969.

Wilson, M., and L. Thompson, *The Oxford History of South Africa*, Vol. 1, 1969; Vol. 2, 1971.


B:  BOTSWANA

Anderson, A., *Twenty Five Years in a Waggon*, London, 1888.

Ansell, D., *Cattle Marketing in Botswana*, Reading, 1971.

Baldwin, W., *African Hunting and Adventure*, London, 1863.

Bawden, M., and A. Stobbs, *The Land Resources of Eastern Bechuanaland*, Surrey, 1963.

Best, A., "General trading in Botswana," *EG*, 46, 1970.

Boocock, C., and O. van Straten, "Notes on the geology and hydrogeology of the central Kalahari region, Bechuanaland Protectorate," *TGSSA*, 65, 1962.

Brown, B., "The impact of male labor migration on women in Botswana," African Studies Association Conference paper, Bloomington, 1981.

Bryant, C., et al., "Rural to urban migration," *AStR*, 21, 1978.

Chirenje, J., *A History of Northern Botswana*, Cranbury, 1977.

Cliffe, L., and R. Moorsom, "Rural class formation and ecological collapse in Botswana," *RAPE*, 15/16, 1980.

Clifford, B., *Kalahari Desert Expedition*, Pretoria, 1928.

———, "Habitability of the Kalahari," *GJ*, 77, 1981.

Colclough, C., and S. McCarthy, *The Political Economy of Botswana*, Oxford, 1980.

*Colonial Development*, Winter, 1954.

Comaroff, J., "Class and culture in a peasant economy: the transformation of land tenure in Barolong," *JAL*, 24, 1980.

———, "Rules and rulers: political process in a Tswana chiefdom," *M*, 13, 1978.

Comaroff, J., and S. Roberts, "Marriage and extra-marriage sexuality," *JAL*, 21, 1977.

Conder, C., "The present condition of the tribes of Bechuanaland," *JAI*, 16, 1886.

Curtis, D., "Cash brewing in a rural economy," *BNR*, 5, 1973.

_____, "The social organization of ploughing," *BNR*, 4, 1972.

Dachs, A., *The Road to the North*, Salisbury, 1969.

_____, "Rhodesia's grasp for Bechuanaland," *RH*, 2, 1971.

Debenham, F., *Kalahari Sand*, London, 1953.

_____, *Report on the Water Resources of the Bechuanaland Protectorate, Northern Rhodesia, Nyasaland Protectorate, Tanganyika Territory, Kenya and Uganda Protectorate*, London, 1948.

Devitt, P., "Drought and poverty," in P. Dalby et al., *Drought in Africa*, London, 1977.

Duggan, W., "The Kweneng in the colonial era," *BNR*, 9, 1978.

Elkan, W., "Labour migration from Botswana, Lesotho and Swaziland," *AP*, 1, 1978.

Erasmus, D., "The national income of the Bechuanaland Protectorate," in L. Samuels, *African Studies in Income and Wealth*, London, 1963.

Ettinger, S., "The economics of the customs union between Botswana, Lesotho, Swaziland and South Africa," Ph.D., Michigan, 1974.

_____, "South Africa's weight restrictions on cattle imports from Bechuanaland, 1924-41," *BNR*, 4, 1972.

Falconer, J., "History of Botswana veterinary services, 1905-66," *BNR*, 3, 1971.

Farrar, D., "Water supply and settlement patterns in Swaziland and Botswana," *Ek*, 43, 1977.

Gaitskell, A., *Report of a Mission to the Bechuanaland Protectorate*, London, 1954.

Gillmore, P., *The Great Thirstland*, London, 1879.

Great Britain, *Basutoland, Bechuanaland Protectorate and Swaziland: Report of an Economic Survey Mission*, 1960.

_____, *The Development of the Bechuanaland Economy*, 1965.

_____, *Economic and Financial Report on the High Commission Territories*, 1954.

_____, *Financial and Economic Position of the Bechuanaland Protectorate*, 1933.

_____, *High Commission Territories: Economic Development and Social Services*, 1955.

Hailey, W., *Native Administration in the British African Territories: The High Commission Territories* (Part 5), London, 1953.

Harrison, A., *Agricultural Credit in Botswana*, Reading, 1967.

Hartland-Thurberg, P., *Botswana: An African Growth Economy*, Boulder, 1978.

Hermans, Q., "A review of Botswana's financial history," *BNR*, 6, 1974.

Hitchcock, R., "Tradition, social justice and land reform in Central Botswana," *JAL*, 24, 1980.

Hjort, A., and W. Ostberg, *Farming and Herding in Botswana*, Uppsala, 1978.

Hodson, A., *Trekking the Great Thirst*, London, 1912.

Holm, J., "Rural development in Botswana," *RA*, 1972.

Ingersoll, J., *Historical Examples of Ecological Disasters*, Hudson Institute, 1965.

Jackson, D., "Income differentials and unbalanced planning," *JMAS*, 8, 1970.

Johns, S., "Botswana's strategy for development," *JCPS*, 11, 1973.

Jones, D., *Aid and Development in Southern Africa*, London, 1977.

Jones, K., "Britain's contribution to Botswana's public debt," *BNR*, 9, 1977.

Kerven, C., "Underdevelopment, migration and class formation in the Northeast District of Botswana," Ph.D., Toronto, 1977.

Khama, T., *Bechuanaland and South Africa*, London, 1955.

Konczacki, T., *The Economics of Pastoralism*, London, 1978.

Kuper, A., *Kalahari Village Politics*, Cambridge, 1970.

———, "The Kgalagadi in the 19th century," *BNR*, 2, 1969.

Lancaster, I., "The pans of the southern Kalahari," *GJ*, 1978.

Landell-Mills, P., "Rural incomes and urban wage rates," *BNR*, 2, 1969.

Lee, R., and I. deVore, *Kalahari Hunter-Gatherers*, Cambridge, 1976.

Legassick, M., "The Sotho-Tswana peoples before 1800," in L. Thompson, *African Societies of Southern Africa*, New York, 1969.

Lever, B., *Agricultural Extension in Botswana*, Reading, 1970.

Lichtenstein, W., *About the Bechuanas*, Cape Town, 1973.

McCarthy, S., "The administration of capital aid," *DD*, 1, 1978.

Mahoney, N., "Contract and neighborly exchange among the Birwa of Botswana," *JAL*, 21, 1977.

Massey, D., "A case of colonial collaboration: the hut tax and migrant labour," *BNR*, 10, 1978.

Massey, D., "Labour migration and rural development in Botswana," Ph.D., Boston, 1981.

Mitchell, A., *The Irrigation Potential of the Soils Along the Main Rivers of Eastern Botswana*, Surrey, 1976.

Nangati, F., "Constraints on a pre-colonial economy: the Bakwena state, 1820-85," *P*, 1, 1980.

Ngcongo, L., "Aspects of the history of the Bangwaketse to 1910," Ph.D., Dalhousie, 1975.

Okihiro, G., "Genealogical research in Molepolole," *BNR*, 8, 1976.

———, "Hunters, herders, cultivators and traders: interaction and change in the Kalahari, 19th century," Ph.D., UCLA, 1976.

———, "Population change among the Kwena of Botswana," in Centre of African Studies, *African Historical Demography*, Vol. 2, University of Edinburgh, 1981.

———, "Resistance and accommodation: BaKwena bagaSechele," *BNR*, 5, 1973.

Osborne, A., "Rural development in Botswana," *JSAS*, 2, 1976.

Parson, J., "Cattle, class and the state in rural Botswana," *JSAS*, 7, 1981.

———, "The political economy of Botswana," D. Phil., Sussex, 1979.

Parsons, N., *The Word of Khama*, Lusaka, 1972.
_____, "The economic history of Khama's country in Botswana, 1844-1930," in Palmer and Parsons, *Roots*, 1979.
_____, "Khama and Co. and the Jousse trouble, 1910-6," *JAH*, 16, 1975.
_____, "Khama III, the Bamangwato and the British," Ph.D., Edinburgh, 1973.
Picard, L., "Bureaucrats, cattle and public policy," *CPS*, 13, 1980.
_____, "District councils in Botswana," *JMAS*, 17, 1979.
_____, "Rural development in Botswana," *JDA*, 13, 1979.
Rains, A., and A. MacKay, *The Northern State Lands, Botswana*, Surrey, 1968.
Rains, A., and A. Yalala, *The Central and Southern State Lands*, Botswana, Surrey, 1972.
Roberts, S., *Tswana Family Law*, London, 1972.
Roberts, S., "Arable land tenure and administrative change in the Kgatleng," *JAL*, 24, 1980.
Roberts, S., and J. Comaroff, "A chief's decision and the devolution of property in a Tswana chiefdom," in W. Shack and P. Cohen, *Politics in Leadership*, Oxford, 1979.
Roe, E., "Development of livestock, agriculture and water supplies in eastern Botswana before independence," Cornell University, 1980.
Russell, M. and M., *Afrikaners of the Kalahari*, Cambridge, 1979.
Schapera, I., *The Ethnic Composition of Tswana Tribes*, London, 1952.
_____, *Handbook of Tswana Law and Custom*, London, 1938.
_____, *Married Life in an African Tribe*, London, 1940.
_____, *Migrant Labour and Tribal Life*, London, 1947.
_____, *Native Land Tenure in the Bechuanaland Protectorate*, Lovedale, 1943.
_____, *Tribal Innovators*, London, 1970.
_____, *Tribal Legislation Among the Tswana of the Bechuanaland Protectorate*, London, 1943.
_____, *The Tswana*, London, 1953.
_____, *Western Civilization and the Natives of South Africa*, London, 1934.
_____, "Economic changes in South African native life," *A*, 6, 1933.
_____, "Livingstone and the Boers," *AfA*, 59, 1960.
_____, "The social structure of the Tswana ward," *BS*, 9, 1935.
Schapera, I., and D. van der Merwe, "Notes on the tribal groupings, history and customs of the Bakgalagadi," University of Cape Town, School of African Studies, n.s., 13, 1945.
Silberbauer, B., and A. Kuper, "Kgalagadi masters and Bushmen serfs," *AS*, 25, 1966.
Silitshena, R., "Changing settlement patterns in Botswana: the case of the eastern Kweneng," Ph.D., Sussex, 1979.
_____, "Notes on the origins of some settlements in the Kweneng District," *BNR*, 8, 1976.
Sillery, A., *The Bechuanaland Protectorate*, Cape Town, 1952.
_____, *Founding a Protectorate*, The Hague, 1965.

_____, *John MacKenzie of Bechuanaland*, Cape Town, 1970.

_____, *Sechele*, Oxford, 1954.

_____, *A Short History of Botswana*, London, 1974.

Spence, J., "British policy towards the High Commission Territories," *JMAS*, 2, 1964.

Syson, L., "Unmarried mothers in Botswana," *BNR*, 5, 1973.

Tagart, E., *Report on the Conditions Existing Among Masarwa in the BaMangwato Reserve of the Bechuanaland Protectorate*, Pretoria, 1933.

Taylor, J., "Mine labour recruitment in the Bechuanaland Protectorate," *BNR*, 10, 1978.

Tlou, T., "A political history of northwestern Botswana to 1906," Ph.D., Wisconsin, 1973.

_____, "Servility and political control: Botlhanka among the Batawana of northwestern Botswana," in S. Miers and I. Kopytoff, *Slavery in Africa*, Madison, 1977.

Truschel, L., "The Tawana and the Ngamiland trek," *BNR*, 6, 1974.

Van Niekerk, D., "Notes on the administration of justice among the Kwena," *AS*, 25, 1966.

Vergroff, R., *Botswana: Rural Development in the Shadow of Apartheid*, Cranbury, 1977.

_____, "Traditional political structures in the contemporary context: the chieftaincy in the Kweneng," *AS*, 34, 1975.

Vivelo, R., *The Herero of Western Botswana*, St. Paul, 1977.

Von Richter, W., "Wildlife and rural economy in southwest Botswana," *BNR*, 2, 1969.

C: AFRICA AND GENERAL

Ady, P., et al., *Oxford Regional Economic Atlas of Africa*, Oxford, 1956.

Allan, W., *The African Husbandman*, New York, 1965.

Allan, W., et al., *Land Holding and Land Usage Among the Plateau Tonga of Mazabuka District*, London, 1948.

Anthony, K., et al., *Agricultural Change in Tropical Africa*, Ithaca, 1979.

Ariza-Nino, E., and K. Shapiro, "Cattle as capital, consumables and cash," in J. Simpson and P. Evangelou, *Livestock Development in Sub-Saharan Africa*, Boulder, 1984.

Baier, S., "Economic history and development: drought and the Sahelian economies of Niger," *AEH*, 1, 1976.

Bailey, H., "Semi-arid climates," in Hall, *Agriculture*, 1979.

Barraclough, S., and J. Collarte, *Agrarian Structure in Latin America*, Lexington, 1973.

Bartlett, H., "Fire, primitive agriculture and grazing in the tropics," in W. Thomas, *Man's Role in Changing the Face of the Earth*, Chicago, 1956.

Bates, R., and M. Lofchie, *Agricultural Development in Africa*, New York, 1980.

Biebuyck, D., *African Agrarian Systems*, London, 1963.

Binns, B., "Cadastral surveys and records of rights in land," *FAOAS*, 18, 1953.

Bloch, M., *French Rural History*, London, 1966.

Bohannon, P., and G. Dalton, *Markets in Africa*, Evanston, 1962.

Boserup, E., *The Conditions of Agricultural Growth*, Chicago, 1965.

———, *Woman's Role in Economic Development*, London, 1970.

Brandstrom, P., *Aspects of Agro-Pastoralism in East Africa*, Uppsala, 1979.

Brekke, O., "Corn dry milling industry," in G. Inglett, *Corn: Culture, Processing, Products*, Westport, 1970.

Brush, S., "The myth of the idle peasant," in R. Halperin and J. Dow, *Peasant Livelihood*, New York, 1977.

Cain, P., and A. Hopkins, "The political economy of British expansion overseas, 1750-1914," *EHR*, 53, 1980.

Chayanov, A., *The Theory of Peasant Economy*, Homewood, 1966.

Clark, C., and M. Haswell, *The Economics of Subsistence Agriculture*, London, 1966.

Clauson, G., "Communal land tenure," *FAOAS*, 17, 1953.

Collinson, M., *Farm Management in Peasant Agriculture*, New York, 1972.

Cooper, F., *From Slaves to Squatters*, New Haven, 1980.

Coulsen, A., "Agricultural policies in mainland Tanganyika," *RAPE*, 10, 1977.

Critchell, J., and J. Raymond, *A History of the Frozen Meat Trade*, London, 1912.

Crotty, R., *Cattle, Economics and Development*, Farnham Royal, 1980.

Curtin, P., *Economic Change in Pre-Colonial Africa*, Madison, 1975.

Dahl, G., and A. Hjort, *Having Herds*, Stockholm, 1976.

Dasmann, R., et al., *Ecological Principles for Economic Development*, London, 1973.

Deane, P., *The First Industrial Revolution*, Cambridge, 1965.

Deare, C., and A. deJanvry, "A conceptual framework for the empirical analysis of peasants," *AJAE*, 61, 1979.

DeCarvalho, E., " 'Traditional' and 'modern' patterns of cattle raising in south-western Angola," *JDA*, 8, 1974.

DeWilde, J., *Agricultural Development in Tropical Africa*, Baltimore, 1967.

Doran, M., et al., "Cattle as a store of wealth in Swaziland," *AJAE*, 61, 1979.

Duckham, A., and G. Masefield, *Farming Systems of the World*, New York, 1969.

Duignan, P., and L. Gann, *Colonialism in Africa: The Economics of Colonialism* (Vol. 4), Cambridge, 1975.

Ehrlich, C., "Building and caretaking: economic policy in British tropical Africa, 1890-1960," *EHR*, 24, 1973.

Eicher, C., and D. Baker, *Research in Agricultural Development in Sub-Saharan Africa*, Michigan State, 1982.

Fielder, R., "The role of cattle in the Ila economy," *ASoR*, 15, 1873.

Fisher, H., " 'He swalloweth the ground with fierceness and rage': the horse in the Central Sudan," *JAH*, 14, 1973.

Fogel, R., and G. Elton, *Which Road to the Past?*, New Haven, 1984.

Ford, J., *The Role of Trypanasomiasis in African Ecology*, Oxford, 1971.

Fornari, H., *Bread Upon the Waters: A History of United States Grain Exports*, Nashville, 1973.

Fortes, M., and S. Patterson, *Studies in African Social Anthropology*, London, 1975.

Frankel, S., *Capital Investment in Africa*, London, 1938.

Fumagalli, C., "An evaluation of development projects among East African pastoralists," *AStR*, 21, 1978.

Fussel, G., "Growth of food production," in Singer et al., *History*, 1958.

Gallagher, J., and R. Robinson, "The imperialism of free trade," *EHR*, 6, 1953.

Gerhart, J., *The Diffusion of Hybrid Maize in Western Kenya*, Mexico City, 1975.

Gonner, E., *Common Land and Enclosure*, London, 1912.

Goodfellow, D., *Principles of Economic Sociology*, London, 1939.

Goody, J., *Technology, Tradition and the State in Africa*, London, 1971.

Greaves, I., *Modern Production Among Backward Peoples*, London, 1935.

Gulliver, P., *The Family Herds*, London, 1966.

Hahn, R., "Dry milling and products of grain sorghum," in J. Wall and W. Ross, *Sorghum Production and Utilization*, Westport, 1970.

Hall, A., et al., *Agriculture in Semi-Arid Environments*, New York, 1979.

Hall, A., *The Improvement of Native Agriculture in Relation to Population and Public Health*, London, 1939.

Hance, W., *The Geography of Modern Africa*, New York, 1975.

Hardin, G., "The tragedy of the commons," *Sc*, 162, 1978.

Haswell, M., *Economics of Agriculture in a Savanna Village*, London, 1953.

Helleiner, G., *Peasant Agriculture, Government, and Economic Growth in Nigeria*, Homewood, 1966.

———, "Smallholder decision-making: tropical African evidence," in L. Reynolds, *Agriculture in Development Theory*, New Haven, 1974.

Herskovitz, M., "The cattle complex in East Africa," *AmA*, 28, 1926.

Heyer, J., *The Economics of Small-Scale Farming in Lowland Machakos*, Nairobi, 1967.

Heyer, J., et al., *Agricultural Development in Kenya*, Nairobi, 1976.

Hill, P., *The Migrant Cocoa Farmers of Southern Ghana*, Cambridge, 1963.

Hobsbawm, E., *The Age of Capital*, New York, 1975.

———, *Industry and Empire*, Hammondsworth, 1968.

Hogendorn, J., "Economic initiative and African cash farming," in Duignan and Gann, *Economics*, 1975.

Hopkins, A., *An Economic History of West Africa*, New York, 1975.

Humphrey, N., *The Kikuyu Lands*, Kenya Colony and Protectorate, 1945.

———, *The Liguru and the Land*, Kenya Department of Agriculture, 1947.

Hunter, G., *Aid in Africa*, London, 1979.

Hyden, G., *Beyond Ujamaa in Tanzania*, London, 1980.

Hymer, S., and S. Resnick, "A model of an agrarian economy with non-agricultural activities," *AER*, 59, 1969.

Jacoby, E., "The interrelationship between agrarian reform and agricultural development," *FAOAS*, 26, 1953.

Jarvis, C., "The distribution and utilization of electricity," in Singer et al., *History*, 1958.

Jarvis, L., "Cattle as capital goods and ranchers as portfolio managers," *JPE*, 87, 1974.

Johnston, B., and P. Kilby, *Agriculture and Structural Transformation*, New York, 1975.

Jones, F., *Farm Gas Engines and Tractors*, New York, 1952.

*Journal of African Administration*, Special Supplements: October 1952; October 1956.

Kao, C., et al., "Disguised unemployment in agriculture: a survey," in C. Eicher and L. Witt, *Agriculture in Economic Development*, New York, 1964.

Katzenellenbogen, S., "The miner's frontier, transport and general economic development," in Duignan and Gann, *Economics*, 1975.

Kitching, G., *Class and Economic Change in Kenya*, New Haven, 1980.

Kjekshus, H., *Ecology Control and Economic Development in East African Economic History*, London, 1977.

Kolawole, M., "Economic aspects of private tractor operations in the savanna zone of Western Nigeria," *Sa*, 3, 1974.

Laut, P., *Agricultural Geography: Mid-Latitude Commercial Agriculture* (Vol. 2), Melbourne, 1969.

Law, R., "A West African cavalry state," *JAH*, 16, 1975.

Lewis, W., "Economic development with unlimited supplies of labour," *MSESS*, 1954.

Lipton, M., "The theory of the optimizing peasant," *JDS*, 4, 1968.

Livingstone, I., "Economic irrationality among pastoral peoples," *DC*, 8, 1977.

Louis, R., *Imperialism: The Robinson and Gallagher Controversy*, New York, 1976.

Lugard, F., *The Dual Mandate in British Tropical Africa*, London, 1922.

McCown, L., et al., "The interaction between cultivation and livestock production in semi-arid Africa," in Hall et al., *Agriculture*, 1979.

McGrath, J., "Explosives," in Singer et al., *History*, 1958.

McLoughlin, P., *African Food Production Systems*, Baltimore, 1970.

Mair, L., "Agrarian policy in the British African colonies," in Afrika Instituut, Leiden, *Land Tenure Symposium*, Leiden, 1950.

Makings, S., *Agricultural Problems of Developing Countries of Africa*, Lusaka, 1967.

Masefield, G., *A History of the Colonial Agricultural Service*, Oxford, 1972.

Massell, B., and R. Johnson, "Economics of smallholder farming in Rhodesia," *SFRIS*, 8, 1968.

Matz, S., *Cereal Technology*, Westport, 1970.

Meek, C., *Land Law and Custom in the Colonies*, London, 1946.

Meillassoux, C., "From reproduction to production," *ES*, 1, 1972.

Mellor, J., *The Economics of Agricultural Development*, New York, 1966.

Miracle, M., "Subsistence agriculture: analytical problems and alternative concepts," *AJAE*, 50, 1968.

Monod, T., *Pastoralism in Tropical Africa*, London, 1975.

Moock, P., "The efficiency of women as farm managers in Kenya," *AJAE*, 58, 1976.

Morgan, W., and L. Stamp, *Africa: A Study in Tropical Development*, New York, 1972.

Morris, T., "Management and preservation of food," in Singer et al., *History*, 1958.

Mosley, P., *The Settler Economies*, Cambridge, 1983.

Nagle, J., *Agricultural Trade Policies*, Westmead, 1976.

Nieuwolt, S., "The influence of rainfall in rural population distribution in Tanzania," *JTG*, 44, 1977.

Norman, D., "Economic rationality of traditional Hausa dryland farmers in the north of Nigeria," in R. Stevens, *Tradition and Dynamics in Small-Farm Agriculture*, Ames, 1977.

Olmstead, A., "The mechanization of reaping and mowing in American agriculture," *JEH*, 35, 1974.

Parsons, K., "The owner-cultivator in a progressive agriculture," *FAOAS*, 39, 1958.

Parsons, K., et al., *Land Tenure*, Madison, 1956.

Pedler, F., "British planning and private enterprise in colonial Africa," in Duignan and Gann, *Economics*, 1975.

Phillips, J., *Agriculture and Ecology in Africa*, London, 1959.

Raeburn, J., et al., *Report of a Survey of Problems of Mechanization of Native Agriculture in Tropical African Colonies*, Great Britain, Colonial Office, 1950.

Robinson, R., and J. Gallagher, *Africa and the Victorians*, London, 1961.

Robinson, W., "The economics of work-sharing in peasant agriculture," *EDCC*, 20, 1971.

Runge, C., "Common property externalities," *AJAE*, 63, 1981.

Ruthenberg, H., *Farming Systems in the Tropics*, Oxford, 1980.

Saul, S., *Studies in British Overseas Trade, 1870-1914*, Liverpool, 1960.

Schneider, H., *Livestock and Equality in East Africa*, Bloomington, 1979.

Schultz, T., *Transforming Traditional Agriculture*, New Haven, 1964.

Singer, C., et al., *A History of Technology*, Vol. 5, Oxford, 1958.

Slicher von Bath, B., *The Agrarian History of Western Europe*, London, 1963.

Sorrenson, M., *Land Reform in the Kikuyu Country*, Nairobi, 1967.

Spafford, W., *Agriculture in the Temperate and Sub-Tropical Climates of the South*, Adelaide, 1936.

Spencer, P., "Drought and commitment to growth," *AfA*, 73, 1974.

Storck, J., and W. Teague, *Flour For Man's Bread*, Minneapolis, 1952.

Swynnerton, R., *A Plan to Intensify the Development of African Agriculture in Kenya*, Nairobi, 1954.

Talbot, F., *The Railway Conquest of the World*, London, 1911.

Thomas, B., "The African savanna climate and problems of development," in D. Brokensha, *Ecology and Economic Development in Tropical Africa*, Berkeley, 1965.

Timmons, J., "Improving agricultural tenancy," *FAOAS*, 35, 1957.

Tosh, J., "The cash crop revolution in tropical Africa," *AfA*, 79, 1980.

Trapnell, C., *The Soils, Vegetation and Agriculture of Northeastern Rhodesia*, Lusaka, 1953.

Turner, M., *English Parliamentary Enclosure*, Folkestone, 1980.

United Nations Conference on Trade and Development, *Special Measures in Favouring the Least Developed Among Developing Countries*, 1971.

United States Department of Agriculture, *Farm Tractors*, Agriculture Information Bulletin, 231, 1960.

United States Department of Agriculture, Economic Research Service, *Food Problems and Prospects in Sub-Saharan Africa*, 1981.

Upton, M., *Farm Management in Africa*, Oxford, 1973.

Vail, L., "Ecology and history: the example of eastern Zambia," *JSAS*, 3, 1977.

Warriner, D., *Land Reform in Principle and Practice*, Oxford, 1969.

Weil, P., "The introduction of the ox-plough into central Gambia," in McLoughlin, *African Food*, 1970.

Wharton, C., *Subsistence Agriculture and Economic Development*, Chicago, 1969.

World Bank, *Accelerated Development in Sub-Saharan Africa*, Washington, 1981.

Yudelman, M., *Africans on the Land*, Cambridge, 1963.

——, "Imperialism and the transfer of agricultural techniques," in Duignan and Gann, *Economics*, 1975.

# INDEX